Jihad!

JIHAD!

The Secret War in Afghanistan

Tom Carew

MAINSTREAM
PUBLISHING

EDINBURGH AND LONDON

First published in Great Britain in 2000 by
MAINSTREAM PUBLISHING COMPANY (EDINBURGH) LTD
7 Albany Street
Edinburgh EH1 3UG

This edition 2001, reprinted 2001

ISBN 1 84018 495 7

A catalogue record for this book is available from the British Library

Typeset in Janson Text
Printed and bound in Great Britain
by Cox & Wyman Ltd

Contents

Acknowledgements

I wrote this book over several months, stabbing away with two fingers at my computer, but I wouldn't have been able to finish it without the help of Nicole; so a big thank you to her.

Having said that, it wouldn't have been possible without the perseverance of my agent, Andrew Lownie, and I'm also grateful for the confidence shown by Bill Campbell and Peter MacKenzie who commissioned it.

List of Abbreviations

AP	anti-personnel
BC	Battery Captain (Artillery rank equivalent to Company Commander)
CIA	Central Intelligence Agency (US)
CQMS	Company Quartermaster Sergeant
DIA	Defense Intelligence Agency (US)
DPM	disruptive-pattern material (i.e. camouflage)
DS	directing staff
E & E	escape and evasion
GRU	Soviet Military Intelligence
HLS	helicopter landing site
IFF	identification friend or foe
KGB	USSR 'Committee of State Security'
MTO	Mechanical Transport Officer
NBC	nuclear, biological and chemical
NCO	non-commissioned officer
OC	officer commanding
OG	olive green (1960s-issue green denim trousers)

OP	observation post
OSS	Officer of Strategic Services
PE	plastic explosive
PJI	Parachute Jump Instructor
PTI	Physical Training Instructor
QARANC	Queen Alexandra's Royal Army Nursing Corps
QM	Quartermaster
RPG	rocket-propelled grenade
RUC	Royal Ulster Constabulary
RV	rendezvous
SAR	search and rescue
SAS	Special Air Service
SOE	Special Operations Executive
TACBE	tactical beacon
VCP	vehicle checkpoint
WRAC	Women's Royal Army Corps

Weapons:

APC	armoured personnel carrier
AGS-17	auto grenade launcher 40mm (same as M19)
AK	Avtomat Kalashnikov - generic name for Soviet rifles
DH-sk	Soviet type heavy machine gun
DPK	Soviet sniper rifle
GPMG	general-purpose machine gun
MI-24	Soviet gunship helicopter
MLRS	Multi-launcher rocket system
RDX	WW2 British plastic explosive
RPD	Soviet type GPMG
RPG-7	Soviet A/T rocket propelled grenade launcher

RPG-18/12	Light anti-tank weapon (same as m72 NATO)
RPK	Soviet light machine gun
SA-80	standard British rifle
SKS	Soviet Simonov assault rifle
SMLE	short-magazine Lee-Enfield standard British rifle from the turn of the century to the 1930s

Author's Note

This is the story of my involvement in Operations FARADAY and FERRET, two operations which took place at the start of one of the crucial engagements of the cold war: the Soviet occupation of Afghanistan. As one of a small number of, mainly British, covert operators, I was tasked to link up with the Afghan Mujahideen resistance movement inside Pakistan, and then to go into Afghanistan itself, to make an assessment of what training and material help they needed.

It went further than that, of course: the SAS has become famous for its counter-terrorist role, but I must be one of the few ex-members of 22 SAS who has actually hijacked an aircraft. I don't suppose all that many have killed Russian soldiers in combat, either.

Obviously, in an account of this sort, security demands that some things remain secret. For security reasons I have agreed to fictionalise the names of virtually all living members of the British special forces and intelligence communities who appear in this book, as well as such real locations as the pubs where SAS men drink and any codewords that we used during the course of these operations. To my mind these are trivialities anyway; and I believe that this book remains the most complete account of a real covert intelligence operation yet published.

Tom Carew
London, April 2000

ONE

I joined the army because I had nowhere else to go. I was a farmboy from Dorset in south-west England, and until I was seventeen I had always assumed that I would take over my uncle's farm when he retired, and stay there.

But things never work out the way you plan them. In my case, a big bust-up with my family coincided with me meeting an old school friend who was serving in the Parachute Regiment. In the course of one catastrophic weekend, I discovered that two years of agricultural college and hard labour on the farm had been a waste – my cousins wanted my uncle to sell the farm off when he retired rather than pass it to me – and I upped and took myself off to Weymouth, the local town, to find out how to join the Paras.

My destination was an office where I'd seen soldiers in the past. I got there at about 9.30 in the morning, and spent the next ten minutes hanging around outside, trying to nerve myself to go in. Eventually, a large, green-clad man came out and asked me if he could help. I went in and sat down in front of his desk. I noticed that sewn onto his jumper was a set of parachute wings. I felt as if I were on safe ground.

'I want to be a paratrooper.'

He began to explain the whole process by which you got to the stage where you earned the wings.

'First off, you do your basic training; then you have to earn the green beret . . .'

I interrupted at this point.

'Er . . . what about the maroon beret?'

'That's the Parachute Regiment, son. We're marine commandos.'

'Fuck! Sorry.'

Twenty seconds later I was back on the street, heading to the army recruitment office. It wasn't far. This time I walked straight in and told the guy at the desk:

'I want to be a paratrooper.'

'All right, son, sit down over there; I'll be with you in a minute.'

I sat down, taking in all the recruitment posters, and then watching as some spotty teenager emerged from the back office, obviously with his mum and dad, and who was all smiles with the recruiter. He looked a smug little git, dolled up in white shirt, tie and blazer, and with his hair plastered down, while I looked unmistakably what I was: straight off the farm.

'Now son, what can we do for you?'

'Er, I want to be a paratrooper.'

'Have a look at these then, and we can talk more in a minute.'

He gave me a sheaf of colour brochures, showing pictures of tanks and helicopters and so on, but none showed what I was after.

'No, look, I want to be a paratrooper.'

He gave a deep sigh. I seemed to be pissing him off but I couldn't for the life of me think why. It was only a year or so later that I came to understand the dislike that many 'crap-hat' soldiers have for airborne forces; and that this could even extend to spotty little sprogs who merely wanted to join the Paras!

Eventually, he gave me a tatty little brochure to read while he went off to the back office to make a couple of phone calls. I flicked through it; it didn't have much to say. The recruiter came back in.

'You can go to the Royal Artillery starting next week. If you want to join the Parachute Regiment, you'll have to wait three months. Don't worry, son, the Gunners have paratroopers as well. I'll put you down as a Para volunteer.'

I didn't really know what he was talking about but it sounded all right and I agreed. Now the only hurdles I faced were a short written test – which I took and passed there and then – a medical and getting my parents' permission, which I needed because I was still under eighteen. I headed home to tackle Mum.

I knew there was going to be a lot of heartache: I was right. My stepfather and uncle played cricket together and knew each other well, and they'd obviously been discussing my 'case' at some length. It seemed that they reckoned they could stitch together a deal whereby I went off and learned a 'trade' and they wouldn't oppose me, but that I had to wait until the harvest was over until I went.

Bollocks to that!

I had a big row with Michael, my stepfather, which ended up with him issuing an ultimatum: either I joined a 'useful' part of the army, or I could fuck off and forget about ever coming home. This wasn't the sort of challenge that I shrank from, and despite a lot of tears from my mother, I told him to get stuffed.

It was a Monday morning a couple of weeks later when my train rattled into Waterloo station, and as I pulled my suitcase from the luggage rack I prepared myself to set foot in London for the very first time. No question, for a quiet farmboy this was a madhouse. I found a British Rail guard and asked for the platform for Woolwich, but he just pointed up at the big departure sign and walked away. I dodged through the teeming crowd and found myself in front of the big mechanical sign, squinting through the gloom of the station to see where I had to make for. Eventually I found what I was looking for, and made my way, suitcase clutched in sweaty, nervous palm, to the grimy commuter train that was carrying me off to the army.

Not much more than twenty minutes after leaving Waterloo, the train pulled in to Woolwich station. I got off, a sinking feeling in the pit of my stomach, and climbed the stairs into the booking hall. I looked around and saw a soldier, dressed in green denims and wearing a dark blue beret with a Royal Artillery cap-badge. He spotted me at about the same time:

'New recruit?'

I nodded dumbly.

'See that truck out there?'

I looked through the dirty glass entrance doors to see a green army Bedford truck, and nodded my head again.

'Jump in the back there then, mate. I'll just wait to see if there's any more of you.'

I walked out of the station and heaved my suitcase into the truck, and then climbed up the tailgate and sat on the wooden slatted bench inside. A couple more lads of about my age came out, and silently followed me into the Bedford, and I sat there feeling miserable, wondering if I hadn't made the biggest mistake of my life so far.

A few minutes later, the driver came out and heaved the tailgate up, slamming it into place with a loud clang and rattling the locking pins into position, and then we set off on the half-mile journey up the hill to the Royal Artillery barracks, my home for the next eighteen weeks.

In 1969, Woolwich was still a thriving garrison town, with a whole bunch of different units based there, not to mention the large military hospital, the arsenal and the old Royal Military Academy building. But without doubt, the most magnificent part of it was the Headquarters Royal Artillery: a long, elegant Georgian façade facing onto a large parade ground and acres of playing fields which then ran on to Woolwich common. Tucked in behind this were the barracks of the training regiment, which took spotty civilians like me and turned us out as trained soldiers – in theory anyway.

I was one of the first to arrive for my recruit intake, and there is no question that it was an extremely intimidating experience. A taciturn corporal took us to draw our bedding, and then led us to a vast, shining barrack room, empty except for iron bedsteads and the carcasses of steel kit lockers. He showed us how to make up our beds and then left us to stew.

Over the next few hours, the room slowly filled up with shiny-faced, nervous new recruits, until there were about thirty of us. Then we began the rounds: haircuts; documentation; kit issue; and the thousand and one little tasks which convert the complete civilian into the army recruit. We started to learn the basics: building up bed-blocks, an arrangement of our blankets, sheets and pillowcases; laying out our '1157' kit so that it could be counted and inspected at the same time; bulling our boots with duster and Kiwi polish so that they took on a gleaming liquid shine so sharp you could see your face in it; and pressing and cleaning our kit so often that the colours began to fade even though it was practically brand new. And we began our military training: PT; drill; weapons; fieldcraft and all the rest of it.

To be honest, I didn't find it that difficult. My years on the farm had accustomed me to hard work and early starts, and I was physically fit from work, rugby and running; I was also used to being away from home, which was certainly a new experience for many of the lads, who I heard crying at night as we lay in our bunks after lights-out. At the end of six weeks we had a drill test and 'passed off the square', meaning we were now deemed to be trustworthy enough to head for the bright lights of downtown Woolwich after work in the evenings, provided we got back before midnight; and as a special bonus I was given a stripe and told I was now a section leader, which meant that I only had to mop the showers, rather than clean out the crappers, which was an improvement.

Except that there was a problem. The first part of training was basically the same thing that all soldiers go through, whether they're joining the Paras or the Catering Corps, but as time went by we started to do more and more of the specialised artillery training, using the basic 105mm pack howitzer. We started off learning all the drills on the gun park at Woolwich and then, towards the end of our training, we had a ten-day live-firing camp at the school of gunnery at Larkhill on Salisbury Plain. At the end of this, I basically knew that I didn't want to be a Gunner. My idea of soldiering centred around close-combat: fighting in trenches; jumping out of helicopters; shooting people; bayoneting them. Naïve maybe, but that's what I thought I wanted to do. But what I knew I didn't want to do was sit at the back of a heavy, noisy, dirty howitzer, shoving shells into the breach and engaging the enemy at ten to fifteen kilometres' range. I went to see the troop sergeant, who was a bit puzzled.

'Well, that's what we do, you silly bastard. If you didn't want to do that, why did you join the Gunners?'

Next stop was the troop commander, a second lieutenant with a pompous voice, a silly haircut and a vacancy for a brain. For some reason he started yacking on about regimental traditions and so forth. I gave up on him and asked to see the battery commander, Major Hall, an officer who had served with 29 Commando Regiment.

I explained my problem to the BC and he was sympathetic, but what he told me froze me in my tracks. As far as he was aware, it wasn't possible to go direct from basic training to airborne or commando units; he understood that you had to do three years with a normal field regiment first. This really screwed things up for me.

20

'In that case, I don't want to stay, sir,' I told him.

By this time I had been in long enough to have enough to buy myself out – or 'discharge by purchase' as the jargon had it – and the price was one hundred and fifty pounds. This was too much for most of the lads still with the squad, but because my pay had been going straight to my bank account, I could afford it. The only formality, after filling out various forms, was an interview in front of a board of officers. I filled out the forms, left my troop and went to the discharge block, awaiting my interview, which was to take place in two days' time.

My final interview began with me being marched into a small office and stood to attention in front of a group of officers, sitting behind a table with a small pile of files in front of them, mine at the top. The senior guy, a colonel, stood me at ease and then asked me to explain why I wanted to leave. I was going through it all again when one of the other board members, a major, I think, interrupted me.

'Excuse me, Colonel. It does actually say on his file that he was enlisted as a parachute volunteer.'

'Really? I've never heard of such a thing. Gunner Carew, wait outside a moment.'

I was marched back out and stood to attention outside, trying to make something out from the murmur of voices in the office. After a few minutes I was summoned back in.

'OK then, Gunner Carew, it is quite clear to us that you were enlisted on the basis that you would go to an airborne unit after you completed your training. Therefore, if we offer you the opportunity to do so, will you reconsider your decision to leave?'

I didn't hesitate:

'Yes, sir, if I can go airborne, I would like to withdraw my application to discharge.'

'I'm glad to hear it.' He tore my discharge forms in half and dumped them in the bin.

'It's time you rejoined your squad.'

I'd only missed two days of training so it didn't take long to catch up. There were only a couple of weeks of the course left and, before too long, we had our final 'passing-out' parade and that was it: we were soldiers.

After eighteen weeks' training, the army rewarded us with a couple of weeks' leave but, of course, I wasn't welcome at home so I stayed at Woolwich for the time being: at least it gave me the chance to explore London a bit. Then, when the leave period finished, I collected my kit together, got a lift from the duty vehicle down to the station and made my way back to Waterloo. From there it was a train to Reading, a change, and then on to Aldershot.

I subsequently found out that I'd gone to the wrong station: my destination was the 7th (Parachute) Regiment Royal Horse Artillery (7 RHA to their friends), and their local station was 'North Camp', but getting out at Aldershot gave me the chance to walk through the town centre, as well as the garrison. In those days, Aldershot was home to the 16th Parachute Brigade – of which 7 RHA was part – as well as a whole host of 'crap-hat' units, ranging from truckies to Gurkhas. After climbing an unpleasantly steep hill, lugging all my kit with me, I reached the top of Queen's Avenue, the main drag through the garrison, and began the long walk to 7 RHA.

Although I'd been in the army for several months now, I could sense that this was different. For a start, a lot of the soldiers were paratroopers, fitter and harder than the average squaddie, and looking the part in maroon berets, Denison smocks and denims. But the whole place had a sense of purpose about it as well; completely unlike a training depot. So it was a little disappointing to finally rock up at 7 RHA's barracks to find them more or less empty.

It turned out that the bulk of the regiment were on leave prior to deploying on an emergency tour in Northern Ireland, working in the IS role as infantrymen, making up the numbers as a result of the sudden onset of the crisis between the two communities. I checked in at the guardroom and was sent to report to a guy called Sergeant McQueenie, who was in charge of pre-parachute selection training while the rest of the staff were away.

McQueenie was a great bloke. As a young man, he'd had to make the choice between professional football and the army: he'd gone for the army. I arrived, straight out of training, to join a bunch of experienced regular soldiers who'd all volunteered for 7 RHA. I was a bit like a lamb to the slaughter; they had me polishing their boots, cleaning up after them and ironing their kit. It was McQueenie who put me straight on all that.

The idea with the 'pre-para' courses run by the major units in airborne forces is to get the 'All-Arms' volunteers ready for P-Company, the selection process for paratroopers. Me, and the others who'd arrived at 7 RHA with me, weren't members of the regiment until we'd passed P-Company, so, in the meantime, we spent our days doing PT of one kind or another and every other night – because the rest of the regiment were absent – on guard. One evening, after finishing my two-hour stag as 'prowler' sentry (a tedious task which meant walking round the barracks clutching a pick-axe handle for protection and a huge A41 radio for communications), the guard commander sent me up to the cookhouse to collect the rations for the rest of the guard, and a container of tea. On my way back, Thommo, the guy who'd taken over from me, grabbed me and told me:

'Okay, Crow, you're back on fucking stag.'

I was hauling the radio back on when I heard a shout.

'Oy! What are you two doing?'

Looking around, we saw Sergeant Mac trotting over from the RHQ.

'Why's he got that radio on again?'

'It's his stag.'

'Bollocks, he's just finished.'

What Thommo hadn't realised was that I'd bumped into

MacQueenie on my rounds and had a chat with him. Mac made him do one hundred press-ups for telling lies, and fifty sit-ups 'for the regiment'.

Next morning, after a run round Long Valley, we were in the gym. Thommo had been falling behind on the run and today he couldn't hack the gym work, even though he was normally one of the stronger performers. As a result, he spent the whole day with Sergeant Mac screaming at him. That evening, Thommo and I were detailed to clean up the gym, which involved brushing oiled sawdust over the floor. After fifteen minutes, Thommo said he was going to the bog; twenty minutes later he still hadn't returned when, unfortunately for him, Sergeant Mac turned up having been running a soccer coaching session for local kids. When he saw me on my own, he went ballistic; he stormed out to the lavatories and kicked the door to one of the cubicles open, where he found poor old Thommo in mid-wank, caught with his trousers very much down.

I was sent back to the block while Thommo spent the next hour or so being beasted round the gym by the sergeant, and then cleaning the floor on his own. I was fast asleep when Thommo got back to the block; unfortunately, really, because he took the opportunity to start filling me in. Next morning, when we paraded in our battle PT kit – red T-shirts, denim trousers, boots, helmets and webbing – my face was a bit of a mess: I had a black eye and a cut lip, along with various scratches and scrapes. Mac obviously saw this, and knew I hadn't been fighting downtown, so I suppose he drew his own conclusions.

The run that morning was a bastard: miles and miles over the Hog's Back, past the old PTI training school, through Ash and back along the old canal, led by Mac and a PT instructor from 23 Parachute Field Ambulance called Long John Pounder. Towards the end I could hear someone getting hell from Mac, and sure enough it turned out to be Thommo, falling behind again as the result of tiredness from being up late.

Back from the run we had time for a quick shower before a session in the gym. Today we were milling for the first time: a one-minute, no-rules boxing match during which, in order to prove that you are aggressive enough to be a Para, you attempt to punch the living shit out of an opponent of roughly similar size. It doesn't really matter whether you win or lose, provided that you keep punching and don't turn away.

The first pair went into the ring and beat the living daylights out of each other, then the second, then it was my turn. As it happened, Sergeant Mac had paired me off with Thommo. I'd done some boxing at school, but I realised that that was irrelevant now: I just had to go for it. I did. The frustration of two weeks of being bullied and fucked around by this guy came out and, in the end, they had to pull me off him.

Beating the shit out of Thommo did me a lot of good. I was no longer the course gopher and, instead, I became accepted as one of the lads. Thommo needed a couple of stitches in his eyebrow and when he got back from hospital I went to see him to shake hands, only to find that he'd decided to RTU himself. Shame.

Around this time, the rest of the regiment began to arrive back off leave and the intensity of our training began to pick up. Partly this was because the rest of the training-wing staff were now back, and partly because, with more soldiers about, we no longer had to do guard duty every other night so we weren't quite as shagged out as we had been. Having said that, one little fringe benefit was that members of the regiment would come down and ask us to do their guards for them at weekends – and pay us for it! This was a nice little earner and also meant that I got to know more of the 'real' members of the regiment (who were nice enough lads, even though you couldn't really be fully accepted by them until you'd earned the maroon beret and wings).

After two weeks' hard-core beasting, WO2 Carr, the training-wing sergeant major, read out the names of four of us who'd been selected to go through to P-Company. Mine was amongst them and, although I was very pleased with myself, I knew the worst was yet to come.

Sunday afternoon at 2 p.m. saw us forming up with our kit outside the block, waiting for the duty driver to transport us the short distance from Lille Barracks to Maida Barracks to begin P-Company itself. Once again we drew kit and then settled into our gloomy twelve-men rooms. One thing I noticed was that the mattresses that we were issued all had plastic covers; when I asked why, the CQMS told me that it was because at the end of the day, a lot of the candidates would be so shagged out that they would simply flop down on their beds in their dirty kit and crash out – or even wet themselves with sheer exhaustion – and that, as a result, the mattress-cleaning bills had become unsustainable!

The whole thing started in a fairly civilised manner on the Monday morning, with a couple of lectures and a visit to the airborne forces museum. That afternoon we had our first run, a fairly gentle affair alongside the old canal, and in the evening most of us were thinking that maybe it wasn't going to be as bad as we thought.

Of course, we were wrong. For the next two weeks we ran our arses off, bunny-hopped 'til our knees screamed and seal-crawled to hell and back; and that only took us to test week! We loaded into coaches and drove to Brecon to spend the next five days running up and down Pen y Fan and the other beacons, carrying various permutations of webbing, forty-pound A-frame rucksacks, stretchers loaded with paving slabs, logs, and all the rest of the paraphernalia. Shagged out at the end of it, we returned to Aldershot on the last Thursday of the course, ready to hear our results in the lecture room on the Friday morning.

The OC of P-Company, a major in the Parachute Regiment, read out the list of passes and fails. Together with about half the course, I'd passed, and to be honest, my reaction was relief more than anything else. I simply wasn't sure I was up to going through that whole experience again: my back was covered in blisters and grazes from running with a rucksack, my legs felt like they'd been stretched on a rack, and my feet were raw and mangled. Still, it was good to know that all I had to do now was the jumps course and I would be a fully fledged Para.

Of the four of us from 7 RHA, two of us had passed: me and Quammie, a black guy from London. In the Landrover on the way back to Lille Barracks, I threw my navy blue beret out of the window – I reckoned I wouldn't be needing it again – and when we arrived back at training wing, we were told to get down to the QM stores to draw our maroon berets and Denison smocks and then to get over to the adjutant's office. After we'd got there, he came out, shook our hands and simply said, 'Welcome to the Regiment', and that was it.

Over the next few days, I turned in all my old crap-hat gear and began to get to grips with all the new stuff I'd been issued. Webbing was a combination of 1944 pattern and the newer '58 pattern, but we also had bergens – which weren't on general issue in the army at that time – special parachute helmets, and all the straps and harnesses needed to secure our kit when jumping. There were two weeks before the next Para course started, so Sergeant Major Carr gave Quammie and me seven-day leave passes. Quammie had some bird in London and was off to the railway station like a rat up a drainpipe but, of course, I had nowhere to go, so I stayed on camp and put my feet up.

Some evenings I would go out on the town with the Parachute Regiment lads who'd been on P-Company with me, all of us dressed the same in maroon sweatshirt, Levi's jeans and desert boots, and all drinking in the special 'airborne' pubs dotted around town or eating hamburgers and chips at the Wimpy bar. Other nights I would stick to the quieter North Camp area where there was less chance of getting picked on by a gang of 'hats' and more chance of finding an available female to attempt to exercise my charms on. This was hard work; the Aldershot area was home to fifteen thousand or so testosterone-heavy squaddies, all on the look-out for a bunk-up. Opportunities with local girls were few and far between and there was a big danger that members of the WRAC or QARANC would turn out to be lesbians. In the meantime, I kept my fitness up with a few runs, even though it just wasn't quite the same without a screaming PTI on your back the whole time; anyway, the hangovers tended to militate against a big effort.

So, two weeks after completing P-Company, Quammie and I clambered back into the duty vehicle to drive up to Browning Barracks, the Parachute Regiment depot. When we got there, we transferred into Bedfords with a bunch of Para Regiment lads and headed off in convoy to RAF Abingdon and the parachute school. After P-Company, the jumps course was like a holiday. We'd go for a run every morning with the instructors, but they weren't trying to beast us, just keep us switched on. Most of the day was spent practising emplaning drills, exit drills, landing rolls, equipment packing and all the safety drills we needed to avoid obstacles like power lines and trees, as well as learning what to do when we had problems like twists and lines over.

After a week of this, the time came for the first jump, which took place from the basket of a tethered balloon at eight hundred feet above the airfield. It was a fine day, with no wind to speak of and somehow or other I got to be the second man out of the first stick. The most unnerving thing about the whole experience was how quiet it was. Apart from the creaking of the basket and the slight whistling sounds from the balloon cables, the loudest sound I could hear was the blood pounding round my ears and the occasional bad-taste jokes of the instructors. The balloon stopped and we waited a few moments while the PJIs made a last quick check that we were ready, then the first man was tapped on the shoulder, took a step forward and disappeared from view. Once they were happy that his canopy was open and everything was all right, it was my turn. My heart was in my mouth and my knees suddenly felt like they were about to buckle as I took up position in the opening at the side of the basket. I felt a tap on my shoulder and stepped out: there was a rush of air as I fell and a crack as the canopy opened. I started to look around, but almost immediately I could hear a voice amplified through a megaphone yelling at me to prepare to land. I started to organise myself but before I could do anything sensible, I hit the ground like a sack of spuds, landing in a great heap of arms, legs and parachute. I'd done it.

Next step was the C-130 Hercules. I'd never flown at all before going up in the balloon, and this was certainly my first go in an aircraft. We had one familiarisation flight, during which the pilot's chief objective seemed to be to make us all as airsick as possible, and then we started jumping. Once again, the procedures were carefully followed, and during the course we always went out with the correct spacing, something that never happened back at the brigade, when everyone would pile out in a big bundle so they didn't have too far to walk back to the rally point on the ground. With eight jumps completed, including a couple with full kit and one at night, we were awarded our wings and sent back to Aldershot.

As soon as I arrived back, I was straight down to the tailors to get my wings sewn on to my smock, shirts, jumpers and Number Two dress uniform. Some of the lads also had them tattooed on their shoulders, and others put them on their pyjamas, or so the story went; personally, I don't think I ever saw a Para wearing pyjamas.

Lille Barracks was strangely quiet when we got back and it didn't take too long too discover why: conditions were deteriorating in Northern Ireland and the regiment's deployment had been brought forward. They'd all gone. Quammie's and my heart sank; we had visions of spending the next four months doing day-on, day-off guard duties, but after we reported to the families' officer, who was acting as OC Rear Party, we were told that we would be joining 2 Para temporarily for internal security training and then going out to join the lads in Belfast.

The IS training was great fun. Basically, the skills we learnt were infantry techniques: setting up roadblocks, patrolling, riot control and so on, and this was really why I'd joined the army; it was what I wanted to do. Of course, I'd naïvely joined the Royal Artillery without appreciating their different basic role, so it was great to finally start doing the stuff I'd been aiming to do all along.

We spent a month with 2 Para and then the pair of us flew out to Palace Barracks at Holywood in Belfast where 1 Para were based. 1 Para were doing a two-year 'residential' tour at this point, as opposed to the four-month 'emergency' tour that 7 RHA were on, so they had the job of training individual reinforcements who came out to the province. After a few days with 1 Para, we were sent off to the Grand Central Hotel (GCH) at the foot of the Falls Road, which was our regimental headquarters and the base for operations in the Markets district, and there I finally joined F Battery as a fully fledged member of 7 RHA.

Once you were through all the training, and had proved that you had what it takes, they were a remarkably friendly bunch. Characters that stuck out in my troop included Sid Burgess and his brother; and two black guys, also brothers, one of whom was well over six feet tall, whilst the other was a more modest five feet four inches, and as result they were known as 'Shaft' and 'Half-Shaft' after the film character.

These were wild times in Belfast. Mostly our job consisted of escorting the RUC on foot patrol round the area, and we rarely got away without being stoned with broken-up paving slabs, bricks and bottles. More often than not, we'd face petrol bombs as well, and every day brought a crop of post office vans and buses being hijacked and burned out. Towards the end of our tour, a big contact took place in the Markets, which ended with our guys killing two provos. For this whole period we lived on our nerves and on adrenaline: we lived in unbelievably crowded conditions, piled up in three-tier bunk beds in tiny cubicles, whilst operations continued around us twenty-four hours a day. Call me crazy, but I loved it.

That first Northern Ireland tour flashed by and in no time we were back in Aldershot for leave and then a short spell of 'normal' duties, followed by a re-training package for redeployment to Northern Ireland and yet another emergency tour. This formed the pattern of our lives for the next two years; most of the time, if we weren't actually in Northern Ireland, we were either getting ready to go there or just coming back, simply because, as the airborne Gunner regiment, we didn't have to take our turn doing tours of duty in Germany or at the other overseas garrisons.

In the odd breaks from Northern Ireland duty, we continued with our training as parachute Gunners and I began to learn my military trade as a driver/signaller. This came about by accident: one day I was reversing a Landrover out of the vehicle hangar when the battery commander spotted me. He went ape! He knew full well that I hadn't passed my test, and if I hadn't held a provisional licence, I would have really been in the shit. Instead, because there was already a shortage of drivers, and after ascertaining that I'd been driving since I was old enough to see over the steering wheel, he sent me to see Major Benn, the MTO, to organise a driving test.

As well as being MTO, it so happened that Major Benn was a 'qualified testing officer', or QTO, and when he learned that I knew how to drive a Landrover, he decided to give me a test there and then. We got in the vehicle and he asked me to drive round camp a little, stop at a junction, reverse round a corner and then asked me a few questions from the highway code. Bingo! I'd passed my driving test at the first time of asking without ever taking a lesson (normally QTOs apply the same standards as civvy driving examiners, but we were fairly pushed at the time; one officer I spoke to told me that he knew he was going to pass his test when the QTO, a Guards colour-sergeant, came to attention and saluted him at the start and finish!).

A couple of weeks later – and after a few lessons this time, I admit – I took my HGV class 3, and passed that too. Next step was signalling. The Royal Artillery has some of the best signallers in the army, and for a good reason: if you start to drop 105mm artillery shells in the wrong place, or MLRS strikes for that matter, people start to get pretty pissed off. Consequently, on artillery radio nets, speed and precision are everything.

I was pulled back from our second Ulster tour to do the B3 signals course back at our training wing in Aldershot. Shortly after it started, I noticed that Sergeant Prentice, our instructor, wore different parachute wings on his shirt. On normal wings, the light blue wings pointed downwards, but on his, the wings were dark blue and light blue and pointed upwards. I asked one of the other lads what this was all about and he told me that it meant Sergeant Prentice had been in the SAS. It meant nothing to me then, but over the next few weeks I saw there were other people in the regiment who had the same thing, including Major Rice, my battery commander, and Sergeant Taff Rogers. I suppose this piqued my curiosity, because a couple of weeks later I was helping Taff Rogers fit a radio in my lightweight Landrover, and I started to ask him about the SAS: what it did, who was in it, and all that sort of thing. To my surprise, he was quite reticent about it, and after avoiding giving me any answers for several minutes told me:

'Listen, son, if you want to know about the SAS, that's fine: put in a couple of years' hard work here first, prove you can do the job properly and then come back and ask me, then I'll tell you all about it.' In other words: fuck off until you're older.

I rejoined the regiment at the Flax Street Mill base in West Belfast and got back to work; but this time, when I was on the street, it was as a signaller, and this, through a series of odd coincidences, led me to finding out much more about the mysterious SAS regiment.

I hadn't been back long when, during the course of an intern-ment arrest, some miserable old bag stabbed me with a knitting needle. This got me five days of tedious light duties back in the ops room after which I was released back onto the streets. However, I'd done about two more days' patrolling when I got caught by a nail-bomb explosion. I wasn't actually badly hurt, much to my own surprise, collecting a few cuts and bruises, but once again it meant more ops-room time for me. The final straw came two weeks after this when, having gone out on riot control duties as radio operator, I managed to collect a big lump of paving stone on my head. Normally this would have been OK, because it would have bounced off my steel Para helmet, but because I was carrying the radio and had to wear a headset, I couldn't wear a helmet and had a beret on instead. The upshot of this was concussion and fourteen stitches: not a good day out!

I was sent back to Aldershot to recover, and after fourteen days of bed rest, I was completely pissed off and desperate to find something to do. Once I'd had the stitches out and got clearance from the medics to do light duties, I was given the job of driving for Major Benn, who was commanding the elements of the regiment that were still in Aldershot.

I hadn't been doing this long when some kind of signals exercise came up at Larkhill. Major Benn was taking part, along with several other officers and senior NCOs, and I went along to drive. Major Benn was yet another of these strange ex-SAS men, and no sooner had we pulled up outside the officers' mess at Larkhill, when he spotted an officer wearing a commando beret and jumped out of the Landrover to talk to him. As I sat there, I saw that he also wore SAS wings, and it began to appear to me that these guys represented a sort of special family within the army. It didn't seem to matter what rank they were, they were always laughing and joking with each other like equals, but at the same time, they were all notably professional and good at their jobs. Later, when I was driving him around on the training area, I asked him about the SAS and how you joined it.

'By working bloody hard, Carew, that's how!' He thought for a moment, and then said, 'Sergeant Rogers said you'd ask me. Didn't he answer your questions?'

'No, sir, he said to wait a few years.'

Major Benn laughed, but didn't add anything, so I dropped the subject.

But the negative responses I got when I asked direct questions didn't put me off – if anything they increased my interest in the subject, and as time went by I did begin to learn what the SAS was all about. I liked what I heard; it seemed to me to be the essence of pure soldiering, elevated to a high level; and it was something I wanted to be a part of. I now knew that fitness played a big part in getting into the SAS, so I began to work on that; and I knew that I would need to be able to map-read at speed and under pressure, so I started practising that as well. Eventually, in September 1972, I formed up in the orderly room, collected the application form for the SAS, filled it out and submitted it. The die was now cast.

It was the first Sunday in February 1973 when I arrived at Bradbury Lines barracks in Hereford for the first time, and although I was somewhat nervous with the anticipation of what I knew was going to be a horrendously tough course, I wasn't over-impressed by what I saw. The reality was that the world's premier special forces regiment lived in a shabby, clapped-out Second-World-War-hutted camp in a suburb of a small West Country cathedral city. It was a nice quiet place, certainly, but it didn't look like the nerve centre of a major operation.

But looks can be deceptive. I'd been given a month off work before the start of the course to get fit, and I'd taken the opportunity to head down to Dering Lines in Brecon so that I could accustom myself to tabbing round the hills. Brecon was like an airborne reunion: together with me and Gordon from 7 RHA, there was Alan Baron, Gordon Hampton and Don Murray from 1 Para; Victor, Mungo, Dan and Ginge Cardew from 2 Para; Martin Duggan from 3 Para; Jock Heron and Ken Morton from 9 Squadron (the airborne sappers), as well as a slack handful from the Guards parachute company and the Royal Armoured Corps parachute squadron.

Over the next four weeks we spent our time slogging around in groups, working on our fitness and, importantly, our map reading. The normal procedure was that ten or so of us would sign out two Landrovers and drive out to opposite ends of the route we were planning to do that day. Then we would arrange to RV in the middle where we could exchange vehicle keys, which meant that we didn't have to do circular routes, and that if somebody broke their leg, we wouldn't have to walk twenty miles to fetch a vehicle.

The pre-training meant that we were about as well prepared as we could be for the course. The advantage of being in the Para brigade was that there were a lot of guys around who'd done selection and failed, for one reason or another, and a fair number who'd passed but had eventually come back. As a result there was quite a broad pool of knowledge about what to expect on the course: for example, when we were at Brecon, we had copies of the routes the guys had walked on the summer selection before us, which was a big confidence builder, but we were also accustomed to pushing ourselves hard and there was a good team spirit to get us over the hills.

The month at Brecon passed quickly – time flies when you're having fun – and in no time at all I found myself checked in at the training wing office and queuing up at the stores counter for kit issue. We didn't get much: a bergen, belt-kit, a wad of maps, a compass, foul-weather clothing, and one twenty-four-hour ration pack in case we got lost in the mountains. I took this lot off to my room, shared with eleven others, then went and collected some sheets and blankets for my bed. The accommodation was pretty grotty: the buildings were what the army calls 'spiders', wooden huts built around a central ablutions block, and these ones had definitely seen better days. In fact, the whole camp was made up of these, but the squadron's were better maintained and more comfortable, and had been personalised by their occupants to give them some privacy from each other.

Once everything was stowed away, there was nothing much to do until we paraded at 08.00 the next morning; so after a big meal in the cookhouse, a few of us drifted down town for a couple of pints and a bag of chips before coming back for an early night. Next morning, there were 120 of us on parade outside training wing. As I said, a lot of us were from 16 Parachute Brigade, but there was a sprinkling of green commando berets, a handful of RAF Regiment lads and a great plethora of navy blue berets from the rest of the army. But most extraordinary of all was the man standing in between me and Martin Duggan.

There were several things that were immediately noticeable about him. Whilst everybody else there was wearing olive green denim trousers, puttees, shirts and camouflaged Denison or combat smocks, this guy was wearing a set of gungey green overalls. Round his ankles he wore a pair of old canvas gaiters and on his head he had a dirty, dark blue beret about the same size and shape as a dustbin lid; where the rest of us wore the relatively new '58 pattern webbing belt, he had an old Second World War belt, stained black with oil.

I was taking this in when a lean, tough-looking soldier, wearing the sand-coloured beret of the SAS, strolled out in front of us, wearing a distinctive camouflaged windproof smock and carrying a clipboard. He started speaking in a soft Geordie accent.

'Good morning, gentlemen, my name is WO2 Lillico and I'm the training wing sergeant major, responsible for putting you through selection. Before we start, there are a few things I want to talk to you about.

'Firstly: discipline. In this regiment, we try not to impose discipline from above; we expect you to be disciplined enough for us not to have to do it. This means that if you are given an instruction or a timing, you will meet it.

'This brings me on to the daily detail: every day we will put the detail for the next day up on the training wing notice board; it is your responsibility to read it; it will contain everything you need to know for the next day. If you can't be bothered to read it, you might as well collect your travel warrant now: you won't last here.'

After this lecture, and various other points, Lillico and the other DS began to walk down the line, handing out white badges with red numbers on them. When he reached the strange-looking guy next to me, he did a quick double take.

'What the fuck are you?'

'Sapper Palmer, sir.'

'When we've finished this parade, you and me are going to have a little talk in my office. You two,' he pointed at me and Martin.

'Sir.'

'You two come with him.'

With everything sorted out we scuttled off to Sergeant Major Lillico's office, together with the strange-looking sapper. We waited outside, unable to hear what was being said within, until the door was opened and the sergeant major stood there, clutching a sheet of paper in his hand; he passed it to me.

'This is a list of what he needs. Take him down to the stores and make sure he gets it, and then make sure he knows how to put it on!' He limped back to his desk: he'd had half his arse shot away in a firefight in Borneo ten years before and was lucky to be alive, let alone still in the army. We went off and got the kit: denims, shirts, combat jacket, puttees and so on, then took it back to the training wing basha to help him put it all on. It turned out he was Tommy Palmer, a Scot who'd come from a

Field Engineer Squadron where he spent most of his time digging holes. Somewhere or other, he did have combats and all the rest of the stuff, but he never had to wear it; as a result, he looked much more like a farmer than a soldier and his general military skills were just as dodgy. Even so, he wasn't stupid, and he was as fit as a butcher's dog. Prior to his tragic death in a car accident in Northern Ireland, he was destined to become one of the SAS's great characters.

The next two weeks panned out much the way I expected; we did runs and marches, interspersed with lessons in map reading and basic military skills, just to make sure that we were all singing off the same hymn sheet. As Geordie Lillico had said, everything we needed to know was written up on the daily detail which was posted up in training wing every afternoon; this told us when we needed to be at the guardroom to draw weapons, when to parade, what we should be wearing, how much weight to put in our bergens and so on. What it didn't tell us was where we were going. Some days we would be in the Brecon Beacons, other days we might go to the Black Mountain or the Elan Valley; and so we always carried the full set of maps.

By the end of the second week we'd lost about a third of the course, as guys dropped out through injury or just decided they'd had enough and jacked their hand in. But then came the real tester, a charming little exercise called 'Sickener'. For most of selection, the attitude of the DS was of carefully cultivated indifference: they didn't encourage or discourage you, they just told you what they wanted you to do, and watched how you did it. This was because we were meant to be self-motivated: if we wanted to pass the course, then we would push ourselves to do it. But Sickener was the opposite of that: over a three-day period we were beasted around the hills of the Elan Valley, often piss-wet through or frozen, getting very little sleep and constantly being shouted at by the DSs – Joe Coulson and Hirohito Jones, in my case – who both seemed to be having a thoroughly enjoyable time. They made a very public bet on who could induce more members of their squads to jack it in.

At the end of Sickener, the squad was down to just thirty-seven lads out of the original one hundred and twenty. We now had one day off before starting test week. I'm not going to bore on about how hard that was; everybody's heard all the stories by now. I reached the end of 'Endurance' absolutely fucked and, in the back of the Bedford that took us back to Bradbury Lines, there were just nine of us left who'd made the time. I was sitting with Ginge Cardew and Spike Baron, and all we could think was: 'Thank fuck that's over with!'

Endurance wasn't the end of it, of course, but it was the beginning of the end. The next phase was continuation training: weapons skills, tactics, first-aid and so on, but if I'm honest, I took to it all like a duck to water. At the end of the course, there were just a handful of us left who'd passed, together with a couple of guys who hadn't quite made the grade but were near enough misses to merit being kept on with the regiment until they could retake the tests they'd failed. Those of us who were already para-trained were now told where we would be spending the next few months: in Dhofar where Operation STORM was in full swing and the regiment was committed to fighting against a full-scale Communist insurgency.

I spent the next six years in the SAS doing a wide range of tasks. These included a couple of tours in Oman on 'Storm' and a long period helping to set up the Northern Ireland cell. My involvement in this came about for the simple reason that I was one of the small number of people in the regiment young enough to have served there: most of the old and bold spent the early '70s in and out of Oman, and contrary to rumour, there was no significant SAS involvement in Northern Ireland until 1976.

But although I enjoyed the work, I can't claim I was altogether happy. There were two major problems, and the first of these was that I got married.

In my case, all the old clichés about getting married were true: we were too young and we didn't really understand the full ramifications of what we were getting into. Debbie, my new wife, was a Scots girl who was living locally. Then, as now, the inhabitants of the town of Hereford have always had a soft spot for the SAS. There can't be many garrisons in Britain, or elsewhere, where the soldiers are so well-behaved. But what the women who marry into the SAS rarely appreciate is the amount of separation that they will have to endure from husbands who are, it has to be said, undeniably enthusiastic about their work and anxious for the next challenge.

The second problem, which stemmed from the first, was money. In those days, SAS soldiers didn't get paid any extra, apart from parachute pay. If you were already parachute qualified, you had to take a pay cut to join the regiment. This led to a ludicrous situation, with people finishing work in the afternoon and then rushing off to do second jobs in the evening in order to earn enough money to pay off the mortgage, or whatever. In my time, lads were working as stewards at the Hereford United football ground, taking shifts at local factories, working as bouncers at clubs across the West Midlands and, in my particular case, operating the slicing machine at a local bakery. Not necessarily the best preparation for a day job which could be somewhat fraught, to say the least.

In consequence, when, in the autumn of 1979, I was offered the opportunity to 'sign off' to work for a private military company doing an outside job in Asia, I didn't hesitate, although I would first need to leave the SAS. The requirement was to train the Sri Lankan Army's special forces to enable them to prosecute their war against Tamil Tiger guerillas. At that point, things had reached such a pitch of brutality that, even if the Sri Lankan authorites had approached the British Government with a request for UK military or SAS training assistance, there was no way that our Government were going to agree. The Sri Lankans realised this, and instead turned to a private company. I left the Army and went out to Sri Lanka soon after.

In practical terms, this didn't make much difference to me: I was still getting paid, albeit from a different source, and I was still working with the same kind of people; and it was undoubtedly an interesting job.

TWO

We got back from Sri Lanka to find that the whole SAS world had changed, more or less overnight. On 5 May 1980, B Squadron had stormed the Iranian Embassy in London, which was being held by a gang of Iraqi-sponsored terrorists, and suddenly we were flavour of the month: no more night shifts at local factories! Within the next few months everything was turned on its head as budgets miraculously increased, special forces pay was introduced and the whole world recognised what we had always known: you don't mess with the SAS!

Pissed off that I'd missed out on it, but pleased for the lads who'd been there, I was now in the market for a new project. I was still a civilian and at home in Hereford, when I received a phone call: would I report to a certain office building in London tomorrow morning in the company of Paddy Egan and 'Darkie' Davidson? I was happy to oblige.

After an early start, Paddy, Darkie and I arrived in London at about 10 a.m. and quickly made our way to our destination:

Roebuck House, a large office building in Stag Place in West-minster, just between Victoria Station and Buckingham Palace. At reception, we were shown to a waiting area and sat twiddling our thumbs for a while until a young female secretary appeared and led us to the lifts. We went up several floors and arrived at a large open-plan office, buzzing with activity. The girl led us past small knots of men and women earnestly discussing Christ knows what; rattling typewriters and humming telex machines; maps and charts.

She showed us into a small partitioned cubicle, shielded from the sight of the rest of the office but not the sound, took orders for tea and coffee and left us sitting round a Formica-topped conference table. A few moments later, we were joined by two men: an Englishman in his late forties or early fifties, and a Middle-Easterner of some sort. The Englishman spoke first:

'Morning, gents! I'm so sorry to have kept you waiting. Journey down OK? My name is Sir William Lindsay-Hogg and I'm co-ordinating Operation FARADAY.'

Without waiting for a response, he continued.

'We've got a bit of a job for you; we want you to put together a training syllabus for us.'

He didn't introduce the Arab.

The tea and coffee arrived and we settled into the briefing. The requirement was to plan a training programme for a group of approximately one hundred 'Middle-Eastern' irregulars so that they could operate successfully in a mountainous environment against a well-trained modern army. Fair enough as a starting point, but we needed more information to go on. Where would this be taking place? The Middle East. Where in the Middle East? Can't tell you, sorry. OK, what about weapons and stores? Whatever you need, within reason, but all weapons will be Soviet-bloc manufactured.

When we'd extracted as much information as we could, the three of us retired to a quiet back office to start work. In the

44

British army, planning a training programme is a pretty straight-forward process: you go from lesson one to lesson twenty (or whatever) in an orderly sequence using the correct training aids and methods of instruction. Unfortunately, this doesn't always work out when you're training guerrillas and the key to it all is flexibility. Darkie had done a lot of this kind of work, and so, for the next four or five hours, he took the lead as we methodically examined the various factors involved and produced an outline plan.

We finished work mid-afternoon and handed over our notes to Sir William. He told us to take an hour's break to give them time to look over our work.

We didn't have much time so the three of us nipped over the road to McDonalds in Victoria Street for a quick burger. Sitting there, watching priests and nuns scurrying in and out of Westminster Cathedral, brought back memories of my schooldays at a Catholic boarding school in Dorset: there's no denying it, cliché or not, it is a funny old world. If you'd asked me then what I thought I'd be doing on a May afternoon fifteen years later, I'd have told you I'd be on a farm in Dorset, not planning mayhem in the Middle East. Well, there you go!

Filled up with burgers and chips, we walked back to the office building. Back in his cubicle, Sir William thanked us for our work, told us that he would be putting our plan up for approval and added that he would be in touch. We left him and made our way back to Victoria station to catch the tube to Paddington and the train back to Hereford.

Back then the train ride to Hereford lasted about four hours and for the typical SAS group would involve the consumption of significant quantities of beer along the way – merely to pass the time, you understand – but on this occasion we were somewhat subdued. The reason for this wasn't difficult to grasp: we were all thinking about FARADAY and was it a 'go' or a 'no go'. The little that we knew about it was tantalising, to say the least. There were several hot spots in the Middle East at that time – the ayatollah's Iran being a good example – and the idea that we might be in on the start of a major operation was strongly attractive.

I got home at about half past eleven to find that my wife and baby daughter were asleep. I thought about bed but I realised I was too wired to get to sleep, and instead I sat downstairs in my living room, re-reading my notes, wondering if we'd missed anything. After an hour or so, I heard footsteps on the stairs and looked up to see Debbie. She saw my notes laid on the coffee table in front of me.

'You're off again then?'

She didn't ask anything else. Like most SAS wives, she knew by now that I couldn't tell her.

I was up at half past six the next morning and straight into a run around my usual seven-mile route along farm tracks and paths. After a shower and a bowl of cornflakes I went into Hereford to call in at the camp and then pick up some stuff in the town centre. When I got home there was a message to phone in.

'Tom, can you get back to London, on your own this time?'

No problem.

I drove to the station and got myself on the next London train, arriving in the early afternoon. Back at the office, I was met by Sir William who now had an American with him:

'Tom, good to see you back. Let me introduce John Miley from the US Defence Intelligence Agency. We're working together on FARADAY and we have a task for you, if you're interested, of course.'

'Sure, what do you want me to do?'

'We're very interested in finding out what is going on inside Afghanistan, and we would like you to go out there and do some reconnaissance for us.'

He pulled back a curtain on the wall to reveal a map.

'There are two areas we want you to look at: down in the south at Ber-Mel near Kandahar; and here, further north, at Wazir, which is close to Jellalabad.'

Afghanistan, I thought. Fucking hell! Just before Christmas, the Soviets had launched a full-scale invasion, leading to one of the major crises of the cold war so far. In the interim six months we knew that they'd been attempting to consolidate their hold on the country against opposition from the 'Mujahideen' resistance, and that what amounted to open warfare was being waged, with no holds barred. This was not going to be a picnic in the hills.

'Well OK, when do you want me to go?'

'We'd like you to fly out to Pakistan on Saturday night.'

It was Thursday afternoon.

'Fine, what do I need to take?'

'You'll be there for a week or two, just take what you think you'll need.'

Their final remarks were about operational security:

'This operation is completely clandestine. Don't mention it to anybody, including Paddy and Darkie. They do not need to know anything about it.'

I got the train back to Hereford, and after I'd collected my car and driven home, I told my wife that I was away on Saturday for about two weeks, but 'expect me when you see me'. It was a routine we'd been through before.

I spent Friday sorting out my personal kit. I took a bergen, a set of windproofs, OG trousers, boots and so on, together with my belt kit and a small medical pack. I had a big civilian duffle bag which I loaded it all in to, and that was it, I was ready to go. That evening, I had a quiet dinner with my wife, too preoccupied about the job to be good company, and early the next morning she drove me down to the station.

I reached Victoria on Saturday lunchtime. First priority was a briefing from the American, John Miley, and an anonymous British man whom I later discovered was called Loughlin. The mission priorities were, firstly, to recce potential training areas, and, secondly – it was now revealed – to try to obtain examples of various items of Soviet equipment. This made sense to me; in fact it seemed more realistic than attempting to set up training camps in hostile territory. It turned out they were particularly interested in any bits I could get of the new MI-24 Hind helicopter, the AK- 74 rifle, the AGS-17 grenade launcher, the RPG-18 anti-tank rocket and any NBC equipment I could locate.

I thought for a few moments:

'Look, what do you really want me to do – recce the training areas or get the equipment?'

'Definitely recce the training areas as a first priority, but try to get as much gear as you can.'

They went on to brief me about contacts on the ground, potential safe houses, cover stories and the rest of the paraphernalia of covert operations. Finally, they gave me a small Olympus Pen-EE 3 half-frame 35mm camera and told me that Sir William would be travelling with me as the operation controller on the ground. And that was it.

'Good luck.'

Well thanks, I thought.

Maybe it's a class thing but for some reason, when we checked in at the British Airways desk at Heathrow's Terminal Three a couple of hours later, I discovered that Sir William had a seat up front in first class, while I was jammed in the back in 'weasel'.

It was a long old flight in a 747 packed to the gunwales with screaming Pakistani children and their parents, all heading home for one reason or another. I managed a couple of hours sleep, but most of the time I spent reading a trashy paperback thriller, trying to keep my mind off the hullabaloo which surrounded me. We had a short stop at Amman and arrived at Islamabad on Sunday lunchtime, in time to get through immigration and make a connecting internal flight to Peshawar.

We travelled into Peshawar from the airport in a rackety old Buick taxi, decorated with strings of beads and brightly coloured pictures. I'm not going to claim that Hereford is the most sophisticated town in the world – far from it – but in comparison to Peshawar, it looked like one of those cities of the future that used to be depicted in kids' comics in the 1950s. The whole town was full of dusty, dirty, amputee beggars, speckled with scabs and sores, as well as being knee-deep in donkey shit and dust.

Peshawar had the bustling purposeful air of a frontier town – which, of course, it is – and was packed to bursting with armed men: Pakistani army, Frontier Police, armed tribesmen and Afghan Mujahideen, all mingling with journalists, film crews, aid workers and all the other testosterone-tourists from the war-groupie flying circus. Passing down the Mall past the glowering red-brick Bala Hissar fort, we took the main Khyber road out towards our hotel, the five-star Khyber Intercontinental which sat, somewhat incongruously, next to an immaculately maintained golf course. We checked in, and after I'd dropped my bags in my room, I washed away the dust of travel with a long, relaxing swim in the hotel pool.

After my swim I lay down for twenty minutes and then got dressed in some clean gear ready for dinner. Being a Muslim country, the rules on drinking alcohol were quite strict: non-Muslims were allowed to drink beer, in the bar only, provided you had a permit, which you had to keep in your passport. If you wanted to drink beer with your meal, then you had to take your meal in the bar. Fair enough. Sir William and I sat down with our ice-cold beers in a quiet corner, out of the way of the various journalists who were knocking around, and began to peruse the extensive menu. After about ten minutes, the waiter asked if we'd made our choice: we had. I wanted a steak; Sir William asked for some chicken dish. Reality brought us back down to earth: there was beef curry, mutton curry or fish curry, all served with rice. I decided on the mutton.

There was no question of a run the following morning, but when I got down to the restaurant at 7 a.m. that Monday, I was surprised to find I more or less had the place to myself. I piled into a big breakfast of cornflakes, eggs, bread and tea, and waited for Sir William to join me. An hour or so later I was still waiting. Bollocks to this, I thought, and went back up to my room. Around nine, there was a knock at my door and Sir William came in, dressed in a rather dapper lightweight suit with a tie: he'd taken his breakfast in his room, every inch the Englishman abroad.

Our first task was to pay a visit to the Mujahideen. We called down to the lobby and ordered a taxi to take us out of town to a place called Fackeyrabad, the headquarters of the Hezb-i-Islami Mujahideen faction. We arrived at their compound, situated close by the bazaar, and within a very few minutes were called in to see the leader, Gulbuddin Hekmatyar.

Hekmatyar was an immensely tall, good-looking middle-aged man, dressed in traditional Afghan clothes, evidently very well educated and able to speak perfect English (I later learned that he had been a professor of engineering at the American University in Kabul). Immediately, he and Sir William began a deep discussion of various issues and, as they continued, it began to become clear to me that operation FARADAY wasn't just some spur-of-the-moment scheme to grab an opportunity to piss the Soviets off: it was big; in fact, very big.

Obviously, it's one of the cardinal rules of covert operations that you don't ask too many questions: if you don't know something, you can't subsequently be made to spill the beans. 'Need to know' is absolute: you know enough to be able to do your job properly, and not an iota more if you can help it. This is counterintuitive: people are naturally inquisitive; but it is essential, and it's a habit you pick up quickly. Consequently, I hadn't made any effort to discover who was sponsoring the operation. The presence of John Miley, the American, and the whole set-up in Victoria made it obvious that this was a major project, and anyway, you didn't need to be Einstein to guess which agencies were behind the whole thing. So, as Sir William and the Afghan leader began to go through the intricate details of operations that were clearly not connected to my task, I slipped out of the way so that I wouldn't overhear anything.

Some time later, while I was dozing in a chair outside Hekmatyar's office, Sir William came looking for me.

'OK, Tom, it's all fixed. Your first trip starts Wednesday.'

I killed a couple of days acclimatising in Peshawar, taking a couple of gentle runs round the golf course, swimming in the pool and looking round the local area until, on the Wednesday morning, William and I piled aboard an F27 for the internal flight to Quetta.

We got there to find that the only good hotel was full – all six rooms of it! Instead, after a bit of faffing about, we came across a 'one-star' (ho, ho!) establishment called the 'Bloom Star'. When I got to my room I found it contained a bed, a tap with a bucket under it and a ceiling fan so rickety it was like trying to sleep under the rotors of a Huey gunship. Pulling aside a curtain, I found the crapper consisted of a hole in the ground with a pair of foot positions either side to assist with the aim. Nice.

There was a knock at the door and William came in. Like most people who travel a lot – and people in his line of business tend to get about a bit – he wasn't that interested in hard-arsing it; he preferred his creature comforts. Still, he brightened up when he saw my room. Evidently it was worse than his.

'Christ Almighty, it's primitive down here!' he laughed. 'Listen, I'm going into town to make contact with Hekmatyar's boys. You'd better keep a low profile, so stay around here, OK.' And with that he was off, complete with straw hat, suit and tie.

I gave him ten minutes and then followed, not for any sinister reason but because I'd realised that, in the overpowering heat, my ensemble of T-shirt and jeans was going to be hideously uncomfortable very soon. I nipped down to the bazaar and was soon kitted out in a pair of light, cotton Afghan pants: just the thing for the debonair man-about-town.

Quetta looked like a scene from a Clint Eastwood spaghetti western: the sun was blindingly bright, but visibility was only about twenty-five or thirty metres because of the clouds of dense dust kicked up by camel trains, jeeps and the occasional large truck. All the men wore a kind of turban drawn across their faces against the dust, and carried Kalashnikovs, or Lee-Enfield .303 rifles, slung over their shoulders on brightly coloured woven straps, along with pistols and daggers tucked into their belts; the women were nowhere to be seen.

I got back to the hotel to find that William had also returned, accompanied by an Afghan, and that they were going over the plans for my first trip into Afghanistan. The idea was that I should wear Afghan clothing, and join up with a group of Mujahideen who would be crossing over the next morning. William was insistent that I should carry no form of identity papers, nor take any kind of western clothing or equipment, with the exception of my camera and a thousand or so US dollars as a float. This bothered me: I was unhappy about leaving my belt kit behind because I knew that in extremis I could live off its contents for a week or so while I sorted out any problems that had arisen. On the other hand, the Afghan assured me that weapons would be available once I was inside the country, which was reassuring: at least I would have some chance of preventing myself falling into the hands of Soviet intelligence. William told me to go back to the bazaar to buy some more Afghan clothes but I suggested that the Mujahideen went instead – he would attract less attention – and I spent the next few hours studying the maps to familiarise myself with my area of operations before turning in for an early kip.

Next morning I was up and about around 2.30 a.m., and by 3.45 a.m. we were ready to go. William had been pacing nervously around as I had my breakfast, looking increasingly agitated, and as I clambered into the back seat of the dilapidated Cherokee Jeep that was taking me into Afghanistan, he grabbed my hand and shook it.

'Look . . . God's speed, Tom. Just . . . just keep out of trouble, OK? Good luck.'

'Sure William, I'll see you in a few days.'

The driver pulled out from the hotel forecourt and away we went.

We weren't very far from the border, but it took us five hours before we eventually crossed into Afghanistan. At this time the war was still hot news and the Pakistani Frontier Police were fighting a small campaign trying to stop half the world's foreign correspondents from making unauthorised border crossings. Every few miles we seemed to run into a new VCP or Police control, where my two Mujahideen escorts had to try to bluff us through. I don't know what they said – my Pushtu was pretty basic at this point – but it worked, and as the Jeep rattled along a dusty track my guide turned round in his seat and told me:

'Now we are in Afghanistan.'

We carried on for a while in the same direction, heading towards a town called Spinboldak, but just before we reached it the driver made a sharp right into some very rough terrain, and we began to make our way towards Shekzi, bumping and bouncing around in the back of the vehicle. Late in the evening, we pulled up at a Hezb-i-Islami base in the foothills of the Kushk-i-Rud.

From what I could see, through the dusty evening gloom, the camp consisted of a series of tents and caves, together with a small collection of clapped-out captured vehicles: three or four Gaz 66 trucks, several jeeps and two BTR-60 wheeled APCs. My two companions and I were taken to what I took to be the base commander's office, a half-tent half-hut. Our letter of authority from Hekmatyar was taken from us, and we were told to wait.

We'd been there a few minutes when a small group of bearded Mujahideen arrived, led by a small man dressed in traditional Afghan clothes, with a webbing belt with a pistol stuck in it and an AKM slung over his shoulder. He was clutching the letter from Hekmatyar in his hand and looking me carefully up and down as he read it. When he had finished, a heated discussion broke out between the leader and my two escorts. As far as I could gather, he was trying to find out what I wanted, what he was supposed to do about me, and why I wanted to do it. It struck me as odd that the letter didn't cover all this, but it seemed that it simply asked Hezb-i-Islami commanders to give me assistance in my 'studies' (whatever they were!). When everybody had calmed down, my guide asked me what I wanted to do at the base and translated my request to be allowed to have a look round in the morning. With this agreed, we were shown to a tent where we could sleep, and left to ourselves.

I was woken next morning, just before 4 a.m., by the call to prayer. I unrolled myself from my bedding and went outside, huddled against the dawn cold, to observe blearily – from a discreet distance – as the rest of the occupants of the camp went through the rituals of their observance, kneeling piously on their prayer mats. When they finished, I went with my two companions to the communal eating area where we were given fresh naan bread and green tea for breakfast and in the early morning light at 5 a.m., we began a kind of sightseeing tour around the base.

It turned out to be much larger than I had thought the night before, spread out over several wadis which gave it some cover from observation from the air. Everybody was armed, almost all with Soviet Kalashnikovs captured in ambushes or presented to the Mujahideen by the many deserters from the Afghan puppet regime's conscript army.

Not far from the commander's shack was a small hut with a group of guards outside. As we approached, they tried to wave us away, but I continued, and Abdul, my chief escort, explained to them that we had permission to go wherever we wanted. Looking through the door, I was surprised to see a group of five young Afghans, all dressed in the remains of khaki uniforms: prisoners.

From the look of them, they'd had a rough old time of it: their faces were cut and bruised, and they stank of shit, sweat and fear. It turned out they'd been captured during a Mujahideen attack on a hill fort. I asked what was going to happen to them and one of the guards explained it to Abdul. He wouldn't translate the guard's answer for me.

'Now they must wait to find out their fate,' was all he would say.

The next structure, a small stone house with a tent appended to it, turned out to be the hospital. Jesus! I'd seen some bad things during seven years in the Regiment, but this was a new low. The patients mostly lay scattered about on bedding rolls on the floor, many with limbs missing, others with huge holes punched through them by bullets, cannon shells and shrapnel; wounds were covered in pieces of cloth, and there was blood everywhere. Surprisingly, there wasn't much noise: I guess most of them were too far gone for that, but there were flies covering everything.

Out at the back, in the tent, was an even more disturbing sight: a group of young men who'd gone as bald as eggs. I asked what had happened and they told me that a Soviet helicopter had sprayed them with a strange liquid which had burned their skin and subsequently caused them to lose their hair. From the way they described their experience, I wrongly assumed at the time that the spray was some kind of defensive countermeasure against missile or ground fire, rather than the straightforward offensive chemical weapon it actually was. Leaving the bewildered Afghans to their suffering, I continued my 'Cooks tour'.

I spent the next few hours looking at their equipment

holdings, and to be honest, they were in a pretty awful state. Most of the vehicles were pretty much unserviceable, weapons had been fired and left to lie around 'sweating' in the heat and dust so that they were rusting beyond use and any radio equipment that they had captured seemed to have been smashed up if they couldn't tune it in to a music station. In one tent I found a heap of old 82mm mortar tubes, lying next to a pile of smashed mortar sights because they simply didn't understand how to use them, even though the mortar is a battle-winning weapon in this type of warfare. I was beginning to get into a conversation with one of the fighters about MI-24 helicopters when the call to prayer came again.

With prayers finished the midday meal was set out: spicy tomato salad with naan and green tea, followed by baked goat's meat and chilli sauce. As I sat eating with Abdul, I casually asked him where the operation's centre was; I don't think I was surprised to find that he didn't know what the fuck I was talking about.

It took an hour or so's argy-bargy with the short fat commander and his Chinese parliament before they managed to work out what I was talking about and then agree to take me there. It turned out that operations were controlled from further inside the country. That didn't surprise me either: the place where we were looked more like a scrap yard than a military base.

While we were waiting for our transport, I asked for a weapon and soon after an old guy came scurrying up with a folding stock AKM and seven full magazines. He started to show me how to use it and, although I'd almost certainly fired more rounds from this type of weapon than him and ten of his best friends put together, I let him continue so that I didn't hurt his feelings; it passed the time anyway.

We set off shortly afterwards in an open-topped Gaz in the direction of Arghastan. We'd only done a couple of miles when we began to hear the sound of heavy fighting over the roar of the truck's engine. We came to a long wadi and the truck halted.

There was a lot of shouting, and as we jumped down from the back of the vehicle, I could see a lot of wounded Afghans lying around, several in quite a bad way.

From what we gathered, it appeared that they had been strafed by a pair of gunships whilst they were at prayer, hitting them with cannon and rocket fire. There was some kind of Afghan doctor scurrying about, but as far as I could see he had jack shit in the way of medical supplies, and all he was doing was covering their wounds with strips of grubby cloth. Medevac appeared in the shape of yet another shagged-out open-backed truck; the casualties were piled on board and it set off in the direction of Pakistan. Treatment was limited to a muttered prayer: if God was merciful, they would make it.

As the Mujahideen reorganised themselves, it became clear that there were more candidates for evacuation, so my transport was commandeered and set off towards Pakistan as fast as it would go. I clambered aboard a tiny, and now vastly overloaded, jeep and we took off again in the direction of Naway Deh.

We didn't get very far: after thirty minutes we encountered a group of somewhat excited Afghan fighters heading in the opposite direction. We stopped for long enough for them to tell us that a convoy of Soviet tanks was heading towards us.

We turned about and headed back the way we had come. About three clicks down the track, we came to a small hamlet and were stopped by a couple of Mujahideen. They asked us, surprisingly politely, whether we would mind helping them, as their commander had decided that he was going to make some kind of stand against the Russians.

As we dismounted, I took stock of the situation. We had a small number of RPG-2s and one or two RPG-7s, but these are close-range hand-held anti-tank weapons, and would probably not have much effect against Soviet T-64s or T-72s anyway. Other than that, it was small arms. Looking at the ground and the likely avenues of approach, I couldn't see us holding the Soviets for more than about ten or fifteen minutes at most: definitely not a good day out. The only plus side that I could see was in the form of a storm drain which ran off to my right: at least I had an escape route when the shit hit the fan.

A thing that struck me at that moment was the discipline and motivation of the Mujahideen: these guys didn't complain, they just got on with it. As time went by, I began to realise that this was the result of their respect for their commander: there was no 'officer-soldier' gap; they all just mucked in, for better or for worse.

The evening started to draw in with no sign of the Russians, and the tension began to ease. Prayers were called at dusk, and afterwards chicken and rice were brought round, together with a bucket of tea which had had camel milk added to it. This made it unpleasantly salty, but it was all we had, so down it went. As night fell, everything was quiet except for our sentries, who would call out 'Allah akhbar!' every thirty minutes or so, to reassure themselves that everything was all right. This gave away our position, of course, but I imagine the Soviets had the same problem with their Afghan soldiers as well.

Dawn brought another call to prayer, but still no sign of the Soviets. After tea and naan, a fierce debate broke out amongst the Afghans over what they were going to do next and where we were going to go. This was curtailed by the sight of a helicopter flying past which sent everyone running for cover.

When we reconvened, it seemed a decision had been reached to send out a reconnaissance party to see what had happened to the tanks. In the absence of any communications system, this seemed a worthwhile exercise, and in the meantime the rest of us were told we were to sit tight.

Around mid-afternoon the recce group returned with the news that the tanks had turned off towards Kandahar and were no longer a threat. This was good news to me because it meant I could continue with my task, pushing forward towards

Kandahar. But when I mentioned this to Abdul, he didn't seem overwhelmed with enthusiasm. I pushed him a bit harder, and made him read Hekmatyar's letter again, and eventually he agreed to go and talk to the commander, who was happy to agree that I should continue, provided it was on foot because he needed the jeep for something else. After a quick discussion, it was agreed that I would leave after prayers and breakfast the next morning.

We set off soon after 5.30 the next morning, plodding along at a snail's pace, but even so, I was soon in trouble, and for a particularly stupid reason: sandals. Like most SAS soldiers, I'd done a lot of tabbing over the years and my feet were well hardened, but the leather thongs that held the sandals in place now started rubbing between my toes, and this was exacerbated by the sand and dust, which burst the blisters as soon as they'd formed. Fairly soon I was hobbling along in considerable pain, and it was lucky that we didn't have too far to go.

Around about mid-afternoon we reached a point from where we could look down onto the main Kabul to Kandahar road quite easily. Unfortunately, because I hadn't been allowed to bring any maps or binoculars, or even a notebook, there was fuck-all I could do about it, other than stare at the big cloud of dust that hung over the road. I took a few photographs, for want of anything better to do, and began the journey back.

My return to Pakistan was pleasantly uneventful. We saw a Russian spotter plane high above us on a couple of occasions, but it didn't appear to take any notice of us and we were eventually able to hook up with a Mujahideen truck going back to Pakistan without any difficulty.

Back in Quetta William had been chewing the carpet with anxiety and frustration, waiting for my return. He was in the same position as the journalists covering the war: he would hear the Chinese whispers version of what had happened, magnified and distorted out of recognition, and when he heard about the gunship attack on the Mujahideen group he had feared the worst.

The first task on my return was the debrief with William. I handed over the three rolls of film I'd managed to take, together with the remaining $700, and then gave him a complete account of what I'd done and seen, working entirely from memory. His response took me aback a bit.

'Jesus, Tom! Is that all you've done?'

'What do you mean?'

'Is that all you've done? It's hardly a bloody basis for assessing the strengths and weaknesses of the bloody Mujahideen, is it?'

I wasn't going to stand for that.

'Don't give me that bullshit, you twat! You sent me in there with both hands tied behind my back. If you need this job done properly, then I've got to take the right equipment with me, and the Mujahideen have got to be told to help me as much as they can. If I've got to ponce around dressed as Gunga Din every time I go in, then we might as well be pissing in the wind, because I'm not going to be able to do the bloody job!'

'Don't you shout at me, Tom!'

'Fuck off! The only reason I'm here is because you need someone like me to carry out these operations. Well, if I'm going to do the ops, I'm damn well going to plan them as well from now on! It's dangerous over there, in case you hadn't noticed, and it's my life that's on the line!'

Our tempers were cooling as we packed up and checked out, ready for the trip back to Peshawar. I'd had a quick shower in Quetta when I'd changed back into western clothes, but when we got back to the Intercontinental, I took a long hot bath, and followed it with a swim, a big scoff and a couple of ice-cold beers in the bar to help me unwind.

Sitting there, feeling the first buzz from the beer, I couldn't help thinking that something had changed. Ireland and Oman were essentially little wars – nasty and vicious certainly – but nobody was coming after you with helicopter gunships or anything like that. Afghanistan was something else again, though. I was up against the Soviets now; I'd been behind enemy lines for the first time, and I'd survived!

And with that thought in mind, I went to bed.

THREE

I was determined that we were going to plan my next operation properly, and it seemed to me that this wasn't going to happen if I let William get too involved. He was a nice bloke who was obviously good at the sort of stuff he was doing, but he simply didn't have the background to organise military special operations, and if I let him try, I was going to be left carrying the can. In fact, I found around this time that he'd done his National Service in an armoured regiment so he had a smattering of military knowledge, and just enough officer 'attitude' to make a nuisance of himself.

The morning after our return from Quetta, we made our way back to the Hezb-i-Islami headquarters to debrief the first trip. As was apparently normal, the place was packed with various Afghans, and stank of stale sweat. We were eventually shown into a meeting room and, after a short period, a group of Hezb head sheds arrived and we got down to business.

My main gripe over the first infiltration was that the in-country commanders didn't know I was coming, and didn't have sufficiently clear instructions in the letter of introduction that I had been given about what I wanted to do. By and large they had all been pretty helpful, even if they were suspicious at first, but I was obviously well down their list of priorities, and they weren't busting a gut to give me a helping hand. As the discussion went on, it became fairly obvious that the Mujahideen didn't really know why I was going into Afghanistan either, and it was only much later in the operation that I discovered that they had been asked to help me as a quid pro quo for the massive weapons shipments that the US and British governments were beginning to facilitate.

The upshot of the meeting was that I would draft the order for the next operation and the Hezb would then translate it and get Hekmatyar to sign it. Together we also decided the location for my next infiltration: the province of Nangarhar, near to Jellalabad, where the Mujahideen were fighting for control against largely Russian opposition, the Afghan army being deemed insufficiently trustworthy to take part in high-intensity operations.

Back at the hotel, William got out the maps and slipped easily back into Colonel Blimp mode:

'Right, Tom, this is what you've got to do. I want you to infiltrate over the border here, near Parachinar, with a Mujahideen escort, and to visit these six camps which encircle Jellalabad. See what's going on at each of them, and bring out as much kit as possible, in accordance with the list we gave you at the briefing in London. The distance is only about one hundred and thirty kilometres, so I would expect you to be able to do it in a maximum of seven days. I'll be giving you $2,000 dollars as a cash float this time, but it's purely for use in emergencies, because I've instructed the Hezb to assist you from their own resources, so you won't be needing to buy anything. Got that?'

He passed me a sheaf of papers which gave the formal outline of the plan.

'William, why does it have to be done precisely this way?'

'Tom, old boy, don't ask questions, just get your gear together and get ready, because you're off again tomorrow.'

'Bollocks to that: you fucking go!'

For a few moments he looked like a lost schoolboy.

'What do you mean?'

'William, we've been through this. This idea is crap; the last one was hit or miss. This fucker is a total waste of time.'

'Why?'

'Have you worked in the Middle East before, William?'

'Of course I bloody have.'

'Well, it's a pound to a pinch of shit you've never worked with tribal guerrillas. This operation might just possibly work if I was visiting the Grenadier Guards, but out here it hasn't got a hope in hell.

'The first reason is the distance: yes, I can cover one hundred and thirty clicks in seven days easily, even in this kind of terrain, if I was navigating and my escorts were people I'd worked with before, knew and could trust. But that isn't the case, is it? The boys I'm going with will want to walk between known points on known routes. We're going to be meeting people the whole time, and it's the way out here, if you hadn't noticed, that they stop and talk to people they meet en route, and change their plans accordingly. Plus, we're not going to be walking continuously, because five times every day they are going to stop to say their prayers, and that is going to take up half an hour each time they do it.

'Don't forget, either, that there are a lot of Russians out there, whose main aim in life is to blitz the Mujahideen, and they certainly aren't going to worry about making my life easier.

'Finally, the money. When you say they're going to help me out of their resources, you have to remember that they haven't really got any resources. If I'm going to bring out piles of Soviet kit, I'll probably have to hire mules: these guys can't afford to just give them to me.'

I knew William was under pressure to get things done quickly from his controllers in London, but to be fair to him, he accepted what I had to say:

'OK, but how long is it going to take?'

'A minimum of two and a half weeks, probably three, and maybe more.'

'Jesus, that's just an impossible time . . . absolutely impossible!' His face had gone white. He thought a bit longer and came to a decision:

'OK, so be it. You'd better get yourself ready, get going and get back a.s.a.p. with as much gear as possible . . . and for Christ's sake don't let the Russians capture you alive!'

'That isn't really in my hands, William, but anything I do collect, I'll send back separately.'

He was still looking stunned as I left to get my gear together.

Freed from the stupid restrictions that were imposed on me last time out, I actually felt reasonably confident as I checked my belt kit, loaded various odds and ends into my bergen, and dubbined my boots. My feet were still sore from the sandals fiasco but I reckoned they wouldn't affect me on the walk because the blisters were in places where the boots wouldn't rub. I loaded my military gear into my duffle bag and then set off for the hotel restaurant and a last big feed before early bed.

I slept well, and was up and ready to go before three o'clock next morning. My taxi rocked up at about 3.15, and in no time at all I was at Hezb headquarters at Fackeyrabad getting ready for the off. This time my escort was led by a tall, slim young man called Ahmed, who spoke excellent English. I loaded myself and my gear onto the back of yet another old Russian lorry and waited for a short period while the Afghans settled down to pray; and then we were off, rattling along at a fair old clip towards death, danger and destruction.

We hit the first checkpoint at Kohat. The convoy pulled over to the side of the road and we sat there and waited while the Police worked their way down the line of vehicles. I'm not entirely sure what they were looking for; we had a shit-load of weapons in the convoy, for example, which they can't possibly have missed; but all we got was a quick eyeballing of our cargo and then we were waved on. With the benefit of twenty years' hindsight I wonder if William hadn't thrown a few hundred dollars in their direction.

Several more checkpoints and controls followed, again without any real problems, and by late afternoon we were passing through the frontier town of Parachinar, heading towards a big Mujahideen camp near Mangel's Post, just on the Pakistani side of the border.

The camp proved to be a large, tented set-up, teeming with Afghan refugees as well as Mujahideen from most of the factions that had formed to fight the Soviet invaders. Ahmed led me through the maze of tents to the Hezb commander, a relatively young man who had been an officer in the Afghan army but had deserted after the Soviet invasion. After he had read the letter of authority from Hekmatyar, he gave out orders for food to be brought for us and a tent prepared for us to sleep in. The food arrived twenty minutes later, together with brand new AKM rifles, a bag of magazines and a box of ammunition. This was a good sign. I gave my rifle a thorough cleaning, noticing that it still bore traces of the maker's packing grease: as far as I could tell, it had never been fired.

I filled ten magazines of thirty rounds, mixing standard ball ammunition with armour-piercing and tracer bullets, but I noticed that my escorts only took three or four mags each. I asked if it was possible to test fire the weapon, but it seemed that the Mujahideen had an agreement with the Pakistanis not to fire weapons on this side of the border, so I was told that I would have to wait until we reached Afghanistan.

I was woken at four the next morning by an Afghan bringing me tea and naan. Outside the tent I could see mules and Afghans forming up into a convoy a few metres away. We were to cross the border with a group of thirty or forty Mujahideen who were going to reinforce a unit near Khogiani, coincidentally one of the areas I had to visit, so the infiltration would be on foot this time, following what was, in effect, an old smugglers' track over Spin-Ghar, a fifteen-thousand foot mountain on the border which was itself one of the foothills of the great Hindu Kush range. My bergen was loaded on to one of the mules and, wearing an old Afghan coat over my shirt, OGs, belt kit and boots, we set off at around 5.15 a.m.

It was a hard old slog throughout the day as we trudged along the trail towards the border. It was difficult to tell precisely where we were, because the only maps I had were 1:250,000 air charts which didn't show the dry stream beds that we were following, or even the many small villages we passed through as the ground became steeper and rougher. The only stops we made were for prayers and to water the mules, and the only time we left the track was to make way for camel trains which came hurtling past in the opposite direction, fully laden with God knows what.

Late in the evening, we reached the foot of the mountain and, to my surprise, a well-used caravanserai where, for twenty US dollars, I was able to buy food for all of the convoy personnel – and the mules – and hire a hut for us to sleep in: not quite the Hilton, admittedly, but better value and at least the food was authentic.

I'd forgotten to bring a book out to Pakistan with me and, instead, William had lent me one: *Flashman* by George MacDonald Fraser. This is a sort of historical comedy featuring a cowardly cavalry officer involved in the First Afghan War of 1842. One thing it didn't pull any punches on was the tendency the Afghans had to carve up any wounded or captured British soldiers they came across, and it struck me as somewhat ironic that here I was, a British soldier, sneaking back into the same area described in the book, to help the descendants of Flashman's knife-wielding maniacs. I didn't ever manage to finish it: I think the atrocity stories were too close to the bone.

Next morning, after prayers, tea and naan, we began the long climb over Spin-Ghar – all fifteen thousand feet of it. I couldn't help thinking about selection and the Fan Dance: humping it over Pen y Fan – three thousand feet high – didn't seem quite such an achievement now, and I was damned glad my bergen was attached to a mule's back rather than mine. The last two thousand feet – with the air getting pretty thin – were hard work, even though we were on a well-worn track. As we reached the summit, around midday, we saw another group coming towards us: fighting men, walking wounded and casualties mounted on mules. As was the custom, we stopped to exchange information and pray together, but I couldn't help noticing that I was getting some distinctly dirty looks from the newcomers.

In fact it turned out that they were members of the Jamiat-i-Islami, a group sponsored by the new revolutionary government in Iran, and a number of them were actually Iranian volunteers. Their hostility seemed to subside as my presence was explained, and before long we were on the move again, reaching the summit, crossing the border and heading down the other side into Afghanistan.

I had half expected a change in procedure once we were over the border. I rather hoped that the group might adopt a tactical formation of some sort, but this turned out not to be the case; they just bimbled on as before, seemingly without a care in the world. Late in the evening we came to a stone hut built round the mouth of a cave and moved in for the night. The Afghans didn't bother to post a guard.

Breakfast the next morning consisted of cold bread and water, and for the first time, I started the march feeling hungry and irritable. The Afghans still weren't making any effort to move tactically, but to be fair there didn't appear to be any need to: there was no sign of the Soviet army at all. So it came as a surprise, soon after mid-morning prayers, when a shot rang out from the rocks in front of us.

I dived to the side of the road to find cover, swiping the safety catch on my Kalashnikov to full-auto as I did so. Looking round the rock I was sheltering behind, I couldn't see who had fired, and I looked over at my group to see what they were doing. It turned out that they were standing on the track laughing at me.

I wasn't quite sure I understood what was happening. I stood up and Ahmed, my guide, came over to me.

'Don't worry, Tom, it's a welcome shot.'

Oh, well that's all right then. Tricky call to make, though, trying to work out whether someone's trying to kill you, or just saying hello. As I was dusting myself down, he smiled again and said:

'Come.'

It turned out we had reached the first camp.

The camp was made up of a small collection of caves, together with a cookhouse-cum-prayer building, protected by a lookout post perched high on one of the mountains above us. The commander was a short, fattish, bearded man – a typical Afghan fighter in many ways – and very keen, once he'd read the letter of authority, to help in any way he could. His problem, he told me, was that he needed every spare man for an operation that was coming up, so how many men did I need for my task?

I'd thought about this quite a lot. From what I'd seen of the Mujahideen, having a big gang of them around was just as likely to be a hindrance as a help when the shit hit the fan. A small group could travel fast and light, and would be less likely to attract unwanted attention from the Soviets or Afghan government forces: they would also be easier to control if anything did go wrong.

'I need three men,' I told him. 'Ahmed, my guide, Mohammed and the mule handler.'

The commander was happy with this, as was Mohammed, a smiling, cheerful guy of about twenty-three who always carried an RPG-7, but Ahmed, whom I called 'Blue' because of the colour of his clothing, was not.

'Tom, no! We can't go with just four of us; it's very, very dangerous out there. If the Communists catch us, we'll be killed.'

A long discussion ensued between me, Blue and the commander, before we eventually compromised on a figure of eight: me plus seven. Blue now selected four more men from our original group to accompany us, and despite his relative youth (he was twenty-eight), his word went unchallenged by the grizzled Mujahideen warriors. In the two days that I'd known him, I'd already got to like him, and it was clear that he was well respected by the Mujahideen. He spoke excellent English, having trained as an engineer and teacher at the American University in Kabul, before leaving to join the Mujahideen in 1979, when he received call-up papers to join the Afghan army.

We passed a comfortable night in the camp and next morning I took a look around. It turned out to be more a stores dump than an operational base, and most of the caves were filled with boxes of 7.62mm x 39 Kalashnikov ammunition, RPG grenades, mortar rounds and so on. One thing did catch my eye, though: a box of small 30mm grenades, a bit like the type we used in the M-79 or M-203. I realised that these were AGS-17 rounds and high on the wants list given to me by John Miley in London. The camp second-in-command was showing me around, and I asked if I could take some. No problem: they couldn't use them anyway. At last I was getting somewhere.

With my tour of inspection over, I got permission to test fire my AKM. The second-in-command was puzzled by this: as far as he was concerned, Kalashnikovs don't need testing because they always work. Which is perfectly true and, of course, completely unlike the situation with the British army's current rifle, the poxy SA80. Actually, I was more concerned with zeroing the sights, and so I took a piece of wood, marked out one hundred metres up the valley, and fired ten rounds to check grouping. I walked back to the wood and saw that I'd achieved seven hits, which was good enough for me, so I emptied the magazine, firing short bursts at a nearby boulder before giving the weapon a quick clean, refilling the magazine and walking back to join Blue who was drinking tea with the commander.

My original plan had been to go from the first camp to a place we had imaginatively labelled 'Camp Two', but Blue now told me that the camp commander, together with the rest of our original convoy, would be heading for Camp Six, near Bald-bagh, to take part in this new operation, and suggested that we accompany them. I thought about it for a while: on the one hand, I didn't want to get embroiled in a slow cross-country trek with a big mob of Afghans; but on the other, this would be a tremendous opportunity to see the Mujahideen in action. After a few moments' thought, I agreed.

We set off soon after midday prayers, in a caravan that had now grown to sixty strong and included many more mules and even a few camels. Looking back from my position near the front of the group, I could see a cloud of dust enveloping the rear of the convoy, kicked up by our feet at the front.

We trudged through the afternoon, and round about last light reached a small village five or six kilometres east of the town of Wazir. The commander sent a couple of men forward to see who was there, and they returned to tell us we would be welcome.

We spent long enough in the village to get some tea and bread down our necks in the meeting hall, but Blue told me that the next phase of our trip was across a flat plain where Soviet helicopters often patrolled, and that we would have to make the crossing by night. It seemed sensible to me. As we prepared to move out, I mentioned something that had been bothering me.

'Hey, Blue, there are no young men here.'

'No, Tom, the woman who brought the bread told me that the army came last week to take them as volunteers; they only left the old and the cripples.'

'What happens if they don't want to "volunteer"?'

'They shoot them as Mujahideen.'

Fair enough; I think I'd volunteer under those circumstances.

We started across the plain at about 9.30 p.m. and sure enough, it was as flat as a billiard table. Just sand, gravel and small boulders: absolutely no cover at all. As we settled in to a steady pace, I gradually became aware of the level of noise the guys were making. Apart from the scuffling of feet and the noise of the pack animals, they were coughing, spitting and talking, and each man seemed to have his own special metallic rattle. Almost all armies which issue Kalashnikovs also issue a webbing chest-rig to hold the magazines, but these guys carried theirs in bags slung over their left shoulders, with the weapons slung over the right, and, as a result, they clattered along like Thomas the Tank Engine.

We kept up a good pace until, at around 3 a.m., it began to get light. Looking around, it seemed to me that we still had some way to go, and I began to worry that we might be caught out in the open in full daylight. In the pre-dawn glow, I looked back and saw the column was now spread out over at least a kilometre, but in front I could see our destination, a rocky escarpment, just some two clicks ahead: maybe twenty minutes' march. Even this early in the morning it was warm and my green shirt and OG trousers were soaked in sweat. My mouth felt gritty with the sandy dust which had washed into it, with the sweat running off my face. Nobody was talking now; we were all moving as if we were on autopilot, pushing ourselves on towards the safety of the hills in front of us.

Walking with Blue, I reached the foot of the escarpment and started up a narrow trail. It was near to full daylight now, and we'd been tabbing for something like twenty hours, with only a short stop for rest and food. We reached a small open area not far up the trail, and many of the Mujahideen dropped to the ground to rest and take a drink of water. But it wasn't safe to stop, and the weary fighters soon picked themselves up and continued along the rocky path.

We'd been climbing for some twenty or thirty minutes when we heard noises in front and a couple of Afghans appeared. Greetings were exchanged, and as we got closer, I noticed several more covering us with weapons from behind a stone sangar. We'd reached Camp Six.

The camp was spread out throughout the mountain, hidden away in caves and tunnels; some ancient, some apparently newly built. I was taken to the camp commander's area: a small cave from the outside which opened up into quite a large area inside. The Mujahideen then went off to say their prayers, and after I'd had a drink of water, I set about cleaning the dust and grit from my weapon, and then from Blue's as well, which he'd left with me.

This was a problem that I was finding difficult to resolve. I'd tried to impress on 'my' team of Mujahideen the importance of keeping their weapons with them at all times, but it was in one ear and out the other. The reason was that most of them hadn't had any military training at all: they were just given a weapon and told to fight for the jihad. They were told that if they were killed, they would sit at Allah's right hand. All very well, but I reckoned they must have a special queuing system in heaven, because these guys were being wiped out in droves, and Allah's right hand must be pretty crowded by now.

The Afghans returned from their prayers and some breakfast was brought in. I was so hungry, I could have eaten a horse (and probably did), and as we sat there filling our faces, the camp commander read through my letter, and through despatches brought to him from Peshawar. When I'd eaten my fill, I scouted out a safe place to sleep, laid my poncho on the ground, put my belt kit down as a pillow, rolled myself and my rifle up in the poncho and fell fast asleep.

Whoosh! Something roared past overhead. I woke up thinking: what the fuck is going on? Where the fuck am I?

I looked around. I was rolled up in a poncho in a rock fissure.

Looking up I could see a bright azure sky. My fuzzy head started whirring into action. The noise was a helicopter – or helicopters – and cannon fire, and explosions. I stuffed the poncho back into my bergen and chucked it into a nearby cave. I clambered up the side of the gully and found a vantage point. A few kilometres away in the direction of the town of Tatang – and partially hidden by a rise in the ground – was a small village, and buzzing around above it three Hind helicopters. Shit.

From my vantage point, I watched as the Hinds swooped down time and again on the village, watching the flash of rockets being fired from the wing pylons, and listening to the rattle of the 12.7mm rotary nose cannon, sounding like a woodpecker attacking a particularly hard tree. The attack continued for half an hour or so before the helicopters peeled off in the direction of Kabul.

As the Hinds swung away, I happened to glance up and catch sight of sunlight glinting on something maybe six or seven thousand feet above us. I took a squint through my binos and saw a small propeller-driven aircraft circling the attacked village: an airborne forward air controller, I assumed, or maybe damage assessment.

Things now went quiet for an hour or more, and afternoon prayers were in full swing when a group of wounded Afghans appeared from the village, several of them badly shot up. There was a lot of shouting, and the Mujahideen in the camp began to saddle-up, grabbing their weapons and packs, obviously getting ready to go somewhere.

'What's going on?' I asked Blue.

'Tom, they've shot down a Russian helicopter on the other side of the village. They're all off to see it.'

Fuck me backwards! This was a turn up for the books. I didn't want to piss on their cornflakes, but there was something they were forgetting:

'Listen, lads, if you've taken out a helicopter, the Russians are going to be back to get the crew.'

Blue translated my warning but the Mujahideen didn't give a toss; their blood was up and they were off to bag some Russians. We set off at high speed, and in less than an hour we had covered the seven kilometres to the village, setting the Mujahideen land-speed record in the process.

The village was a total mess. Many of the buildings were still burning fiercely and wounded people lay scattered about as their friends and relations ineffectually tried to help them. Shortly after we arrived, a small girl was brought to us and I was asked to help her. Looking down, I saw there was little I could do: she had a chunk of shrapnel the size and shape of a banana protruding from her abdomen. Even with a medevac she would have been lucky to make it but there was fuck all I could do. I put a field dressing around the wound, but within minutes she was dead and her weeping father carried her body away. She wasn't more than six or seven years old.

Looking around, there were a lot of people who needed help but all I had was a small medical pack. There was enough work here for a large hospital. It occurred to me that as we were trying to treat the casualties, we had no kind of security or early warning sentries out at all and, after a quick discussion, I did persuade the commander to send a team out to the village perimeter.

My priority now was to reach the crash site. Blue was pumping the villagers for information and quickly produced an old man who agreed to take us there. We made the three kilometres in about twenty-five minutes and, as dusk began to fall, I was able to begin my inspection of the helicopter.

The first thing I noticed was the body of one of the crewmen. He'd obviously survived the crash and attempted to crawl away from the wreckage. He hadn't got very far. Angry villagers had found him and attacked him with knives and agricultural tools. His head was completely severed, whilst the rest of his body, which lay in a large damp bloodstain, had been hacked and mutilated. It was a disgusting sight. From the depths of my memory, a few lines of Kipling's poem *Young British Soldier* popped up.

> When you're lying out wounded on Afghanistan's plains,
> and the women come out to cut up what remains, you roll
> to your rifle and blow out your brains, and go to your God
> like a soldier.

My first thought was that the helicopter was a Hind D, but after looking carefully at the tail and seeing a group of antenna pods beneath it, and then checking the external weapon pods, I was sure it was the newer Hind E. Inside the cockpit there had been a small fire, but it was largely intact. I told my team to spread out and cover me, and then took a long look inside by the light of my small right-angle torch.

The first thing I noticed was that both seats were empty. This meant that one of the crewmen, and maybe more, was lurking around somewhere, possibly with some kind of TACBE to bring in search and rescue aircraft, and certainly armed. I would have to move fast: I didn't know if Soviet SAR operated by night, but they would certainly be around at first light.

The fire had taken place in the instrument panel, apparently destroying the radio sets, so I assumed that it was either the result of some sort of automatic self-destruct or due to a simple short circuit on crash landing. But just next to the aircraft was a small pile of charred ashes where paper appeared to have been burnt, and I guessed that that would have been the maps, codes, orders and so on, destroyed by the surviving crewman. There appeared to be nothing of any great interest left inside the cockpit.

But what was interesting was that the aircraft was largely intact. It had come down under some degree of control and landed upright, shoving its nose into the sand. It seemed to me quite likely that the weapons' sights and other sensor equipment were still extant, buried underneath it. I began to pull away some of the loose, dented panelling around the nose, and soon exposed the front armoured plate, designed to protect the crewmen. I had a small toolkit with me, which included an adjustable spanner, and I used this to undo the bolts on the armour, before applying brute force and a series of sharp kicks to break the welds which held it finally in place.

After half an hour or so of effort, Blue and I finally managed to work it free from the side of the aircraft, where we encountered our next problem: it weighed a bloody ton! I stood up and looked around, and saw to my annoyance that the rest of the team were sitting around watching us and having a chat rather than occupying the sentry positions I'd put them in. I gave them a bollocking but I knew as I was doing it that the whole thing was falling on deaf ears: they simply had no real idea about proper soldiering.

The armour plate was about four feet long, two feet wide and quarter of an inch thick – a good two-man lift. But it wasn't going to be easy to get it back; firstly to the village, and then to the Mujahideen camp. I asked Blue whether we might be able to get a mule or donkey, and he passed my request to the old man, but he was sure that nobody would want to come out now. Instead, I got two of the team to lift it up and load it onto my back, and I walked back with it, holding it by the edges while Blue carried my bergen and Kalashnikov.

When we reached the village I was wet with sweat, but we got some sweet tea down our necks while our guide found an old guy prepared to let us hire his donkey to transport the plate to the base camp. We agreed a price of $30, lashed the sheet of metal to the unfortunate moke and he set off, as I began to explain to the team that we had to return to the site to see what else we could salvage. I wasn't entirely surprised that this suggestion didn't go down at all well, but after yet another Chinese parliament they finally agreed.

We got back to the helicopter at about 2.45 a.m., as the pre-dawn glow was beginning to appear above the mountains to the east. My guess was that we had about an hour and a half to get what we could from the aircraft and get into cover before full daylight and the appearance of Russian search and rescue teams, and possibly a retaliatory mission as well. We weren't going to have time to get back to the base camp, but I calculated that I had enough food and water in my bergen for the eight of us, so we could sit tight for the day and make our move the next night.

In the early light the dead Russian was even more of a mess than he'd appeared the night before, and I made a mental note that there was no way I wanted to be around when his friends found him. Taking a closer look I realised that he wasn't more than twenty-one or twenty-two, and from his blond hair, pale northern skin and blue eyes, I guessed he'd died a long way from home.

Looking at the wreck I realised that several pieces which had been there earlier had now gone – the nose cannon, for example – but there were no signs of any bootprints apart from my own, so I concluded that another Mujahideen group must have been here in the couple of hours we'd been away and taken them. I took my camera out and began to photograph anything I thought was of interest, and to pick up any fragments which happened to be lying around, when Blue ran over to me, his eyes wide with fright. For a moment I couldn't think what was wrong, then I heard them too: rotor blades.

We had to move, and fast. We couldn't go in the direction of the village because that was where the helicopter sound was coming from, but I had earlier spotted a ditch which ran off towards some higher ground to the south, and this was where I wanted to make for. I got my team together and told them what we were going to do: for once they didn't argue. We kept low and well spaced, crouching as we ran along the bottom of the dried-out watercourse, but we had hardly got two hundred metres from the crash site when the first helicopters appeared overhead. Now we had to freeze. I didn't imagine the recovery team would want a firefight on the ground, but the Hind escorts would be itching to hose anything that moved, and the last thing we wanted to do was attract their attention.

Over the roar of the engines and the thump of the rotor blades, I heard the hydraulic whine which signifies rotors changing pitch for landing, and although I couldn't see it, I gained the impression that at least one of the helicopters had set down. Then it started.

Somebody nearby had opened fire on the Russians with an automatic weapon, and several others had joined in: Christ knows why; I had no intention of mixing it with a flight of Hinds. There was a roar as a gunship came over us at no more than a hundred feet, and before I could stop them, three of my crew had switched their Kalashnikovs to automatic and opened fire on it. Stupid bastards, they might as well have thrown tennis balls at it. There's a slight possibility that if you get a lot of rounds into the tail boom you might fracture a hydraulic line or an oil pipe, but hit anywhere else and it will just bounce off the armour plating. I shouted to Blue to tell them to spread out and get into cover, but he was in such a panic he wasn't understanding a word I said.

In the maelstrom of dust and noise, my three idiots continued to loose off round after round, firing now in any direction in abject terror rather than in any hope of hitting anything. There was a lull followed by frightened shouting, and I called to Blue to see what was going on.

'Tom! Tom! They have run out of bullets!' he shouted back.

'Oh yes?'

'What can they fight with now?'

My obscene reply was drowned out by the scream of incoming 12.7mm cannon fire, as a cloud of dust and bullet fragments boiled around us, and another Hind roared over. What the fuck were we going to do? If we stayed put, the Hinds would eventually move in close, winkle us out of our cover and kill us. We had to take the risk of moving.

I explained this to Blue and tried to impress upon him that they must not fire their weapons on automatic: they'd already used a third of our ammunition and had jack shit to show for it. I then gave each of the guys who'd used up their rounds one full magazine in return for one empty one of theirs. They looked a bit put out by this, but they were going to have to learn fire discipline if they wanted to stay in this war – and to stay alive.

As Blue finished explaining to them what we were going to do, another burst came in, impacting well to our left, but showering us with gravel and stone fragments. This galvanised the boys into action and they followed me like sheep as I led them along the ditch towards some boulders.

As we squeezed in amongst the rocks, a troop carrying MI-8 clattered directly overhead and flared out for landing at the crash site. The Hinds seemed to have lost interest in us and were concentrating their efforts on a small hill to our north-west, where most of the ground fire seemed to be coming from. I could see some activity on the ground by the wreck, about four hundred metres away, and with difficulty persuaded my crew not to open fire, as the MI-8 lifted off and flew back over us. There was a momentary lull, followed by a loud explosion as demolition charges on the Hind detonated, showering us with dust, stones and small pieces of metal. Then all was quiet.

I kept my crew in the ditch, sitting quietly, as the dust began to settle, literally and metaphorically. Everything was silent for several more minutes, and then I heard the sound of voices, coming from the direction of the hill to our north-west, and before very long, a group of 25 or 30 Mujahideen appeared, jabbering excitedly to each other as they walked along a cart-track towards the remains of the downed Hind. I told my group to get ready to move, but as they did so, there was a roar and clatter of

rotors and the Hinds were back, swooping down on the Mujahideen with cannons screaming.

It was all over in a few moments: the Hinds thudded away to
the east and all went quiet again, apart from the screams and
moans of wounded Afghans. I noticed sunlight glinting on something in the sky, and once again saw the little spotter plane,
circling high above us. In a sense it was reassuring: it meant that
the Russians used airborne OPs rather than putting troops on the
ground, which would be an advantage to us in several ways.

The other Mujahideen group was a mess. The track was dotted
with bloodstains and severed body parts, not to mention dead
and dying fighters. I took off my bergen and got my medical pack
out but Blue sidled over to me.

'No, Tom, don't help them.'

'Why ever not?'

'These are bad people, Tom. We should go.'

'I don't understand.'

'Tom, they are Jamiat-i-Islami, bad people . . .'

'Blue, we can't just leave them like this, all shot to pieces, and
besides, there is meant to be an alliance between the Mujahideen
groups. You're all supposed to be on the same side. If you don't
want to help, fine: go and wait over there with the others, but I'm
going to do what I can.'

I began to give what treatment I could, tapping antibiotic
powder into bullet and shrapnel wounds and covering them with
field dressings, and after a while Blue began to help as well. There
were fourteen dead and nine wounded, but two of them died very
quickly, and by the time a donkey cart arrived about four hours
later to begin the casevac of the seriously wounded into Pakistan,
I can't say I had a high expectation of their chances.

With the wounded gone and the dead left in the care of the
villagers, we began the trudge back to the Mujahideen base. It
occurred to me that none of us had eaten for about thirty hours
– and even before that we'd had little but bread and salad – and

the constant activity was beginning to tell. I had little energy left and had to concentrate hard just to make the relatively short distance 'home'.

Evening was drawing in as we entered the camp and there was much hugging and glad-handing as my escorts bragged about their encounter with the Hinds. Sitting eating my supper with Blue, I realised that this had been the first encounter with the enemy for almost all of them; they were the heroes of the moment. For my part, there was work to be done. When I'd eaten my fill, I went to the commander's hut and refilled the three magazines from a crate of loose rounds, and then gave my weapon a quick clean. Even though I hadn't fired it, it had nonetheless managed to fill with sand and grit. I then asked whether the sheet of armour plating had arrived at the base and was told it had.

I spent the next fifteen or twenty minutes trying to find the armour, before eventually discovering that it had been incorporated into the roof of the commander's bunker for protection. I started to remove it but a guard came up to me and gestured to me to stop. Blue wandered over and I told him what was happening. He spoke to the guard for a while, then turned to me and said:

'He says you must have the commander's permission to take this, but the commander has gone to a wedding in another village.'

Great. Still, I supposed it was as safe here as anywhere, and I decided instead to get my head down for a while.

FOUR

My sleep was disturbed that night by various comings and goings around the camp, and by the sound of the guards shouting to each other and chopping wood for their fires. I finally got up around 4.30 a.m., when the first call for morning prayers came, and sat alone for a while, drinking a brew of tea and thinking through the events of the last few days. I was disturbed a short while later by Blue and the rest of the boys, who had eaten their breakfast elsewhere and were now keen to find out what we were to do next.

'So, Tom, when will we be going to the other camps?'

'Today, mate. We should leave here at about 0800 hours . . .'

This went down like a fart in a spacesuit, and yet another Chinese parliament started up, as it did every time I said I wanted to do something they weren't keen on. To be honest, it was beginning to piss me off, but it occurred to me that there might be a way round it.

'Look, Blue, I don't mind discussing things, but if you want to be paid, you've basically got to do what I tell you . . .'

This was an aspect he hadn't considered.

'You will pay us? How?'

'I will pay you cash when we get back to Pakistan. Come with me a second . . .' I led him a little to one side. 'Blue, if we're successful, I'll pay each of the boys $100 and I'll give you $150. It's only fair.'

He nodded sagely and went back to the group. There was a short discussion followed by a series of near ecstatic smiles. $100 was about six months' wages for the average Afghan in 1980. Suddenly they were keen to make a start and after I'd made arrangements to shift the sheet of armour back to Camp One, we got going.

We made about thirty-five kilometres that day, stomping through the mountains at a fair old clip and climbing, I guess, about four thousand feet en route. When we made our midday stop, I made a brew for the boys as they prayed, and gave them each a sweet army oatmeal block from a tin I kept in my bergen, which gave us all an energy boost. In the early evening we reached the main Kabul–Jellalabad road, which we crossed with ease via a culvert, and beyond that the Darya ye Kabul river where we waded the chest-deep water (which gave us our first wash for some days). These were the kind of choke points that any military security force worth the name would have been picketing, and it began to occur to me then that maybe the Russians weren't all they were cracked up to be: we weren't just being lucky.

We continued to trudge through the evening gloom until it became too dark to continue, then we stopped and took shelter amongst some rocks, dozing until about half past two in the morning when it was light enough for us to move on. In fact, after only two hours or so we reached Camp Five, a small collection of caves and trenches, much less extensive and better concealed than the previous bases that I'd visited.

The commander of Camp Five was Abdullah, a young, lean fighter of twenty-seven who was very different to any of the previous Mujahideen leaders I'd met. He'd been trained by the Russians as a member of the puppet Afghan army but had deserted and immediately joined the Mujahideen. The most obvious difference was the way he and his men dressed: he wore an old American combat jacket rather than traditional robes, and boots rather than sandals. They were also armed with Heckler and Koch G3 rifles rather than the ubiquitous Kalashnikovs. The G3 is a high-quality German-made weapon which was standard issue with the Bundeswehr and several other armies, and which is still popular in the SAS because of its accuracy and reliability, and because it can fire its powerful 7.62 x 51 Nato rounds in bursts reasonably comfortably. Looking at one of the rifles, I noticed that many of the markings on it were in Arabic script (or rather, I suspect, Farsi) and I assumed that they had come from Iran. I didn't bother to ask Abdullah because I doubt if he would have known how they got there. Although the G3 is in many ways a better weapon than the Kalashnikovs that everybody else had, it struck me that Abdullah and his guys were likely to have problems sourcing the different calibre ammunition that they would need, and they would have done better to have stuck with the AKs.

Once Abdullah found out what I was there for, he was keen to help as much as possible, and particularly to show me round his little camp. One thing that struck me straight away was that they had acquired a large number of mortar rounds, which were piled up in caves, still in their Soviet-marked crates, but that they appeared not to have any mortar tubes to launch them. I asked Abdullah, who spoke some English, why this was and it turned out that they got them after attacking a convoy on the Kabul-Jellalabad road. The Russians had made no attempt to recover the rounds and, indeed, hadn't even mounted a follow-up after the ambush, so Abdullah had been able to scoop up a considerable amount of kit.

Much of the rest of it was junk, but looking in one cave I

noticed an orange plastic box which appeared to be some kind of chemical warfare countermeasures kit. Abdullah had no objection to me taking it, so I slipped it into my bergen: another target achieved.

With the tour of the camp complete, it was time for prayers and lunch. I was quite surprised to find that as well as the usual naan and salad, we also got chicken and rice. With this finished, Abdullah asked me whether I would mind taking a look at a plan he was working on. I followed him to his cave where, to my even greater surprise, he produced a map and a sheaf of notes. This quite took me aback: up to this point I hadn't seen an Afghan use a map at all, let alone show any inclination to plan ahead. From what I could gather, the typical Mujahideen assault took place when they had worked up enough of a head of steam to go out and take a poke at the Russians, but they rarely had much of an idea about how it would work out; they just did it. I put this down to their lack of military training and the fatalistic Islamic culture: 'God will decide'. Fair enough, but someone was going to have to persuade them that God would decide in their enemy's favour unless they started to think ahead.

Abdullah's scheme turned out to be somewhat ambitious. He wanted to sabotage the hydroelectric plant at Oluswah Sorubi which supplied a lot of the electricity for Kabul and also for the Soviet Bagram airbase.

'How do you plan to do that then?' I asked him.

'We'll need to blow up the sluice gates on the main dam wall.'

'Do you have enough explosives?'

'Oh yes, we've got plenty. Come and see.'

I followed him to one of the other caves and he showed me a bunch of long, sausage-shaped, cellophane-wrapped packages containing some kind of plastic explosive. Each of the packages weighed about four or five kilos, and they had plenty of them.

'Does it work?' I was suspicious because I'd never seen explosives packed that way before.

'Oh yes, we used some to build the mine when we ambushed the convoy.'

Fair enough, but I wondered how he envisaged mounting the operation.

'I'm not sure yet, but I thought that tomorrow I would go and look at the dam.'

I was intrigued by this because Abdullah's approach was absolutely right: a reconnaissance was precisely what I would have done under these circumstances. I thought for a few moments, imagining William chewing his fingernails with anxiety back in Peshawar, and then decided. Fuck it! I'll go as well. My reasons were simple: Abdullah was the first Mujahideen leader I'd met with the brains and the balls to attempt something constructive, and if I didn't help him achieve it, nobody else was going to.

That evening, over supper, I told Blue that the next day we would be going to look at some water. He gave me a strange look, as if I'd flipped my lid, but raised no objection: the money was obviously still working.

We set off next morning around 5 a.m. and soon made the ten kilometres to the target. We followed a feeder stream which came down out of the mountains, then forked up onto a small plateau which gave us a good view over the whole area. Yet another surprise: as we settled into our OP, Abdullah pulled a large pair of naval binoculars from his jacket and began scanning the area, making notes and beginning a sketch of the area with guard positions marked in.

It was clear that the Soviets had identified the dam and its reservoir as a vulnerable point and there was a considerable guard force deployed throughout the target area. From our position it was possible to identify pillboxes, barbed wire and trenches running off the access road, and as we watched we heard an engine start and saw a T-55 tank pull out of a hull down position and drive down to the road where it refuelled from a bowser. Realistically, I knew that Abdullah's small force wouldn't have a hope of mounting a successful attack here; or, at least, not with their current level of military training.

But that didn't mean we couldn't do anything. The dam was out of the question, but the power lines that led from it seemed much more vulnerable and, according to my compass, went off in the direction of Kabul to the west and Bagram to the north. During the several hours we spent in the OP, several MI-8 helicopters appeared, apparently either patrolling the power lines or using them as a navigational aid, but security on the cables appeared far less intensive than on the dam. Hmm!

We left just before midday and headed back towards the town of Yakhdand which was close to Abdullah's base. We arrived there in the scorching heat of the early afternoon and settled in the shade of a tree while two of Abdullah's group went into the village to check that it was clear of enemy.

They came back to tell us everything was OK and in we went. First stop was a kind of barn from which the noises of heavy hammering and sawing were emanating. Abdullah ushered me in, and what I saw there nearly made me wet myself. Two Afghans with a large home-made hacksaw were sawing the end off an unexploded Soviet bomb. Every now and again, they would stop sawing, insert a steel chisel into the cut they'd made and give it a good hard whack. After a few minutes of this, the end of the bomb did indeed come off, and the Afghans began to pull out the characteristic sausage-shaped packages of explosives. No wonder they had so much!

'Have you never had an accident getting these explosives?' I asked Abdullah.

'No. Why?'

'Sometimes these bombs can be very sensitive, even though they didn't go off when they were dropped.'

'Oh, really?'

Abdullah didn't sound very interested and I decided not to point out that if one of the bombs went off, it would take most of the village with it. By now, the bomb casing was empty. The two Afghans lifted it off the trestle they had perched it on and placed it against the wall, then they began to eye up another one: a 250kg high-explosive iron bomb, bent, battered and unstable looking. I decided to make my excuses and leave. I returned to the tree by the stream bank, trying to look casual and not break into a run, and after a few minutes Abdullah joined me.

As we sat there, I explained to Abdullah why I didn't feel that an attack on the dam was feasible now, but I pointed out that he would get just as big an effect, in the short-term at least, if he blew up the power lines. We argued the toss back and forth for a while and eventually Abdullah came to his decision.

'Okay, Tom, we will attack the power cables.'

'That's a good decision, Abdullah. When you've had more time to train, and you have a bigger force, you'll be ready to take out the dam itself.'

He nodded; the Afghans were very proud and touchy, but they could also be pragmatic. Every time I made a suggestion I was walking a tightrope between helping them and offending them. Fortunately Abdullah had enough military training to be realistic about his own weaknesses, and positive about his strengths.

'Tom, come with me tonight to look at the cables.'

'Abdullah, I'd like to do that, but my job here is to find out what help you need and then to report back, not to get involved in attacks on the Russians.'

Now I'd said the wrong thing. Abdullah was becoming angry.

'Tom, you must understand that we are not fighting the Communists as a joke. Let me tell you something: I have a wife and a little boy who is two years old, and they live in a village near here with my family. In April, a convoy of Communists, Russian and Afghan, came to the village. They took two of my three brothers as conscripts to join the Afghan army. Then they decided to rape my wife and my two sisters. My father tried to stop them so they shot him dead.

91

'The convoy left my village and travelled on towards the next one, but on the way it was ambushed by Mujahideen. Rather than be slowed down by their new "conscripts", the Communists shot them, and my two brothers were killed.'

I'd seen that he carried a piece of wood with notches cut in it, and now he flourished it again.

'These cuts in the wood, there are eleven of them and each of them represents a dead Russian. Not an Afghan traitor: a Russian. This war is a jihad, a holy war against the Communists, but it is also a war of honour against these murderers.'

I sympathised with him, of course; how could I not? But this was no basis to fight a serious shooting war.

'I understand you, Abdullah, but if you let revenge overshadow logic, you'll get into trouble . . .'

I was getting worried about the direction the conversation was taking. I didn't want to piss Abdullah off too much, but I was saved by the timely arrival of Blue who had brought me some bread, at which point Abdullah went into the village to organise something.

After I'd eaten the naan, I took the opportunity to clean my rifle and then headed down to the stream for a wash.

When I'd finished, I went back to find Abdullah with a group of the village elders preparing for prayers in the mosque which doubled as a village hall. I pulled a sharp U-turn and went back to the shady tree, accompanied by six or seven children, where I made a good brew of compo tea with sugar and powdered milk, and handed out a few boiled sweets to the kids.

I leaned back against the tree, feeling fresher and more relaxed after my wash, and closed my eyes. In the far distance I could hear the thud of rotor blades – an ever present noise when I was in Afghanistan – but other than that, the only sound to disturb this hot, tranquil afternoon was the plaintive bleating of the village goats. It was hard to believe I was in a war zone.

I lay there dozing for an hour or so, until I was woken by Blue and Abdullah who were keen to find out what I wanted to do next. I would actually have liked to get on towards camps Three and Four, but Abdullah still wanted me to check on the plans he was making for the power-line attack and, as it was too late in the day to make a start for the camps, I reluctantly agreed.

We set off after nightfall, guided now by the light of a full moon, following the same track we'd used earlier in the day. We didn't use the same OP, however, because I wanted to get eyes on the guard compound, which would give us an idea of how many enemy soldiers there were and what their routine was. Instead, we settled into a small cave beneath an overhang in a low cliff face and waited.

By dawn we were all frozen and shivering. The only sound I could hear was the uncontrollable chatter of teeth: my own and the Afghans'. While it was still reasonably dark, I got Abdullah to send most of the guys back to a safer position beyond the skyline, while two or three of us maintained watch in the OP. There was still very little movement from the guards.

But around 6.30 a.m., things began to stir. First of all, a couple of soldiers came out of the guards' building and walked around the wire of their compound, then a patrol appeared, walking towards the compound along the line of the power cables.

From what I could see, the patrol consisted of about fifteen soldiers, mostly Afghans but including three unmistakable Europeans. They quickly entered the building and all was quiet again.

Twenty minutes later, the patrol came out once more. Looking through the binoculars I could see there had been a change of personnel: the same three Europeans were present, but a different set of Afghans was accompanying them, and I guessed that what we had just seen was a guard changeover supervised by the Russian advisers.

When the patrol had moved off a little, Abdullah detailed two guys to remain in the OP and the rest of us headed back, crouching low as we quickly crossed the ridgeline behind us. We picked up the rest of the group and made our way back to the village in time for a late breakfast of tea and naan.

We spent the rest of the morning discussing various aspects of the attack. Although we had plenty of PE and detonators, we only had one exploder – a plunger-type like you see in old films – which worked perfectly well but meant that we would only be able to take out one pylon. Never mind.

At midday the plan was as ready as it was ever going to be, and I reflected ruefully that I seemed to be certain to be taking part, no matter what I wanted to do. Abdullah and the rest went off to pray while I sat down under the shady tree to eat stale naan and tomatoes, and drank more tea. Despite the noise of the children playing near me, my lack of sleep during the past forty-eight hours was beginning to take its toll and I soon dozed off.

I don't know how long I'd been sleeping, but I was woken by the sound of a helicopter landing on the other side of the village and with a sudden sick feeling in the pit of my stomach, I realised that we were deeply in the shit. Jesus Christ, this was not good at all!

I jumped up, picked up my Kalashnikov and ran over to where I could see Blue and the rest of my group assembling outside the mosque. Abdullah was herding the children of the village into a basement and a few others were running around, but it was clear that the Afghans didn't have a clue what to do and that I was going to have to take charge. I wasn't going to Moscow if I could help it!

I did a quick count and saw we had twenty-three fighters in all, armed with a mixture of AKs, SKSs and G3s, together with Mohammed and his RPG-7. We didn't have a huge amount of ammunition, and my first instruction, via Blue, was to shoot single shots only.

'Only fire when you have a positive target to aim at; and only

94

fire single, aimed shots – we can't afford to waste ammunition.'

I pointed out some likely avenues of approach for the enemy and positioned the Mujahideen in a series of covered, inter-locking fire positions. As I was doing this, an old man ran up to us, dragging a case of 7.62mm x 39 ammunition, which was quickly distributed. Apparently the Afghans routinely buried ammo where it could easily be retrieved in time of emergency. Whatever, I was grateful for it now, because there was a possibility that this might turn into a Rorke's Drift situation, at least until the gunships arrived.

Leaving Blue in temporary charge, Abdullah and I hurried back through the village to set up our depth position. En route we met two ancient guys carrying .303 SMLE rifles, now rushing forward to grab themselves a piece of the action. At the rear of the village, Abdullah and I stationed a couple of his men as a rearguard, trying to impress on them the need to stay where they were to give us defence in depth, then we began to make our way forwards again.

We hadn't got far when there was an almighty outburst of automatic rifle fire from our front. Abdullah was looking a little wild-eyed by now, chanting something to himself, but he was sufficiently together to accompany me, and just as pissed off as me when we found out that the shooting had been a response to a couple of the enemy breaking cover to run across a track five hundred metres away – well beyond the useful range of the Kalashnikovs.

'For Christ's sake, boys! Don't shoot until you've got a clear target; you'll give away our numbers and position and you'll piss away our ammunition!' Abdullah shouted (a rough translation, minus the profanity).

One of our guys had an RPK, a section light machine gun, and I got Blue to take him back to the rearguard to beef up our depth position. Now looking around I was trying to work out some kind of scheme of manoeuvre, but nothing sprang immediately to mind. I wished we had just one GPMG or mortar, but these things happen, and one thing the SAS had taught me was that when the shit hits the fan, you've got to go with what you've got.

I called Abdullah over and told him that him, me and two others would form a small reserve, moving to reinforce areas which came under heavy pressure. At the rear of the village was a small re-entrant leading up into the hills, and close by it was an odd-shaped boulder about two metres in height. I pointed it out to Abdullah and told him:

'That rock there, that is our emergency rendezvous if the village is overrun. Anyone who is still alive and gets away should go there and regroup.' This information was quickly passed around, but as Abdullah's man rejoined us, there was a loud bang as an RPG round, I believe, hit a building just down the street from us, showering us in dust and grit.

By now there was a steady volume of fire coming in from our front and our left flank as the enemy soldiers tried to work their way round to an assault position. Our boys were returning fire, but mostly in single shots, and I think this was disconcerting for the enemy who weren't accustomed to the Mujahideen standing their ground or exercising any kind of fire discipline.

Around this time, a runner came up from the rear group to tell us that they were under heavy machine-gun fire. I went down to take a look and before I was even close I could see green tracer rounds bouncing and clattering all over the place. Shit. I sent the runner back to fetch Abdullah and the rest of the 'reserve', but almost as soon as he left, a group of thirty or forty enemy rose up from the area of the stream where I'd been sleeping only half an hour before and charged towards us. I opened fire at the leading section and together with our 'depth' position managed to drop a few, but we were in real trouble now, not least because I could clearly see a number of Europeans amongst the enemy. I dropped back down behind a low wall.

At this point Abdullah appeared with three guys, moving in

close, even though rounds were hammering against the wall and some were coming through.

'Abdullah, we've got to support the rear defence team. On a count of three, we'll all pop up and open fire on the enemy group by the stream.'

I counted three and we opened up, firing bursts to try to break up the momentum of the enemy advance. To my surprise they did stop shooting back for a few seconds, but we soon discovered why when, with a whoosh and a huge bang, an RPG grenade hit the wall just in front of us, blowing a huge hole but, miraculously, not injuring any of us.

'Fuck me, that was close!' I shouted, but Abdullah just looked uncomprehendingly at me.

We couldn't stay there any longer. That one had missed but the next one might get lucky. I was with Abdullah on one side of the hole, Blue and the other two lads were on the other, but in between, the enemy were pouring a hail of fire through the breach in the wall.

'Abdullah, if we work our way round through that alleyway, we should be able to link up with Blue.' He nodded and followed closely as I set off. We got round the corner and made eye contact with Blue, who began to work his way towards us, but there was too much fire coming in: there was no way we would be able to join up. Bollocks.

Still, it was clear for the moment that the attack had faltered a little. As far as I could see, the enemy weren't trying to overrun us but were trying to suppress the position with fire from their support machine guns. I told Abdullah that we had better check on the fighters at the front of the village, and after we'd filled an old bucket with ammunition from the crate, we made our way forwards, keeping low to avoid the rounds which were still cracking overhead.

In fact the group at the front had held out very well, and the two old men with their .303s were still popping away at any enemy soldiers foolish enough to show themselves, and cackling merrily while they did it. Even so, two of the fighters had been hit, and one of the wounded was in poor shape. I dragged him back into cover to get a good look at him and discovered that he'd taken a big round right through his chest. As I pulled back his shirt to get a better look at his wound, he simply expired then and there.

We left the bucket of ammunition with the forward group and headed back to where the crate was so that we could replen the guys at the rear. Rather than trying to find another bucket, Abdullah and I dragged the crate between us down the dusty alleyways, but as we got closer, we literally had to get down on our bellies and crawl, as so much fire was coming in.

It was clear when we got there that the rear position was on its last legs. Out of the five, one was dead and three were wounded, including Blue, who had received a gash across his cheek from a piece of flying metal. The other two had bullet or shrapnel grazes, but neither was particularly serious. I quickly sluiced Blue's wound with a surgical wipe and some antiseptic and stuck a dressing on it, and then told him to pull his guys back into the cover of another stone wall.

There was a lull in the firing and the Mujahideen took the opportunity to start refilling their magazines, but I was concerned: were the enemy moving forwards again? Leaving one guy with Blue, I took Abdullah and two others back along the street towards a house built round a courtyard where one of the village elders lived with his wife and daughter. As we got there, we heard shouting and screams from within, followed by a jumble of shots and other noise. We crouched low behind the courtyard wall and I looked across at Abdullah who was covering the rear of our group.

When I glanced back I saw the muzzles of three Kalashnikovs suddenly appear, poking over the wall. Almost immediately I realised that the closest of the three had a strange flash-hider of a type I had never seen before. I turned again, wildly gesticulating to attract the attention of my own team, and as I did so the owners of the Kalashnikovs made their move over to our side. Even now I can clearly remember thinking: 'What the fuck did you want to do that for, you fucking idiots?'

Two Afghan conscripts and a European came over the wall, only noticing us as they were momentarily poised in mid-air. The butt of my own Kalashnikov was already pressed into my shoulder, and I let go a long, violent burst at less than two metres' range, struggling to maintain my aim, switching fire between them as the weapon bucked and climbed. They had no chance; one of them did manage to pull his trigger and fire a couple of rounds, but they were nowhere near me. They were close enough for me to hit each of them several times in one burst and, without doubt, all three were dying as they flopped awkwardly into the dust.

There was no choice now but to try to deter any immediate follow-up. I put my Kalashnikov over the wall and let the rest of the magazine go. There was shouting, screaming, a few returned shots, but then silence. Shit, shit, shit; the smart money now had to be on a grenade coming our way: time to go.

I executed a quick magazine change and scuttled across the alleyway towards the partial cover of the next house. In my peripheral vision I caught an impression of the area beyond the wall: a dead body, maybe an Afghan soldier, and greasy, thick smoke rolling out through the smashed door of the old man's house. I signalled Abdullah to come with me and told the rest of the group to cover us. Move again.

I hopped over the wall, ran to the door and quickly scanned inside. A pool of blood covered almost the whole floor area, and in the middle of it was sprawled the body of the old man, his dead fingers loosely clutching a huge, ancient Webley revolver, worn silver with age. He had paid the price for trying to defend his home and family.

Now I moved inside to see what else was there and to shelter from a renewed storm of firing from a nearby building. Crouching low to avoid being seen through the windows, I shuffled towards the rear, and as I did so, I heard a curious sound: someone outside was blowing a whistle, as if for half-time in a football match.

Reaching the back of the house, I came across another body, this time a young woman. I could see the smooth skin of adolescence on her neck and forearms, but her face had been entirely shot away. As I stared down at her, I became aware that Abdullah was shouting excitedly at me in Pushtu, and, although I couldn't understand a word he was saying, he was obviously asking for instructions.

I ran back to the doorway and called the rest of the team in. Once they were assembled inside the entrance – and Abdullah had calmed down enough to speak and understand English – I explained to them as best I could that we needed to recce the rest of the village to try to ascertain who was in control. When I'd got this through to them, I checked that we all had full magazines fitted to our AKs and led them past the two corpses to the rear of the house.

The bullet-riddled back door was hanging open so I took a risk and grabbed a quick look out to see what was going on. There was no movement, but off to the left a column of bright red smoke was rising steadily above the wall which surrounded the rear courtyard. My stomach sank. Jesus! They're using gas. But after a few moments' terrified consideration I realised that none of the soldiers, Russian or Afghan, that I'd seen had been wearing or carrying gas masks so I reckoned we were probably OK. I took a deep breath to calm myself down and then crossed the courtyard, running bent double, to the rear gate. This was also burst open, probably broken down by the Afghan soldiers as they came in to clear the old man's house, and just outside lay the body of another dead Afghan infantryman, his teenage face frozen in an agonised grimace, rigid fingers clutching at an ugly chest wound: probably the old man's revolver.

I glanced out through the gate and caught a glimpse of movement in the cloud of smoke. I brought the AK up to my shoulder and let go a series of double taps, and a few rounds were returned in my direction. By now Abdullah and the other lads were with me and we all fired into the smoke which, in the absence of any breeze, was rising slowly straight up into the sky.

By now the enemy's firing was dying away and I guessed that they were probably withdrawing under cover of the dusty, opaque plume of smoke. We began to skirmish forwards and almost at once I came face to face with Blue and two of his team. It was a close call – we nearly shot each other – but fortunately we recognised one another in time to prevent a nasty accident.

We crouched down in cover and Abdullah tried to pump Blue for information about what was happening. He had no more idea than we did, but I took the opportunity to check that they were OK for ammunition, and Blue sent one of his two boys back into the old man's house to scavenge ammunition from the dead soldiers.

Blue's lad came back quickly with a pouch containing about ten full mags and after we'd distributed this, the seven of us carried on towards the centre of the village. On the way, we met three more from our group who had a terrified-looking prisoner, an Afghan boy of about seventeen with a face drained grey with shock and fear. It surprised me that they'd kept him alive this long after the way they'd dealt with the airman from the crashed helicopter; I'm not a betting man, but I'd have put a week's wages on this boy dying a painful death within twenty-four hours. Matey here had missed his chance for a quick way out, and he was going to regret it.

So now there were ten of us, together with the prisoner, and I began to feel slightly more confident that we would be able to protect ourselves if everything went tits up in the next few minutes. We could hear the sound of the Russian helicopters on the other side of the spur now, and it occurred to me that if the soldiers really were going to pull out, it was likely they were going to bomb the living shit out of the village before too long. With this in mind, I told Blue to send his boys round the village to start an evacuation, while the rest of us continued towards the centre.

As we moved forwards, we came across three more dead civilians and a cow which had been riddled with gunfire, and there were a further five or six corpses lying sprawled around the central area. It was only when we reached the village entrance that we began to meet the living. The first we saw was one of the old guys with the .303. He told us that the soldiers had made off over the hill towards the dam – which explained the noise of the helicopters – and as he was telling us this, women, children and old people began to emerge from the houses to survey the debris and to try to help the injured.

At this point, the other fighters from our group began to appear. Their news was not good: we had a total of four dead and nine wounded, and two of the wounded were in a really bad way. The priority now was to get everybody clear of the village before the gunships and bombers came to flatten it, but before I could organise that, I had one other task: to get the strange Kalashnikov from the dead Russian. I grabbed one of Abdullah's group to escort me – I didn't want to be mistaken for a stray Russian in the failing light – and headed back to the old man's house.

The Russian was still lying where I'd shot him, face down in the dust, a dark stain spread beneath him. I could see claw marks in the sand by his hands, so I presumed he'd lived for a few minutes after I'd shot him, but hadn't had the strength left to move himself at all. I guess he was doing the same kind of job as me: an advisor of sorts, maybe from Spetsnaz or the GRU. I was expecting to come across Russians, but it must have been a shock to him in the brief moment between seeing me and the first rounds hitting him to see a white face at the wrong end of a Kalashnikov.

I pulled the weapon out from underneath him and examined it. Apart from an extended flash-hider, which was similar to a CAR- 15, it looked much the same as my AKM. With my left hand I removed the magazine and put it in the pocket of my smock, then I pulled back the cocking handle and out popped a small round like a 5.56mm Armalite bullet – certainly very different from the usual stubby Kalashnikov round. Great. So this was an AK-74, the new Russian rifle: another of my objectives achieved. I slung the weapon across my back and briefly searched his pockets. Nothing. I took his spare ammunition from his pouches and cached it in my bergen, which I had left nearby, then I turned to leave. I didn't turn the Russian over; I didn't want to see his face.

By now Blue and Abdullah had organised the villagers for evacuation and we led off up the mountain slope to a point a couple of kilometres from the village where the civilians wanted to say prayers. As they organised themselves, I got behind a rock and began to brew up some tea over my hexamine stove, keeping a poncho close by which I could use to shield the flames from view. After I'd stirred in a sachet of sugar, I sat quietly by myself with my back to a rock. In the far distance, I could see flares being dropped from helicopters, along with the occasional flash of tracer ammunition and rockets. Another village getting it, almost certainly, and most likely the reason why they hadn't come here yet.

By now the villagers had finished their prayers and had begun a dialogue with Abdullah. This seemed to go on and on, with Abdullah haranguing them at considerable length and various members of the group energetically answering. By now the days' march and the aftermath of the firefight had caught up with me, and as the argument continued I dozed off.

I woke a little later to find Abdullah squatting next to me. The debate had evidently ended and the villagers were picking up their belongings.

'Where are they going?' I asked Abdullah.

'Back to the village.'

'But they can't . . . if they go back there, they'll be bombed for sure.'

'We both know this,' agreed Abdullah, 'and I have told them many times. They understand that the Communists will come back, but they say that the village is all they have and they must trust God to protect them. Where else can they go?'

There was no answer to that. Their whole way of life and all they owned was centred on the village. They had no alternative but to accept their fate and to hope that reprisals would not be too severe. The villagers bade their farewells and set off back down the slope whilst we prepared to head back to the Mujahideen camp.

We reached the base at about 3.30 a.m., after a slow exhausted march. One of the most severely injured had died on the way, but we carried him along anyway. After we'd arrived, I did what I could for the wounded, but what they all needed, above everything else, was rest, food and clean dressings. It was the same for the rest of us: I was so tired I could hardly stand upright, and Blue looked pretty much the same. The rear party, mostly older men, now set about preparing food and tea for us, and boiling water so that we could clean up the men's wounds, and when I'd got them as comfortable as I could manage, and after Abdullah, Blue and the other fighters had gone off to pray, I wrapped myself in my poncho, flopped down in an empty cave and went to sleep.

FIVE

I was woken by Abdullah at about 4.30 p.m. with the news that the village had been bombed. There wasn't much to say; we knew it was going to happen. I got a mug of tea and began to pull myself together. I picked up my rifle and my medical kit and walked over to the hut where the wounded were being looked after. Most of them seemed much better after a good sleep, but one was in poor shape and I guessed he was on his way out. As I was checking them, Abdullah wandered over, and together we went to find Blue.

We tracked him down in a small hut where he and the rest of my escort were lying flaked out on a pile of old straw, covered by a blanket. They were sound asleep and snoring loudly, but they still looked completely shattered, and I knew that there was no chance of going anywhere until they'd had a decent rest, and at least one more night's sleep.

As we walked back to the centre of the base, I asked Abdullah how far it was to camps Three and Four. His answer was not encouraging. It turned out that Camp Three was about thirty-five kilometres north-east of Jellalabad – about fifty kilometres from where we were as the crow flies – while Camp Four was well to the south-east of Jellalabad. A total march, if we managed to walk in straight lines, of around a further two hundred and fifty kilometres to get to them and back to the border via Camp One. Thanks a fucking bunch, William, I thought.

After evening prayers, we ate and then hit the sack again. As I was settling down, I caught a whiff of myself. Wow! I hadn't managed a proper wash or to get my boots off since we'd left Pakistan, and you could more or less see the noxious fumes coming from me. I made a note that the next day was going to be a proper admin day: I'd get myself cleaned up and back on the road again, ready for the off the day after.

I stayed in bed the next morning until about 6.30, and then I made myself a brew of English tea, with milk and sugar, and some porridge out of an oatmeal block, which went down a treat. When I'd heaved myself out of my pit, I grabbed my wash kit and walked down to the stream to sort myself out.

The relief at getting my boots off was extraordinary: my socks were stiff with dust and sweat and the gaps between my toes had become a painful mixture of athlete's foot and gunge. I stripped off my stinking shirt and trousers, pulled away the remaining shreds of my underpants and then jumped into the chilly water, letting it sluice away all the aches and pains of the last few days. I cleaned myself up, without bothering to shave, and then put on spare pants, shirt, socks and trousers and began the process of washing out my old ones.

When I'd laid my clothes out to dry, I went off to find Abdullah and discovered that he had left to visit another village about fifteen kilometres to our east. Blue told me that Abdullah had come to see if I wanted to go with him but that they couldn't wake me up. I found that hard to believe but decided to make the best of the situation and had another look around the base.

Tucked away in one of the grottier lean-tos was an interesting discovery: a completely unused 82mm mortar tube. I poked about a bit more and came up with an old but serviceable base plate and a new sight. I asked Blue about this, and he asked a couple of the others, and it turned out that nobody knew how to use it. I started to set it up, and soon a small crowd had gathered, anxious to see how it worked.

With Blue translating, I explained the workings of the mortar to this group of increasingly excited Afghans. When I'd finished telling them how to adjust fire onto a target and made a move to begin packing it up, there was storm of protest:

'No, no! You must fire it to show us how!'

'I can't, we need to have a safe area for the bombs to land.'

'Just shoot it at the mountain, it will be OK!'

I couldn't help thinking: why the fuck did I start this then?

I picked up a bomb and fused it, then attached the charge bags and primer and, warning the Afghans to get out of the way, dropped it down the tube. It launched with the characteristic metallic whoosh, and then there was silence. The Afghans looked disappointed, until suddenly: BOOM! The bomb exploded roughly where I'd aimed it, at the top of a rocky mound on the other side of the valley, showering birds, rocks and grit down the hillside, terrorising the mules and delighting the Afghans.

'Do it again, do it again,' they all shouted, like little kids on Guy Fawkes night. I could see a fuck-up looming.

'No, if we make too much noise we'll attract the Soviets . . .' It was the best excuse I could come up with at short notice. I whipped the sights off the mortar and began to remove the tube from the base plate. The Afghans mooched off like a bunch of children whose football has just burst. The birds were still squawking an hour later.

Abdullah returned during the late afternoon. I was surprised to learn that he had been taking the prisoner, captured during the firefight, down to his home village where he had volunteered to join the local Mujahideen group. It seemed that, like many Afghan soldiers, he had been press-ganged into joining the army and was now happy to have escaped. It struck me that the Mujahideen were very trusting to allow people to change sides so quickly and I mentioned this to Abdullah, but he simply remarked that they could always spot the liars and we left it at that.

After prayers that evening Abdullah introduced me to a fighter who was travelling to Camp Three and who would act as our guide, and then Abdullah, Blue and I sat down by the stream that ran through the camp to eat the chicken, tomatoes and rice which had been prepared for supper. It was a quiet, peaceful setting, and as we sat there, we fell into conversation about our lives. I knew already that they had both had a hard time, but listening to their hopes for the future made me suddenly feel very protective of them, and I resolved to do what I could to help them after I returned to Pakistan. Both were fantasising about a time when Afghanistan would be free from foreign domination, although they seemed sanguine about the likelihood that they would have to die to achieve it; but they also looked forward to being able to live in peace with their families. It was a nice thought for a quiet evening in the mountains, though, to be honest, I couldn't see it happening any time soon.

I asked Abdullah whether there was anything I could bring him – personally – to make life easier when I returned. All he wanted, he told me, was a camouflaged smock like mine, a rucksack and a belt with a water bottle and ammunition pouches. Really that summed up the Mujahideen. If you asked a British soldier the same question, you'd get a list as long as an army-surplus catalogue, but these Afghans were actually going at it, head-to-head against one of the most powerful armies in the history of the world, on a shoestring.

I turned my attention to Blue and, particularly, the gash he'd acquired on his face. With the dressing off I could see it was healing well, so I cleaned it up a little more and applied a new dressing. While I was doing this I remarked to him that if we didn't move the next day, I would be in deep shit. He laughed.

'Yes, Tom, sometimes it's good to move on.'

I drank a last mug of tea and then went to get my head down, leaving the Afghans to talk amongst themselves.

I woke at 4.30 the next morning to find that the weather had changed: it was cold and overcast and clouds were rolling along the valley. I pulled on my windproof and went in search of some breakfast, shivering in the unaccustomed morning chill as I ate naan and drank green tea. As I was finishing off, Blue and the boys came back from their prayers, accompanied by Abdullah who had come to say his farewells. I promised him that I would return in about a month with the equipment he needed.

We set off at 6.15, making slow progress through low clouds and drizzle as we climbed steadily into the mountains, heading in the direction of Camp Three at Panj Likhla. From the summit of the range at seven thousand feet, we could clearly see both the dam that Abdullah had wanted to attack, and a second dam and power plant at Chahar Bagh-e-Laghman, which supplied Jellalabad and a number of other places with their electricity. From this point, it was a steady downhill slog to the Kabul–Jellalabad road, which we would have to cross, and then back into the mountains for the approach to Camp Three.

But this proved easier said than done. As we got closer to the road, it emerged that this was the first time our guide had followed this route, and try as he might, he could not locate the storm drain or culvert which we were supposed to use to cross the road. We spent an hour or so farting around, dangerously exposed to the view of anyone on the road who happened to have their eyes open, before I reached the conclusion that we would be better off simply waiting until darkness and crossing then. We retreated a few hundred metres and settled down to wait as the rain became increasingly heavy.

The Afghans are proud men and our guide was despondent

that he'd failed; so much so that he wouldn't – or couldn't – look me in the eye. I decided that we needed to cheer ourselves up and so I moved in to a sheltered spot and made a brew over my hexamine cooker which we shared round. This probably would have lightened the mood had it not really started to piss with rain. Instead, we huddled together under my two ponchos and tried, unsuccessfully, to stay dry as darkness slowly fell.

Traffic slackened on the road as the evening progressed, and at about 6.30 I decided that we needed to try to cross, even though it was by no means fully dark. We closed up to the roadway and sheltered in a ditch and then, one by one, scuttled across and into cover on the other side. No sooner had the last man got across than we heard the sound of engines being revved and the squeal and clatter of tank tracks coming along the road from the direction of the dams. As I poked my head up to see what was happening, a searchlight beam stabbed out of the gloom, purposefully probing the shadows at the side of the road. I told my team to stay still – nine times out of ten it's movement that gives you away – and we waited for twenty minutes as eight or ten tanks rolled slowly past, evidently doing some sort of patrol.

We crossed open ground until we arrived at the river which fed the reservoirs. In the twilight we could just make out a bridge a few hundred yards away but, as I was debating with myself whether we should take the risk of using it, a door opened from a nearby hut and someone came out. That settled the matter. We followed the river until we came to a point where it narrowed slightly, and then waded through the waist-deep water to the other side.

There was a road parallelling the river on the far bank but no traffic and we soon skipped across and began our ascent into yet more mountains. It was getting close to 11 p.m. and completely dark, and we needed somewhere to stop for the night. After a brief search, one of the Afghans spotted a rocky overhang which would protect us from the elements, and after Blue and the boys had said their prayers, we huddled together for the night.

We were up at first light, and I made us a brew while Blue and Mohammed held up my poncho to shield the flames from view. We ate a few compo biscuits, the boys said some prayers and then we were off, following a goat drover's path up into the hills.

We stopped in mid-morning for a quick break and as we sat there, a huge flock of goats ambled past, followed by an old man who greeted us cheerily as if it was completely normal to find a group of armed men lurking around his grazing. Mind you, this being Afghanistan, it probably was. We carried on through the day and eventually, in the late evening, we arrived at a stream where two Afghan men were sitting. There was some shouting, and I slipped the selector lever on my Kalashnikov to automatic as a precaution, but after a short wait, a huge man, at least six foot six inches tall, appeared and invited us to enter his cave. We'd arrived at Camp Three.

The cave was large and deep, and there were a good number of Afghans sheltered inside. After prayers had been said, we were brought a stew of goat meat, with rice and salad, and as we ate, we spoke with the commander.

It soon emerged why they stayed inside the caves. Some weeks before, Russian helicopters had landed troops at two positions near the summit of the mountain we were sheltering on. The Russians had started to construct forts – not unlike the hilltop observation posts the British Army put in along the Irish border – but the Mujahideen had launched repeated attacks against them and eventually the Russians had abandoned the position. Instead, they now flew repeated Hind sorties over the mountain in the hope of drawing ground fire; and when they did, they retaliated with rockets and bombs.

He was also surprised that we had managed to get through so easily. Apparently the Russians were patrolling extensively, and there had been several ambushes in recent weeks. It didn't surprise me.

111

'Look, basically the Russians know that you're here. For them, it's a question of priorities: when they have the time and the manpower, they're going to come and get you. If you make too much of a nuisance of yourselves, then it will be sooner rather than later.'

Blue was a bit hesitant about translating this, but the commander didn't seem put out. Now, shagged out after a hard day's walking, it was time to get my head down. I found an empty nook inside the cave and rolled up in my poncho, with my belt kit as a pillow and my rifle next to me. I didn't want to take any chances.

I walked out next morning just after five to find that the clouds had blown away and the sun was shining. It was still cold, but I knew now that it would be warm again within a few hours. Blue and the boys came back from prayers as tea and naan were set out for our breakfast, and I told him that I wanted to see round the camp and be out again by 2 p.m. at the latest. He didn't exactly dance with joy at this news and I began to realise just how tired the Afghans were: it wasn't that they were unfit – far from it – but they had had months of poor nutrition, anxiety and constant travel, and they were getting close to the ends of their tethers. The commander had sent a young Mujahideen to show me around the camp and we did the usual tour of caves filled with ammunition, weapons and rusting equipment. There was nothing of intelligence interest that I could see, and so we prepared to continue our journey.

We left soon after midday prayers, accompanied by two guides courtesy of the giant commander. As we followed yet another goat track, we encountered a group of twenty or thirty Mujahideen, stumbling exhaustedly towards the camp. We stopped briefly to exchange gossip and learned that they were *en route* to the Panjshir Valley from Pakistan to join the Mujahideen band led by the then little-known Ahmed Shah Massoud, later to be recognised as the great guerrilla commander of the Afghanistan war. To be honest, they looked completely chin-strapped, staggering dazedly uphill under crushingly heavy loads, an easy prey for an ambush. We let them continue on their way, and we followed our own path towards Camp Four at Shahi Kowt.

Towards last light the terrain began to level out and we arrived at a road junction. Normal procedure would have meant that we would observe the road for twenty minutes or so before attempting a crossing, but the need for speed was pressing now and we piled straight over. The map showed that we were about to cross a marshy area followed by three streams but it turned out that the summer heat had largely dried out the marsh, making it easy to get through. But the same wasn't true of the streams: they were deep, fast and dangerous. The first guide got in and was straight up to his armpits in water; I followed him, and being slightly shorter got ice-cold water up to my neck. Aaargh!

Still, it was a good sluice-down and my bergen, packed with a waterproof dry-bag, kept me buoyant while I held my AKM above my head and kept my map tucked into my bush hat. I got out of the water and stood for a few moments as the water poured off me, then turned to assist Blue and his gang as they came over. Unfortunately, of course, most of the Mujahideen couldn't swim and it took more than an hour to get them across, and the best part of four hours to get us all over the three streams. There was now a slight climb up to yet another road which headed off towards Jellalabad, and across this into more mountains.

We climbed all night, into the crystal-clear, starlit sky. From the first summit we could see, far in the distance, the twinkling lights of Jellalabad, and as we trudged through the darkness, they continually reappeared to remind me how close to a form of civilisation we really were. As the first light of dawn began to break – around 3 a.m. – we came across a disused goatherd's cave. This would have to be our home until the next evening; it was impossible to cross the plains around Jellalabad in daylight.

We got inside and set up a poncho close to the entrance to

shield us from any chance sightings, then I got the stove on and brewed us some tea and handed out a few compo biscuits. Fed and watered, I opened my bergen to find that a lot of the contents had, in fact, got wet: shit! I unpacked it all and arranged it to dry out as much as possible, then got myself rolled up in my second poncho for a kip.

I suppose I'd been asleep for two hours when the sound of a low-flying helicopter woke me. I looked around groggily, as the sound of the chopper faded into the distance, and tried to settle down again. Somehow, I couldn't get back to sleep. The cave was full of fleas and I felt as if I was crawling with them; I was also thirsty, and worried that I was down to my last half bottle of water. One gripe I had with the Afghans was that they would only carry half a plastic pop bottle of water: they wanted to keep the weight down, and they knew I had three one-litre bottles in my belt and bergen. I was scrupulous about keeping my bottles topped up from any stream we crossed (and sterilised with two Puritabs), but Blue and the Mujahideen would just drink straight from the streams, and as a result they were all afflicted with chronic diarrhoea from gut infestations.

It was a long, hot day in the cave, but it gave me the chance to clean myself and my kit a little, and to doze on and off for twenty minutes or half an hour at a time. In the late afternoon I repacked my bergen properly and got a brew on, scoffed down a few biscuits and suddenly found myself feeling fighting fit again; ready for the off and raring to go. I suppose I'd just needed the rest, but there was no doubt that I was feeling the strain of isolation a little. The Afghans were great guys and we got on fine, but there's no question that it helps to have one of your own kind along, if only so you can take the piss a bit or crack a joke. It helps you get through the day.

Blue and the boys said their evening prayers and with the light fading fast we set off, heading quickly down the track towards the flat plains which surround Jellalabad. Our target was a road and it wasn't hard to spot it: a ribbon of yellow light in the gathering dusk where vehicles had been halted at a checkpoint. I soon found that our guides were parallelling the road, taking us towards the checkpoint, and this bothered me. I grabbed Blue and the two guides and asked what we were doing. It seemed that they needed to find a particular junction which would indicate to them a crossing point on the Darya-Ye-Kabul river.

'How often do you use this crossing?' I asked as casually as possible.

'Oh, there are groups going over every two or three days,' was the calm reply.

I had a nasty sinking feeling in my stomach: one day they were going to walk into a terminal ambush there. I hoped it wasn't going to be tonight.

It turned out that the checkpoint was being mounted at the road junction we were looking for. Perfectly normal but a pain in the arse for us as it meant a detour of a kilometre or so as we boxed around it. Once we were across the road – and across a second, minor one – we arrived at a swampy area which apparently led all the way to the river. The Afghans removed their boots and sandals but I stupidly decided to keep mine on, a decision that I started to regret almost immediately.

We spent the next hour and a half slopping through the stinking mud, being bitten and eaten by virtually every mosquito and leech that ever lived. When we got to the river, it was to discover that it was actually quite fast-flowing, and chest deep in places, though this was in some respects a relief as it got the gooey, shit-smelling bog mud off us fairly efficiently. When we reached the far bank, we were soon climbing again, skirting the village of Gardi Kac to the sound of barking dogs. After a stiff climb, the ground levelled out at around fifteen hundred metres and in the distance we could make out our next obstacle, the Kabul–Peshawar road which snaked off towards the Khyber Pass to our south. This was a road along which at least two

British armies had marched to destruction and it was now just as militarily important, picketed night and day as the Soviets used it as a main conduit to carry men and material to the border in their – so far – vain attempts to stop Mujahideen infiltration.

It was now about 1.30 p.m., but the road was still busy and from a kilometre or so we could see some evidence of security procedures in operation: a huge, powerful searchlight was being shone on the mountain slopes on the other side of the road; and we could hear the distorted boom of orders being shouted through a megaphone. The guides stopped and I went forward to discuss our next moves with them. As we debated, a stream of green tracer was fired into the air from a few kilometres to our left, drifting into the sky and burning out behind us. A jumpy sentry probably, but also a warning to be careful.

The reason we had stopped, it emerged, was that one of the guides thought he had seen movement on the route that we needed to take, while the other was sure that it was all clear. Through Blue, I urged them to make up their minds.

'If we're caught out in the open here at daylight, we will be in deep shit!'

At this point, I saw movement as well. We passed the word quickly back and, as quietly as possible, settled down into fire positions. As the seconds passed, I could see that there was a group of people walking towards us, coming back along the route that we were taking, the tension mounting until one of the guides muttered something to Blue.

'Tom, Tom, it's OK, they're Mujahideen!'

Thank fuck for that! Still, I was half expecting some kind of balls-up as the two groups came across each other. I was wrong; they passed us without spotting us and carried merrily on their way. But I was concerned that the other group's passage might have been what provoked the shooting we'd seen just before. If we had been dealing with the British or US armies, then they would have undoubtedly followed up with a patrol, if only to reassure themselves that it was only nerves. Nothing came.

We reached the road – a broad, modern blacktop – at the favoured Mujahideen crossing point, close to a set of power lines, and ran across; fast, low and as a group. We got to the other side without incident, crossed a low ridge and found ourselves on flat, open countryside, completely devoid of any worthwhile cover. It was now about quarter to three in the morning, just before dawn, and we had about ten kilometres – six miles – to go to reach the relative safety of the mountains. We were going to be caught in daylight.

We began to pick up the pace. Nobody was beasting us; we had no choice. The warm magenta light of early dawn began to surround us, and the sweat was pouring from me. I was carrying a bergen weighing around fifty pounds, together with my belt kit and weapon, and the weight was beginning to tell. Even some of the Afghans, who were carrying much less, were flagging. Close to full dawn, we reached the outskirts of a small village and one of the guides went to check whether we could stay there. Fifteen minutes later he returned. Unfortunately, it seemed the Afghan army were regular visitors and we wouldn't be safe, but on the other side was an area where we could lie up for the day to rest and shelter before continuing on to Camp Four.

It turned out that the lie-up area was a dried-up streambed with steep sides, into which a number of small caves had been dug. We were all pretty hungry by now, having not eaten substantially for a couple of days, but we were short of food. Checking through my bergen, I found I had three packets of dehydrated mutton curry with rice, a couple of tins of compo chocolate, half a tin of oatmeal blocks and some boiled sweets. Not much between ten of us but it would have to do.

I only had two mess tins and one spoon, but everyone took their turn and got a fair share. When the food had gone, I took the mess tins to the stream and washed up, and then repacked my cooking kit, making a mental note that I only had enough hexy left for three or four brews at most. Once I'd washed my face and neck, and refilled my water bottles, I went back to the little dugout to get my head down.

Sleep wasn't easy: it was scorching hot, there was no wind, the air was full of flies and the mud floor of the cave was thick with ticks. I could feel the little fuckers burrowing into the skin on my legs and arse. What's more, there was a constant level of air activity nearby; not only helicopters, which were ever present, but fixed-wing Antonov transports, and high-flying Migs as well. All in all, I think most of us were glad when evening came and we were able to continue.

It was only fifteen kilometres further to Camp Four, in the hills above the town of Shahi Kowt, and we covered the ground in a few hours, arriving just before midnight. As usual, we got some food down our necks, and then Blue and I went to speak to the commander.

This particular commander was in his forties, and even after he'd read my letter of introduction treated me with a certain circumspection. From what I could gather he was very pro-Iranian, which meant that I had to be extra careful about everything I said, even though it was a strict rule of mine never to discuss politics or religion with the Mujahideen. He also understood English, although he claimed not to be able to speak it, and when I enquired how he could do this, he told me that he'd learned it from listening to the BBC World Service and, as a result, was also perfectly able to talk about British and American politics – a somewhat unusual talent among the insular Afghans. At this point he told me that his name was Salim, a detail which I had avoided finding out from previous commanders (except Abdullah), on the basis that I didn't really need to know, and he began to unwind and talk in a much more relaxed and friendly manner.

What emerged from our conversation was that he'd held quite high rank in the Afghan army (a major or colonel, from what I could gather) and he had a sound military brain. We chatted for a while about Soviet tactics, then I got myself a brew, rolled myself into my poncho and turned in.

Tired as I was, though, I couldn't get off to sleep. For some reason I kept on thinking about all the events of the last couple of weeks and, I suppose, trying to impose some order on them. I'd done a lot, no question, but there was much still to do. I thought of William and his idea that I could visit all the camps in a week and how lucky it was that we'd eventually agreed to leave the timetable open. The reality of life with the Mujahideen was that time had little or no meaning: we moved when it was reasonably safe to do so, but my operations were largely constrained by what the Soviets were doing, not by a fantasy schedule imposed by some spook in London or Washington.

I must have drifted off at some point because the next thing I heard was the morning call to prayer and in the dim pre-dawn half light I could make out the shapes of the fighters as they went outside. I hauled myself up and looked out, watching early morning mist rolling through the valley as I automatically went through the motions of getting a brew on. Sitting drinking my tea, I decided that the next move must be to get back to Pakistan, via Camp One where I needed to retrieve the armour plate from the Hind. With prayers finished, Blue came over and sat with me. After I'd checked the wound on his face, which was healing very nicely, he asked:

'Tom, what do you want to do next?'

'I think it's time to head back to Peshawar. Tell me, will it be possible to hire mules or donkeys to carry the armour plate from Camp One?'

'I don't think it will be a problem, but it will take a day for them to get here because they need to be brought from another camp.'

'That's fine; we need the rest. You get us some mules, then, and we'll move out to Camp One tomorrow.'

119

I spent the rest of the morning giving my rifle a thorough clean out, and then unloading, disassembling and cleaning my magazines, which had managed to attract a good deal of sand and grit. It occurred to me that I hadn't seen a Mujahideen ever clean his weapon, let alone the magazines, and it struck me what a good rifle the Kalashnikov is to still be able to function after the kind of abuse it gets from the average Third-World soldier. In comparison, the British SA80 gives up the ghost as soon as you see sand or snow, let alone leave it uncleaned for three months.

After midday prayers, a light lunch of meat, chicken, tomatoes and naan was laid out, and when we'd finished, I took myself off to the nearby stream for a good wash. I felt like an old stray dog: in addition to the dirt, I was now hosting a thriving colony of fleas, as well as a few ticks, lice and other nasties. I was half-way through my ablutions and soaking wet when I heard Blue calling my name. I quickly pulled my wet clothes back on and hurried over to see what was the matter. When I found Blue he was flapping like a budgie.

'What's the matter, Blue?'

'A messenger has come from Abdullah at Camp Five. There is a big force of Communists approaching his camp and he needs help.'

We walked over to Salim's hut and found him deep in conversation with a young man I recognised from Camp Five. Salim looked up and nodded at me as I entered, and I took a place on the rug in the corner from where I could observe what was happening. As I sat there, several more fighters came into the hut, and soon a big Chinese parliament had started, with all of them talking ten to the dozen.

After a few minutes, the debate had become quite heated, and when Blue came and sat next to me, I was at last able to discover what the fuck was happening.

'Tom, Salim says we must all go to help Abdullah defend his area. Salim says that because it is an emergency I must go, as well as all the rest of your escorts.'

That left me with a simple choice: accompany them or stay behind with the sick, lame and lazy. Oh well, it would be nice to see Abdullah again.

It took about an hour for the Mujahideen to get themselves ready. They loaded up a few mules with cases of ammunition, RPG-7 rockets, a complete 12.7mm Dshk machine gun and a few anti-tank mines, got a little speech from their mullah, and then set off. It was about 2.45 and with thirty-odd kilometres to cover, I reckoned we ought to arrive at about 9 p.m., give or take, which would mean a final approach to Camp Five in darkness, but at least we shouldn't be visible to the Soviets.

I'd thought that Salim knew his stuff, but the move was a complete gang-fuck. We made the first ten kilometres in good time, but then they stopped to pray. We set off again half an hour later, but now we were going much slower and I could see that we certainly weren't going to get there before 10 p.m. hours. We stopped for more prayers at 7 p.m. as dusk was beginning to descend and when we moved off again there was some confusion about which way we should go. After an hour or so of farting around, it was decided that we should stay where we were for the night. We stopped and the mules were unloaded, then the Chinese parliament went into full session. Even worse, someone lit a fire.

Fuck this, I thought, and I took myself off to find somewhere sheltered to sleep, as far from the fire as I could get while still remaining within our notional defensive perimeter.

Once again, sleep was difficult, though this time only because every fifteen or twenty minutes the sentries would yell out 'Allah Akhbar!' at the tops of their voices, in order to reassure themselves as well as, presumably, to help the enemy vector in his mortars on our position. If the Soviets were any good, we should have been hit hard that night.

But we weren't.

At about 2.30 I gave up trying to sleep and walked over to the fire where I made myself a brew. One of the sentries came over and sat with me. He spoke no English, so we simply sat there, staring mutely into the fire, waiting for the first signs of dawn.

Dawn arrived at about 4 a.m. and my silent companion went off to wake the others for prayer. After a rushed breakfast, we set off, mincing along in the same stupid gaggle as before like a bunch of schoolgirls on a day out at the museum. Around 7 a.m. we heard the first sound of helicopters. Looking about me, I could see fuck all cover to speak of, and I can't say I was all that pleased when Salim and his second-in-command stopped, with the rest of us out in the open, to discuss this interesting development. I was having really serious doubts about the wisdom of my decision to accompany this bunch: there was a good chance that we were going to have a contact at some point, either with ground troops or with helicopters, yet these boys made no effort whatsoever to move or even think tactically. Although I'd impressed on Blue and 'my' team the need to keep well spaced out at all times – and they were keeping to it – the rest of the gang were walking in a mob that would be a machine gunner's wet dream. Fortunately, whoever the helicopters were after, it wasn't us on this particular day, and we were able to continue – even if we did look like Fred Carno's army on their day off.

Soon afterwards we arrived at the road which had caused us so many problems when we left Abdullah's camp. In broad daylight, it was busy enough for me to wonder at the sanity of the Mujahideen for stopping where we did the night before, rather than continuing under the cover of darkness. We parallelled the road for a couple of hundred metres and then swung down into a culvert which led to a storm drain – evidently the crossing point we'd failed to find last time out. It was big enough to get the loaded mules through – the rest of us went through with ease – and after we'd climbed a few hundred metres from the road, we stopped for prayers and, in my case anyway, a nice cup of tea.

By the time we resumed our climb, the sun was much higher

in the sky and the day was turning into a scorcher. There was no wind, and the dusty air simply hung around us like a warm blanket. Although I knew there were only about four kilometres to go – an hour or so's walk at most – it was hard not to switch off and go into autopilot. My smock, trousers and shirt were soaked in sweat, and my boots were white with salt. When you do SAS selection, you get your head down, your arse up, put one foot in front of the other and park your mind in neutral – it's the way to get through – but on operations that kind of attitude will literally be fatal. You have to stay sharp. I was glad, then, when a challenge was shouted and an old man in his sixties or seventies popped up from behind a rock, waving a Kalashnikov. We were back at Camp Five.

SIX

The only problem was that, apart from a few old men, and some women who were washing clothes and cooking, there was nobody else there. Certainly Abdullah was nowhere to be seen. I thought to myself: this'll be interesting, what are they going to do now? Most of the lads I'd come with were completely fucked. They just stood around, gasping at the hot, dusty air, watching blankly as the senior men convened yet another useless bloody discussion group.

I wandered over to the cooking fire and poured myself a mug of tea from the Afghans' pot. It must have been brewing since the early morning; it was so stewed it was like drinking liquorice, but it was hot and wet, and just what I needed right then. I sat down in the shade and rested as a couple of women set out a salad and some naan for our lunch. When it was ready, I stumbled over, with the rest of the group, and began to wolf it down: it was excellent, and by now they'd made some fresh green tea as well which really took the edge off our thirst.

When we'd finished, Blue and I walked over to the commander to find out what was happening. He was talking animatedly with his second-in-command, and it turned out that he wasn't at all sure what to do next. The problem was that Abdullah had gone off with his fighters, and nobody had had any word from him for at least twenty-four hours. This wasn't a worry in itself – they didn't have any radios after all – but it meant that, although we were supposed to be supporting Abdullah, we had no idea how to do so. I left them to it and went off to Abdullah's shack to get my head down for a much-needed nap.

I was woken an hour or so later by the whoosh of a jet flying over, low and fast. By the time I got out of the hut, it was a small dot, dwindling in the distance. Probably air recce, I reasoned, or maybe a bombing run. Blue came over, from where he'd been talking to the old man who'd been left in charge.

'He says that it has flown over many times in the last week, always alone, very fast and very low. He wonders whether it is lost and trying to find its way back to the airfield.'

'I think that's unlikely, Blue. These aircraft don't get lost; and they don't operate alone. He'll have a mate around someplace . . .'

I wondered momentarily whether he might be trying to draw ground fire, but then dismissed the idea: you only need one lucky shot to bring one of these fuckers down, and it would not be a good day for the pilot to fall alive into the hands of the Mujahideen.

I walked over to where the commander's debating society was still in session. He exchanged a few words with Blue, who turned to me and said:

'The commander has decided that tonight we will go to find Abdullah's group.'

'What, all of us?'

'Yes, Tom.'

This was daft.

'Blue, tell him that if we all go wandering around at night in a big group, we will almost certainly get in the shit. What he should do is send out several small groups of two or three to particular places, and get them to return here by a set time – say midday tomorrow – whether they've found him or not.'

Blue translated this and there was a short discussion.

'The commander agrees with you, but says they do not have watches so they won't know when it is midday.'

'Well, tell them last light tomorrow then.'

When this was agreed we got my map out and got the old man to point out where he thought Abdullah had gone, then identified a couple of places about ten kilometres from us where we could send our scouts. Around 4.30 p.m., the two teams left and I went back to Abdullah's hut to get a brew on, thinking to myself: these boys have got to get organised.

Later in the evening, I was sitting outside the hut, watching the last rays of the setting sun as the Afghans prayed. I must have drifted off, because the next thing I knew, Blue was squatting next to me, asking in an anxious voice if I was all right.

'I'm fine, Blue, just thinking. Even the British think sometimes.' He laughed and sat next to me. Considering everything they'd been through, they were a cheerful bunch and very friendly once they had accepted you. We sat quietly together for half an hour or so, making the occasional comment, then I decided to clean my AKM and get my head down.

It seemed I'd only been asleep a few minutes when I was woken by a commotion outside (it was actually nearer five hours). I grabbed my belt kit and weapon and peered out to see what was happening but it was so dark I couldn't make out jack shit. On the assumption that as there had been no shooting, it probably wasn't the enemy, I went out to see what was going on.

It turned out to be a small group of Mujahideen who had just come from Abdullah's position at a village called Zirani. They had been sent back to escort a couple of casualties. The name rang a bell and I took a quick look at my map to see where it was.

Bollocks! We'd bypassed it on the journey here from Camp Four.

I took a look at the two wounded lads and quickly realised there was very little I could do. Both had taken rounds through the guts, and needed a very quick helicopter evacuation if they were going to make it. They weren't.

The problem with a bullet through the abdomen is infection. Obviously, you get a lot of damage to organs like the liver, kidneys, intestines and so on, but you can overcome these with skilful surgery. What will finish you off – particularly in the conditions we were operating in – is the infection caused by all the shit that a bullet takes into your body with it, and which leaks out of your alimentary canal when it's been pierced in several places by the passage of the bullet. I put some water on to boil, and with Blue holding up an oil lamp – it must have looked like something out of the Crimean War – set about cleaning them up as best I could.

Once the wounds were bandaged, I pulled out my drugs pack to sort out some medication. I had courses of penicillin and tetracycline capsules, as well as streptomycin which I could inject, but I was reluctant to use the injections because I was worried that if they pegged out – and I was fairly sure they were going to – I would get the blame. In the end I decided, wrongly, to just give them the tablets.

I went out of the hut to see what was happening, and found that the guy who had come back from Abdullah, Mahmoud, had taken charge and was getting everybody organised to go to help Abdullah. He wanted me to help him formulate a plan to get to Abdullah, and he wanted to borrow my map, which I reluctantly gave him. As we were talking, the young woman who had been nursing the two wounded fighters came out to say that one of them was making strange noises. Blue translated this and asked if I would take another look. Of course I agreed, but as I was making for the hut, Mahmoud quietly asked me what their chances were.

'Not good,' was all I could say. He nodded.

We went in to find that the more badly injured of the two was delirious with pain, sucking in whistling breaths and whimpering, sweating with the infection that was already setting in. I doubt he had the strength for more than twenty-four hours. I thought for a moment, and then decided to give him one of the four syrettes of morphine I was carrying. From both medical and tactical points of view, this was wrong: morphine depresses respiration and shouldn't be used for abdominal and chest injuries; and the morphine was supposed to be only for me, a last-resort painkiller which might let me slip away if we got ambushed and I was injured, as Jock the Clog had once done in Borneo. But it seemed to me the only thing to do: I was the only one around with either the knowledge or the equipment to ease his pain and I wasn't going to leave him to die in agony. I injected the morphine into the fleshy part of his thigh and we waited as he, quite quickly, drifted off to sleep. I hoped he would die soon. Looking at his face, he couldn't have been more than twenty-four or twenty-five.

The other one was still holding out, though. I delved into my pack for a couple more tetracycline capsules for the 'nurse' to give him in six or seven hours when he woke up, but as I turned to explain this to her, she shrieked and ran away.

'What the fuck's wrong with her?'

'I'm sorry, Tom, these people in the mountains are very primitive,' explained Blue. 'She believes that if she looks into the eyes of an infidel, then she will become infertile. If she is infertile, she will never bring her family a dowry, and she will be cast out or sold as a slave.'

I laughed.

'Shit, I thought it was something I said!'

Blue laughed at this as well.

'Do women always run away from you, Tom?' he joked.

'Only when they get to know me.'

I didn't want to go too far down this particular conversational route: there were too many ways in which I could offend Blue. I told him to make sure to tell the girl to give the capsules to the wounded guy in six hours, then went outside to see what was happening.

Mahmoud had got the whole bunch formed up in a mob outside, and was standing on a pile of logs giving them the run-down on what they were off to do. He hadn't got very far when an old mullah limped up, and started jabbering away in a combination of Pushtu and Arabic, clearly getting the boys all psyched up. As he reached his crescendo, the only words I could catch were:

'Jihad! Jihad!'

I turned to Blue.

'What does that mean then?'

'Jihad is the holy war against the infidel Communists. If you are killed in the jihad, you are blessed in the eyes of God and you will sit at his right hand in paradise.'

'Can't be bad.'

The mullah had finished now and everyone was ready to go. Well, everyone except me: I didn't have a clue what was happening. I asked Blue what we were doing; he didn't know either. Oh shit; I sensed that a big fuck-up was just entering its early stages. There were thirty-two of us, including me, in this group, and I don't think one person had a real idea about what we were going to do next.

I'd taken the precaution of acquiring six extra magazines for my AKM and even Blue had got hold of a few more. I wasn't sure if that was a good sign or not, and I was wishing that I'd taken the time to teach him and the boys some anti-ambush drills. I had a feeling they might come in handy over the next few days. We set off in a bunch and made good speed, but I can't pretend I wasn't feeling extremely nervous: these boys had Islam and a promise of eventual paradise if they were killed or captured (which out here would amount to the same thing), but if anything went wrong and the Soviets got hold of me, a European, I was going to Moscow, dead or alive.

After an hour or so of hard tabbing, we started to hear the distant sound of a loud bang every few minutes. I put this down to an artillery piece, or possibly a mortar, firing somewhere way down our line of advance, but as time passed, we could also discern the sound of heavy machine-gun fire, and what might have been grenades as well. I jogged forward to Mahmoud and asked whether he had a plan or whether we were just going to charge forward and pile in. He told me that we were due to meet up with another group from a different area and that we would join up with them. I'm not sure that this cheered me up very much.

We'd come to the end of this particular range of mountains. Zirani – where Abdullah was supposedly waiting with his merry crew – was some twelve kilometres to our front across the plain, while the town of Shahidan was four clicks to our right. By now, the sound of the explosions was getting quite loud and, although it was impossible to see clearly through the heat haze, we were evidently about to encounter their source.

Surprise, surprise! At this point, the Chinese parliament reconvened for a plenary session. Too late, though. As they talked, a T-55 tank rumbled out of the haze about two clicks from where we sat, its gun pointing at something out on the plain, and then fired a round. The haze was too heavy to allow us to see what it was shooting at but it did persuade the Mujahideen to get down into whatever cover they could find.

I scuttled across to where Mahmoud was trying to spread out his map. He was a bit short on ideas about what we should do next, but I was quite keen to make sure it wasn't anything stupid. We saw some shapes moving in the haze a few kilometres in front of us. The tank fired again, and we saw the impact of a shell a couple of hundred metres from the shapes. As the minutes passed, the shapes resolved themselves into the forms of six men, jogging along in our general direction across the plain. We heard the slow throb of a 12.7mm Dshk machine gun being fired from the tank, but now we could see that its rounds were dropping well short of the little group.

It was a pound to a pinch of shit that these boys were Muja-hideen so I suggested to Mahmoud that he send someone to attract their attention: if he didn't, they were going to pass by several hundred yards from where we were hiding. He im-mediately sent two guys forward, warning them to keep low so that they didn't attract the attention of anybody on the road. There was another big bang as the tank fired its main armament, and the six figures disappeared for several minutes in a swirl of dust and smoke as a round exploded close to them. When it cleared, they were quite close to us but there were only five of them: either one of them had copped it in the last explosion, or he'd run off somewhere else.

When they got to our position, they were on their chin-straps, soaked in sweat and covered in dust and sand. We gave them water, which they gulped down, and then Mahmoud began to question them.

I couldn't follow much of what was being said until Blue came over and joined us, but it soon emerged that these guys were from another Mujahideen group which was converging on Zirani. They also told us that the enemy column which we had understood to be heading for Abdullah's camp was actually trying to break through Mujahideen-dominated territory towards the town of Tirgari, about thirty kilometres north of Zirani on the river Alishang. The enemy were now bogged down fighting various groups of Mujahideen situated between Zirani, the town of Agharabat and a village called Qarghay.

The enemy operation now began to make sense. Looking at my map, it seemed clear that the operation was aimed at seizing control of an area around the junction of the Kabul–Jellalabad road and the Tirgari road. This would enable them to move substantial forces into Laghman province and from there into Kunar province, effectively disrupting Mujahideen infiltration and supply routes to most parts of the country. The tank patrol on the road was clearly intended to stop substantial reinforcements from getting across the plain.

We questioned the Mujahideen some more and their leader, Haji Ahmed, gave us a vivid picture of what had befallen them. They were originally part of a group of twenty-six but they had come under attack in a village called Darunto a couple of days before and had retreated after heavy fighting. For the next few days they had been under severe pressure from Soviet tanks and helicopters, falling back to Agharabat then Qarghay. His group of six had become separated from the main body the night before in a Soviet barrage in Zirani, and now he was simply trying to get the fuck out of it all. Hard to blame him for that, really.

It was about 12.30 now, and scorching hot. We were faced with an uncertain tactical situation and a water shortage. Mahmoud's plan, such as it was, was to head for Zirani and find out what was going on, but this struck me as a bit silly. Far better, in my view, to get the main body of the group into cover close by the river, where they could obtain water, and send a small light-order reconnaissance into Zirani to see whether it was in Mujahideen or Soviet hands. Mahmoud didn't appear to be overwhelmingly delighted by this idea but, after a bit of huffing and puffing, he finally agreed. We sorted out a place where he would take the group to shelter, and then I told him that I would do the recce into Zirani with Blue and two others. He agreed to this as well, and after I'd passed my bergen over to a member of his group, set off across the plain towards the town.

I'd warned Mahmoud that we should be back at around 9 p.m, which gave us a good eight hours to cover the ten kilometres to the outskirts of Zirani, do our recce and get back, without busting a gut. We didn't need to do a fast tab, which would have been hard work in the blinding heat, and instead we made off at a good patrol pace, covering the ground reasonably quickly, but carefully as well. These were 'my' Mujahideen, and I was pleased to see them maintaining proper spacing and all-round observation as we moved, rather than bimbling along holding hands with their mates, which was the normal style. This was no more than a sign of friendship but I suppose my years in the testosterone-charged atmosphere of the British army made me uneasy about it and I generally forestalled any hand-holding attempts by carrying my weapon in both hands. It sounds ridiculous now, but if I was spotted by some journalist, I didn't want to appear in the world's press holding hands with a big, hairy Afghan.

We made good progress and soon came across the body of the sixth member of Haji Ahmed's group. Something – a 12.7mm round or a big shell splinter – had removed most of the top of his head, and what was left was covered by a seething mass of ants. One of my guys went forward to search his body, but I called him back: bodies are classic sites for booby-traps and simple anti-personnel mines, and quite a small mine could kill or wound most of us.

By mid-afternoon we'd reached the outskirts of Zirani to find that nothing was stirring. At the end of the street I could see what appeared to be a couple of bodies, but nothing living. I took the lead as we began carefully to patrol between the buildings, Northern Ireland-style, looking in through any open doorways we came across in an effort to find out what had happened to the inhabitants.

As we got further in, I swapped with one of the Afghans so that, if we did meet anyone, we wouldn't be taken for Russians. We now started to home in on the sound of a barking dog. In any village throughout Asia or the Middle East there will normally be hundreds of dogs – pets and strays – yapping and growling at you as you pass. When one starts barking, the rest join in. But not here: there was just the one.

Increasingly, we could see signs that a firefight had taken place around us. There were empty 7.62 x 39 cartridge cases scattered all over the place, bullet holes in the walls, stinking dead donkeys and mules, and even dark bloodstains in the dusty earth, where men (presumably) had been shot and wounded. But still no people, and just the sound of the single dog barking. It was weird and worrying.

We crossed an open square and came to a large house built around a courtyard, from which the barking was emanating. I looked in through a hole in the wall. Sure enough, a great big mongrel was in there, straining at a chain which held it securely to the wall. There were blood trails all round the courtyard, where bodies had been dragged about, but still no sign of any people. One of the lads found a bowl and filled it with water for the dog, which at least stopped the noise, while Blue took the other lad into the building to see whether they could find anything of interest.

After a few minutes he came out again. Sheltering inside the house he had found a small group of women. This was good news: I was worried that everyone had done a runner, or even that we were going to find a big heap of bodies somewhere.

'They won't come out, Tom, they're too scared.'

There was no way I could go and interrogate them – they wouldn't talk to an infidel – so I sent him back inside to find out what had happened, while the other lads and I kept watch outside.

About twenty minutes later, Blue emerged again, looking grim-faced:

'The Government army came. They rounded up all the men and put them on trucks. Some men tried to fight or escape but they shot them. The women have been raped and beaten.

'Some men got out before the soldiers arrived: they have gone to the hills.'

Shit! It was getting on for 6.30 now and the daylight was beginning to fade fast. We needed to be back with Mahmoud by 21.00 but I felt we couldn't just leave the women here unprotected. On the other hand, with just the four of us, we weren't going to make it back on time if we took them with us. I sat down with Blue to discuss what we were going to do, when we spotted movement down the street from us.

We moved fast into fire positions. In the twilight, we couldn't identify the new arrivals, but their lack of any tactical formation suggested to me that they weren't soldiers; Mujahideen possibly, or maybe the escaped villagers returning. I told Blue to wait until they were reasonably close before challenging them and we settled down to wait.

When they were ten or fifteen metres from us, Blue spoke out. There was a short exchange of words and then Blue turned to me, a grin splitting his face from ear to ear.

'Tom, Tom! It is Abdullah!'

And it was, and what a piece of good news! We greeted each other like long lost brothers, with hugs and much back-slapping and hand-shaking. I suppose more than anything else I felt relief: sure I was a big, tough SAS soldier, but I was largely at the mercy of the decisions that the Mujahideen commanders were taking on the ground; I had neither the knowledge nor the contacts to survive for long out here on my own. But Abdullah was the nearest thing I'd seen to a proper soldier out here and, what's more, he had a sound tactical brain, and we shared the bond of having been in combat together. Altogether, I was damned glad to see him.

Together with Blue, we had a chat to update ourselves on the situation, explained the problem of the women to him, and made an arrangement to RV at the same place the next morning, unless there was a serious change of circumstances. Then we headed back.

Back at training wing, I suspect they would have questioned the haste with which we headed back to Mahmoud's group, but my judgement was that if we were late, he would take it as a good reason to do something stupid. We speed-marched back and dragged ourselves in with ten minutes to spare. We drank some tea and ate a little stale naan, then back-briefed Mahmoud on what we had seen and heard, ending with the arrangement to meet up with Abdullah. It was clear that while we'd been away, the group had somehow increased in size; apparently other Mujahideen had appeared during the course of the afternoon and elected to stay with Mahmoud.

Mahmoud accepted the outline we'd given him and declared that we would move out at 4.30 the next morning and, in the meantime, I decided to get my head down. The lack of uninterrupted sleep was beginning to get to me.

I hadn't had much more than four and a half hours' kip when I was woken to move out. I had a drink of water from the bottle on my belt kit and we were off, making a good pace back towards Zirani in the pre-dawn cool.

We arrived just before 7 a.m., and met up with Abdullah in the same courtyard we'd seen him in the previous evening. He was his usual cheery self but, in the light of day, his face betrayed the effort and strain of the last few days and he looked tired and drawn. We made a light breakfast of tea and hot naan and, when we'd finished, the inevitable Chinese parliament began. Rather than get involved, I took the opportunity to slip away to sit down for a little while by myself with a mug of tea.

I remember thinking about William back in Peshawar. I had no doubt that he'd climbed the walls of the Khyber Intercontinental many times over by now, and that the telex machine would be close to meltdown. I wondered whether he'd had any news of me at all. Probably yes: the Mujahideen grapevine seemed to work reasonably well, even if not entirely accurately. I also kept on getting little whiffs of myself. It was several days since I'd had a proper wash, and my clothes were absolutely heaving, seemingly a combination of dirt, blood (not my own, I hasten to add), sweat, salt and sand. Everyone else was in a similar state, so I don't suppose they noticed, but it was quite a stink.

I heard footsteps behind me and turned to see Abdullah and Blue approaching. Abdullah was looking worried.

'Tom, you didn't stay for the meeting. Have I offended you?'

'No, Abdullah, of course not, and I would tell you straight away if you had. I felt that as the commander, you should be in charge of the meeting, and you don't really need any help from me.'

He accepted this, and he and Blue went on to outline the plan that had been agreed by the group.

Their scheme was to attack the enemy column at a road junction and river bridge near to Tirgari. If they could hold the bridge long enough, they would destroy it, thus cutting the column in two. We looked at the map and I agreed that it seemed a good idea. As we continued to discuss the plan, Mahmoud came over and joined in, but somehow I got the impression that he wasn't so keen. We finished up by agreeing, at my prompting, that what was needed was a good recce.

'You can never tell, the situation may have changed since you were last there,' I cautioned them, in schoolmaster fashion. 'It would be usual practice for the Soviets to anticipate this kind of attack and to have put in defensive positions around the bridge. You always need to have the most up-to-date tactical information before you can proceed with a plan like this.'

To my surprise, Abdullah responded to this by pulling out of his satchel a letter from his headquarters. Blue translated the gist of it, which was that every effort was to be made to stop the enemy from entering Nuristan by launching harassing attacks, that Mehtariam was already under Soviet control, and that a ground assault was expected on Alingar today.

'Tom, any attack that we launch will take the pressure from these places, so it is our duty to attack.'

'That's true, Abdullah, but if you do it properly you will live to fight another day. If you go in without reconnaissance and a proper plan, you will be lambs to the slaughter!'

We talked around it for several minutes, but they saw the logic of what I was saying and eventually agreed to do it my way. I was lucky in that both of them had previous military experience: a lot of Mujahideen commanders would have just shouted 'jihad!' and piled in regardless of what was there.

The Mujahideen didn't believe in hanging about and we set off shortly afterwards, stringing out across the plain in a great, long line of seventy or more fighters, along with mules and donkeys. It was only about ten or twelve clicks to the operational area and we were in position and in cover by 10 a.m. I couldn't believe that we hadn't been sighted, but it seemed we'd got away with it. I went forward with Blue, Abdullah and Mahmoud to take a look at our target from a suitable vantage point.

It was then that I saw the most immediate snag: there wasn't just one bridge, there were two in parallel, one for each direction. As I pointed out, even if they were able to seize control and hold one span long enough to blow it, the Russians would still be able to use the other one, albeit at lower traffic volumes. But capturing both spans long enough to blow them would be a tall order for a group of seventy. In plain sight we could see two T-55 tanks, several BTR-60 wheeled APCs, along with various trucks, jeeps and so forth. My guess was that the area was held by at least a hundred, and probably many more, enemy troops. From the map, we could see that there was a second bridge, further along the road at Nuristan itself, and my advice to Abdullah was that this should be their target.

But Abdullah didn't think this was a runner.

'Tom, if we attack here, how can we succeed?'

'You've got to get the basics right: firstly, you will need good co-ordination so that everything happens in the correct order; secondly, everybody will need to know exactly what his part in the plan is; and thirdly, you will need to achieve total surprise.'

'I understand this, but you know it won't happen: the fighters just don't understand these things; they only want to attack. And they know I have orders to relieve the pressure on Alingar.'

'Abdullah, you won't relieve the pressure anywhere if you launch an attack without proper planning. They will kill all of us, and then go on to kill everybody at Alingar. This is a major assault that we're contemplating: you can't just launch it like that.'

We walked back to the main group to find that yet more Mujahideen had turned up and that a Chinese parliament was in full swing. Abdullah tried to explain what we were going to do, but to my surprise, and his frustration, he was shouted down by the new arrivals. Once again, in the tumult of Pushtu, I caught the words 'Jihad! Jihad!'

The commander of the new arrivals, Ilderim, was openly hostile towards me. He made no secret of the fact that he hated all Westerners and that the last thing he believed the Mujahideen needed was help from Britain and America.

'My father fought the British army, and beat them!' he told me, as if I gave a flying fuck. I kept my thoughts to myself, but I was 100 per cent certain that this clown was going to get the surprise of his life when he attempted to take on the Soviets.

Ilderim had the mob on his side and had ordered Blue and my escorts to take part in the attack, whatever I was going to do. I wouldn't have had a problem navigating back to Pakistan – I could probably have managed it much better than most of the 'guides' I'd been given so far – but I didn't fancy roaming around on my own through Mujahideen territory, at the mercy of anyone who took me for a Russian. Instead, I decided that the best thing I could do would be to exert some influence to stop Ilderim doing anything too thick. Blue and I wandered over to where he was sitting with Mahmoud, Abdullah and some muppet called Mohammed who appeared to be Ilderim's second-in-command.

Through Blue, I asked what they were intending to do and Abdullah unhappily sketched out a plan in the sand. In essence, they would take the whole group along the banks of the Alishang and attempt to hit the two bridges simultaneously, then blow up the bridges with anti-tank mines. A head count showed we had ninety-six fighters, together with a motley collection of weapons, ranging from a single Dshk to a collection of Indian-manufactured .303 SMLE rifles from the 1930s. The biggest problem that I could see was that we would have to walk along the fringes of the town of Tirgari to reach our target. Inevitably, the barking of the village dogs would alert every Afghan and Soviet soldier for miles of our presence. When they were on the bridge, they wanted to blow them up by using four anti-tank mines on each, linked by equal lengths of detonating cord to obtain simultaneous detonation.

Most of this was crap. I suggested that they might try two separate routes for the approach march, thus achieving some mutual support, and that they might want to try using electrical detonators to fire the charges when they were on the bridge, to achieve genuine simultaneity; but Ilderim wasn't listening. He wasn't going to change his plan at my suggestion The only good part of the plan was that they would wind up on the other side of the bridge after they'd blown it, giving the group the chance to disperse into the Kashmund mountains before the follow-up could start.

It was now mid-afternoon and time for prayer. I made a brew and sat down, wondering what the fuck I was doing with this bunch of cretins. At that moment, I felt I'd had it up to my back teeth with the Mujahideen. I couldn't believe that these fighters would rather follow an ignorant, superstitious peasant like Ilderim, rather than seasoned, successful soldiers like Abdullah and, to some extent at least, Mahmoud.

About this time, yet more Mujahideen appeared, though members of a different faction: Ahmed Shah Massoud's Tajik Jamiat. They were clearly of a higher military standard than the Hezb-i-Islami fighters I was with. They moved tactically and automatically took up an all-round defensive position as their commander discussed matters with Ilderim. But soon after they arrived, they about-turned and fucked off. I asked Blue what had happened, but either he didn't know or wouldn't tell me. For the first time, I sensed that the Mujahideen weren't taking me into their confidence. I began to get a nasty sinking feeling in the pit of my stomach.

In the early evening some food was produced and we quickly ate it. I gathered from Blue that the attack was due to start at 11 p.m. but to my surprise nobody was making any great effort to get ready. The Mujahideen took their lead from their superiors, and Ilderim's attitude was very much Im'shallah – it's God's will – so there was no point planning too much. I cleaned my weapon and magazines and got my head down. I was still pissed off with them all: fuck 'em!

Just before eleven o'clock, I was woken by Blue. Even in the dark I could see how nervous he was, and he stumbled over his words as he asked whether I would be going with them.

'Blue, Ilderim hasn't asked me and I don't think he wants me to come . . . he certainly hasn't given me a task.'

'You must come, you can't stay here on your own!'

To be honest, I wasn't so much worried about coming along with them as getting the fuck out of there when the shit – inevitably – hit the fan. The group began to assemble and, after a short talk by their mullah, headed for the river bank. I decided that I would follow along; I didn't actually fancy staying on my own. So I tagged on at the back, listening to the usual clanking and rattling of a Mujahideen group on the march.

I was at the back, so I've never learned what the precise sequence of events was. We had followed a dry watercourse which cut through the plain and gave us cover from view of, if not fire from, anyone in our immediate vicinity, and made our way along the river bank, reaching the outskirts of Tirgari. Suddenly, a flare shot up into the sky, and the world's supply of automatic fire came thumping in at us.

I ducked down behind a low sandbank and rolled over to watch green and orange tracer flashing past overhead. Beneath the high-pitched crack of 7.62 rounds was the slower hammering of 12.7mm Dshk, like a woodpecker taking on a hard tree, and the occasional percussive bang of grenades and RPG rounds. I poked my head up for a look round: whoever was winning, it wasn't us. I could see dead and wounded Mujahideen all around. Surprise, surprise; we were completely fucked.

How did the Soviets know we were coming that way? I suppose it could have been an alert sentry, or the chance triggering of a trip flare, but I'm pretty sure it was an ambush; and I'm pretty sure it happened because when the Mujahideen put the word about that this attack was going to take place, the wrong people got to hear about it.

But the immediate problem was how to get away. The sand-bank I was lying behind wasn't going to provide much protection from the Dshk and I reckoned that our only route out was to try to suppress some of the incoming fire. Our RPG-7 operator was busy trying to dig through to New Zealand a couple of yards away from me, so, through Blue, I persuaded him to have a shot at the Dshk which was about one hundred metres from us, firing at a group further forward.

With a loud bang, the RPG shot off towards the enemy position and exploded with a bright flash and a shower of sparks. Shit! He'd missed by about ten metres. Close enough to wound some of the people round the Dshk – we could hear them screaming – but not close enough to stop them. Blue screamed at him to reload and have another go – and his number two was just slotting a second grenade onto the launcher – when, in a shower of dust and gravel, a 12.7mm round hit the earth bank in front of him and ploughed straight on through his chest, hurling the RPG man backwards to land in a stone-dead heap five metres back from where he'd been kneeling. The number two picked up the launcher and scrambled back up the bank to fire it.

'Blue, Blue!' I yelled. 'Tell him to take his time and get it right.'

Blue turned to pass this on, and we both watched as the second man's head snapped back as a round took the top half of it off. We were now the focus of most of the incoming fire, but even so, a third Mujahideen got to the RPG, knelt and fired it before he too dropped dead. This time, the rocket was close enough to the Dshk to silence it temporarily.

'Blue, it's time to fucking go! I'll cover you, while you fall back.'

A small group of us pepperpotted back, covering each other over short ten-metre bounds as we tried to extricate ourselves from the ambush. I'm not sure how many came with me, but we certainly lost a few over the next couple of minutes, and by the time we'd got out of the immediate ambush area, we were down to five.

Nice one, Ilderim.

SEVEN

I t was about 2 a.m., we had jack-shit cover and a long way to go. You learn about escape and evasion on continuation training but I had never really thought that I would end up doing it. There was still a good deal of shooting, and flares whizzing up into the sky, but we had extricated ourselves from the worst of it and had time to pause in a small depression in the ground while I took stock.

Looking around, I could see that Blue and the other three lads were dazed and shocked by what they'd just been through, functioning on autopilot at best. From the map, I quickly plotted a course to take us to Wazir and then on to Camp Two, a distance of about fifty kilometres as the crow flies though considerably further on the ground. I grabbed Blue by the shoulders and gave him a quick shake to wake him up. I looked straight into his eyes.

'Blue, listen to me. We have two hours before daylight. In that time we have to get as far away from here as possible.'

He nodded dumbly.

'Come on, Blue, you need to get a grip of yourself now. We've got work to do.'

He seemed to be snapping out of his reverie. He passed on my orders to the other boys and we set off across the plain at a fast tab.

We'd covered about a kilometre when we saw movement ahead. I got Blue and the boys to lie down while I cautiously went forwards to see who it was.

Whoever was there seemed to be milling around in a chaotic fashion and clearly hadn't noticed my approach. I wasn't in the mood to take any chances and I kept them covered with the AKM while I moved in closer. I can't have been more than twenty metres from them when one of them made a sudden movement. My finger took the first pressure on the trigger and I just managed to stop myself firing as I realised that they were our mules. They'd obviously fled as soon as the firing had started.

I called Blue forwards as I tried to decide whether it was worth taking them or not. After a few moments' thought I decided not: they would be too difficult to hide, and that would outweigh any movement advantage they gave us.

We pushed on until about 4.30 a.m. when it was getting quite light and we could clearly see our destination, the beginning of the mountains, just four or five kilometres from us. By now we were all pretty much parched: I had a couple of water bottles on my belt kit but one had already been drunk. I took a drink from the other and passed it round: it came back empty. After a couple of minutes we set off again on the last leg.

We were about a kilometre from the foot of the mountains, and completely out in the open, when we heard the sound of helicopters coming up fast. There was no cover.

'Blue, tell them to lie on their stomachs and make sure they don't look up!'

Pilots become used to seeing the flash of upturned faces as they go past.

We got down in the dirt, and through the crook of my elbow I watched three Hinds skim past, moving fast towards Tirgari, presumably mopping up the rest of the Mujahideen. I made sure there was no spotter aircraft and then got them up and pushed on towards the relative safety of the foothills. Our main immediate problem now was water; we didn't have any and I was the only one with any water bottles, so I decided that we might as well push on a further couple of clicks to the river where we could replen, get some sleep and then cross when it was dark. The exhausted Afghans weren't entirely happy about this but I wasn't taking any shit from them now: this was a survival situation.

We made it to the river and Blue and I went forwards to fill the water bottles. Bugger! The water looked like sewage soup – as far as I could see it contained everything you could possibly imagine – but without water we were up shit creek anyway so I filled the bottles and doubled the dose of Puritabs. It wasn't going to taste very nice, but it was drinkable at least. I made a good strong brew for everyone and we sorted ourselves out to get a little kip.

Around 2.30, the Afghans went off to pray and, after I'd had another drink of vile water, I rolled over for a bit more sleep. I hadn't had my head down more than thirty minutes when I was rudely awakened by gunfire. I squirmed into cover and tried to shake myself awake as bullets cracked overhead and ricochets pinged off the rocks. What the fuck was going on?

I poked my head up to see a group of Afghan soldiers on the trail just below us and my guys huddled behind a large rock. Only one of them seemed to be armed and the soldiers were closing in fast.

I quickly checked my rear, and seeing it was clear, began putting down fire towards the soldiers. It seemed to take them by surprise – it was like shooting ducks on water – and they quickly withdrew into the cover of some overhanging rocks, leaving a couple of mules which they had with them stumbling towards us. I now had the chance to see what had happened. It turned out to be a typical Mujahideen fuck-up: they'd posted a guard while they were praying, as per my instructions, but when they'd finished their prayers, they'd gone into a huddle to discuss the previous evening's festivities and the guard had joined them, thus allowing an Afghan army patrol to walk right into the middle of them.

I don't doubt the soldiers were just as surprised as the Mujahideen. Only the guard had his weapon with him, and he'd got off a burst at the soldiers, but the big problem was that my merry men had all taken off their boots and sandals and left them in a big pile with the rifles, and they couldn't get near them. One had made the attempt, but he'd been hit as soon as he reached them.

My intervention gave the Afghans the chance to scamper back to their footwear and rifles, and Blue and I carried the wounded man back into cover. He was lucky: although there was a lot of blood, the bullet had hit the fleshy area above his knee and gone straight through without breaking the bone. We ripped his pants open and I stuck a shell-dressing on, binding it tightly to the wound. At this point one of the Afghans ran up with the good news that several military trucks had appeared down by the river and a whole load of troops were debussing from them.

The only option that I could see was to head further up into the mountains and hide up until dark, then try to slip away. Blue had grabbed one of the Afghan army mules and we got the wounded man onto it and detailed one of the other lads to lead him off, while I pondered how to delay any follow-up.

By now it was pushing on for four o'clock but there were several hours of daylight left before we would gain the cloak of darkness. There was no option but to begin climbing.

We were shagged out and hungry, but there's nothing like a hostile enemy snapping at your arse to motivate you to further efforts. We had plenty of cover from the rocks but from time to time the soldiers below obviously caught sight of us and fired a few rounds up, fortunately without effect. After twenty-five minutes hard labour I looked up to see that the mule was still going strong with the wounded man on board and that we seemed to be moving out of trouble. Around this time a Dshk opened up from the trucks, but although we were getting showered with little splinters and fragments of rock, it wasn't all that accurate and I guessed they had lost sight of us and were trying to provoke a response.

We were actually less than ten kilometres from Abdullah's Camp Five and I calculated that if we kept up this rate of march we could be there in three hours or less, give or take. Except, of course, that if we did go straight there, we would take half the Afghan army with us. We were in need of water, food, ammunition and medical aid for our wounded guy. My medical pack was in my bergen, no doubt even now being examined by a Soviet intelligence officer. All I had with me was a small pocket pack of basic items and the fact was that in this situation, I was saving them for myself.

At about five o'clock we heard the sound of rotor blades. Oh shit, I was thinking, please just go away. But they didn't. As they got closer and closer, I got everyone apart from the mule and the wounded guy down as deep into cover as I could. From between a couple of large boulders I watched as two MI-8 'Hip' troop carriers flew slowly past, evidently looking for a suitable HLS. Bugger!

The two helicopters passed slowly overhead and crossed out of sight over the ridgeline but from the sound of the rotors I could tell that they were flaring out for landing. This threw me into a quandary: if they'd landed troops in front of us, would they try to sweep back down to catch us between them and the guys below us, or did they think that we'd got further on and they were in hot pursuit? If they were going to come down towards us, then we should put in an ambush, but if we did that, we risked being trapped between the two groups. On the other hand, if we carried on, we might well walk into an ambush ourselves. The only fixed element seemed to me to be daylight: there was about an hour left before nightfall, before which the helicopters would have to piss off home.

At which point, a little light bulb came on above my head: of course! The guys who'd landed from the helicopters would be sweeping down to link up with the trucks down by the river because they wouldn't need to worry about getting picked up before last light. Having reached this conclusion, the solution was obvious. I got the wounded man and the mule under the cover of an overhang and set the rest of us out in ambush positions.

We lay there for thirty minutes, watching as the sun sank slowly into the west, turning the mountains a rich, golden colour. Apart from a few eddies of dust in the warm breeze, nothing was moving. I looked around at the rest of the group; all were wide-eyed and strained. I supposed I looked much the same. As the sun finally set, I knew there wouldn't be more than fifteen minutes or so for the enemy to make their move, but nobody came.

As darkness fell, I got Blue to bring the group in closer together, and then explained through him that our only option now was to send a patrol forward to clear our route and then carry on. Strangely enough, there wasn't a huge rush of volunteers. I looked across at Blue and raised my eyebrows: he agreed to come with me. I explained to the boys that when we returned, I would raise my rifle in both hands as a recognition sign. For some reason this seemed to amuse them.

I took point as Blue and I set off slowly along the path. It took us twenty minutes to reach the ridge, where we came across a small open area, largely surrounded by crags and big boulders. This would be a classic ambush site: cover from fire and view but with less than fifty metres to the killing ground. We settled into cover on our side of the area and waited, but everything was quiet and still. There was no sight, sound or scent of the enemy. Under normal circumstances, I would have looked for some way of bypassing the area but there seemed little point, and with Blue covering me I made my way across. There was no reaction and, looking about me as I crossed, no sign of the enemy either: no anti-personnel mines, not even a bootprint.

I called Blue over and we carried along up the path as it got steeper and more precipitous, reminiscent of Jacob's Ladder on Pen y Fan. We reached another ridgeline and sat down for a breather. Another light bulb came on above my head: this couldn't possibly be the right path; you needed to be a mountain goat to follow this one. By accident, we might have stumbled across a way out of our problems.

We headed back quickly. I left Blue at the open 'plateau' and went back down to get the group ready. The recognition sign worked – they didn't shoot me anyway – and after the usual twatting around, the Mujahideen were ready to move. We arrived back at the plateau and I was shocked to find Blue sprawled on the ground. Oh shit, he's had his throat cut, was my immediate reaction. Then he snored; he'd fallen asleep. I shook him awake and he sat up in a confusion of embarrassment.

'Don't worry about it, Blue, I know you're very tired. Look, can you explain about the path to these guys?'

Blue explained what we'd discovered and we continued on-wards. About five hundred metres past where Blue and I had reached on our recce, our rough track joined up with a much wider trail. We were close to Camp Five now, and I told Blue to take the group forward to find it. Meanwhile, with one of the other fighters, I waited in ambush for twenty minutes to see if anyone was following us.

Nobody appeared, and when the time had elapsed, we followed on after Blue. Sure enough, no more than twenty minutes later we heard a shout and looked up to see a group of Mujahideen training their rifles on us from amongst the boulders. We were back at Camp Five.

I'd hoped we were reaching some kind of safety, but looking around I could see I was wrong. The Mujahideen had ready-use ammunition piled around, and talking to the old man Abdullah had left in command, we discovered that they expected an attack within the next forty-eight hours. Some food and tea was brought as we discussed the situation. The old guys were anxious because they didn't have clear instructions about what to do if the camp was attacked, but they knew they would be in the shit if it all went wrong. They were also worried about Abdullah. All we could tell them was what had happened at Tirgari; Abdullah was either dead, captured or evading, in which case he might well turn up in due course.

I got the food down my neck, cleaned my weapon and crashed out. I was so shattered I think I was asleep before I was fully horizontal.

But I didn't sleep for long. Around 2.30 a.m. I was shaken awake by an old Afghan. I jumped up and put my belt kit on, but I felt absolutely numb with exhaustion. I staggered out of the hut to where a gaggle of Mujahideen were assembling. They looked like I felt: fucked. There was a communal water butt nearby and I splashed some of the icy cold liquid on my head; at last I began to wake up.

It turned out that one of the old guards had seen movement down below and heard some noises, and now they were all discussing what to do. The consensus, according to Blue, was to open fire with everything they had.

'No, that wouldn't be a good idea. It could be anything down there. It may be the enemy, or it might just be an escaped mule milling around waiting for daylight before it comes in. Either way, I doubt whether anything will happen before first light.'

We sat down to wait and someone brought round some green tea. As I drank it, an overwhelming wave of depression and exhaustion swept through me. I was thinking that I ought to get the Afghans to do some kind of 'stand to', but I couldn't be bothered getting off my arse to do it. Living on the edge like this was really getting me down, physically and psychologically. I'd never had to work for so long on my own; even one other white face would have eased the burden considerably. I'd recently read a book about Lawrence of Arabia. I thought to myself: I'd love to see how far you'd get with this fucking lot, mate.

Blue came over and sat next to me. He could see I was pissed off.

'Tom, what do you want us to do?'

I snapped out of it.

'Okay, Blue, I'd like you to make sure that everybody's weapon is clean and ready. I'm going to the guard position to see if I can see anything.'

I took up position looking out over the approaches to the camp. In the darkness before dawn I couldn't see anything unusual. After a few minutes, Blue came and joined me.

'Everything OK, Blue?' I asked.

'Yes, fine, Tom.'

'Will the group be ready to go in twenty minutes?'

'No problem.'

We lay there quietly for a few moments, when the silence was suddenly broken by the sound of a rock falling below us. First and last light are the most dangerous times of day, militarily: the light conditions favour attackers who can use the cover of partial darkness to infiltrate close to defensive positions unseen. Now Blue, me and the Afghan guard strained our eyes to see what was moving below us. There was another rustle of movement in the bushes below and the culprits broke cover: a small rabbit jinked through the scrub and rocks below us, pursued by a large golden-brown wildcat.

With that excitement over, we got on with our preparations to move on. I wasn't prepared to use the old route. With the amount of Soviet activity in the area, I was sure it would be ambushed; so I worked out a new one which should get us to Camp Six at Bald-Bagh in approximately two days. We couldn't expect to find any food on the way, so we each loaded up a little sack of naan and I got the Afghans to fill their plastic bottles with water as well. We set off just before 7 a.m. in perfect tabbing weather, cool but dry, and were soon making good progress down the track.

I wasn't too concerned at this stage by the soldiers we'd met the evening before. We were travelling away from where I thought they would be, so I was concentrating more on the map and compass when I happened to catch sight of bootprints in the dust of the trail in front of me. I stopped everyone and had a good look.

They were definitely boots with heavy treads but there was nothing conclusive about that: quite a few of the younger Muja-hideen wore them. Having said that, I'd never seen a Mujahideen group with everyone in boots so my suspicion was that they had been left by a Soviet or Afghan patrol. But on the plus side, I couldn't imagine the enemy planning to ambush this trail and then leaving bootprints all over it. I called Blue over and explained that I was going to patrol forward on my own to the next bend in the trail, and then give them a signal – holding my weapon above my head – to indicate that it was safe to come forward. If there was somebody there, I would hold the AKM out to my side and they should get the fuck out of it, sharpish.

I headed on at patrol speed, following the bootprints along the trail. I didn't want to go so slowly that I spooked my group, but natural concern militated against pushing the pace out too fast. I reached the bend and stopped, watching and listening, sniffing the air for the scent of tobacco smoke or soap. Everything was quiet, I gave the signal and the boys came jogging up.

We carried on doing this for six or seven more legs, and every time it remained quiet and clear of enemy. After a while, some-thing on the ground caught my attention: it was a small piece of paper. I quickly inspected the ground around it for signs of AP mines and, as everything appeared to be OK, picked it up. It was a sweet-wrapper. To me this confirmed the fact that the boot-prints had been made by Russian or Afghan soldiers.

We carried on down the trail as it slowly levelled out towards the river. We still had no idea who was up ahead or where they were, just that it was likely that they were enemy. As we came out onto the flat ground, I decided that I wanted to get a better view of the route in front of us, so I climbed up onto a large boulder nearby and tried to spy out a reasonably safe route down to the river so that we could get there and then lie up for the rest of the day. There wasn't much to see, the thick scrub and rocks made it difficult to see the shape of the ground in detail, so I decided that we would continue along the trail for a while.

No sooner had we moved off than we heard shooting behind us. It wasn't aimed at us, and it wasn't particularly heavy – just AKs being fired in bursts – but it was certainly puzzling. We pulled off the trail and went to ground while we waited to see who showed up.

The firing stopped and we waited in silence for twenty minutes or so. It was so quiet and peaceful that I was beginning to think about putting a brew on, when I heard the sound of marching feet on the trail. We all froze absolutely still. From my position, I couldn't actually see how many there were but the amount of noise led me to suppose ten or twelve. For some reason, it occurred to me then how incredibly difficult it must be for the Soviets to develop a strategy to win this war: they were actually fighting against six major Mujahideen groups, several smaller ones and a number of little private armies, none of which co-ordinated their operations according to any kind of system. It must have been mindblowing trying to concoct an intelligence picture; still, that was their fucking problem!

Soon after the soldiers had gone past, we heard the sound of rotor blades and an MI-8 came over and landed further up the trail, near where we'd heard the sounds of shooting coming from. This was turning into one of those days when anything that can go wrong does so. A few minutes passed and the helicopter took off again, flying low directly overhead as it returned the way it had come. As far as we could tell, we remained undetected.

It was just after midday and Blue asked whether he and the lads could go and pray. This was fine so long as they kept reasonably quiet, and I moved a little way over towards the trail to give them some privacy. Almost immediately I noticed movement, and saw a group of men, not more than three hundred metres away, slowly advancing along the path. Prayers would have to wait. I slowly crawled back to Blue and shook him by the foot. He looked over at me and I pointed down the trail and gave him the walking fingers sign: he immediately understood and passed it on to the rest of the group, who carefully and slowly settled down into cover.

The soldiers walked slowly past; the only sounds they made were from their boots. When they were about a hundred metres down the trail, I wrapped a camouflage face-veil round my head and crawled down to get a better look at them. At first I did a double take: they were all wearing bush-hats with one side of the brim folded up and looked just like Australians. Through my binoculars, I could see that the entire group consisted of Europeans – Russians presumably – though we later discovered that special forces from Poland, East Germany and Czechoslovakia did go to Afghanistan in small numbers. A deep tubercular cough from one of my guys caused me to freeze. The Russians were too far away to have heard, but I decided not to take any further chances and crawled back to the team to let them know the score. I found most of them doubled up with hysterical laughter. Apparently the face-veil made me look like a woman. Now wasn't the time to bollock them, but I angrily told Blue to make sure they kept the noise down and then crawled back.

I was just in time. The group of Russians had now divided in two and one patrol was coming back along the trail while the first continued in their original direction of march. I crawled back to the group and we watched as the Russians patrolled by.

I was beginning to lose my sense of humour about this. We

now knew for sure that there were two separate groups of Russians patrolling around the area and we could also hear the sound of rotor blades, higher up in the hills, but too close for comfort. I let everything settle down for half an hour or so and then gave out my instructions. We needed a good brew and a fill up with our naan-packed meals, and then to get the fuck out of it!

As dusk surrounded us, I got the boys out onto the trail and organised them to make our way down to the river. My assumption was that the Russians would be home and tucked up in their beds by now. From the way they were equipped they clearly weren't planning to spend long out in the cuds. We got down to the river bank without incident and, as the only swimmer, I led the way across.

No question: it was bleeding cold! At the bank it only came up to my knees, but very soon I was in up to my armpits and suddenly, with no warning at all, I stepped into a hole and was completely submerged. Somehow I managed to hold onto my rifle and half swim at the same time, but it wasn't a comfortable few moments.

Now there was a problem: none of the Afghans were prepared to make the attempt. At one time I'd had twenty metres of Para cord in my belt kit, but it had taken a walk and I didn't have any kind of substitute. Now I was on one side of the river, piss wet through, and my fearsome escort was on the other, afraid of getting their heads wet without a substantial helping hand from me. At this crucial juncture came the sound of rotor blades. A couple of kilometres away, a Hind was dropping flares and lighting the area to such an extent that I had no option but to tell the boys to get down into cover. By now I was shivering with the cold and, for thirty minutes or so, I lay there cursing everything and everybody while the Soviets finished their task.

The departure of the Russian helicopter coincided with moonrise. In the steely blue light everything seemed much easier, and

I waded out into mid-stream again without going above my waist. I wondered briefly why I hadn't had the luck to find this place earlier. I got the boys over one by one and we then made our way to the road, which was actually only about three hundred metres away.

Once we were across and in all-round defence at the top of the bank at the other side I had a chance to take stock. Out to our left was darkness, but to our right, in the direction of the dam that Abdullah had been so keen to attack, was the orangey-yellow glow of sodium lighting. In front of us we faced a rock wall and a small trail up into the mountains and relative safety. We took it.

We'd been climbing for an hour or so when we stopped for a breather. Far back we could see the road, and even as we sat there, nibbling our naan, a convoy of BTR-60 APCs slowly rolled past where we'd been, before pulling up. Through the binoculars I could see that they'd met up with a large foot patrol. I motioned Blue over to me.

'Take a look at that.'

'Yes, Tom. Many Communists . . .'

'The point I'm making is this: last time we came across this road, a week ago, there was no security; now they have foot and vehicle patrols.

'It's like football. If you guys carry on like you are now, then you might get the occasional lucky win, but these boys are like Manchester United: in the end they're going to crush you. The Mujahideen have no option but to train and prepare, otherwise these boys will beat you.'

Blue nodded glumly and we got up to continue our climb.

We were all pretty shagged out, to put it mildly. The climb was steep and within fifteen minutes of starting again we were strung out half way down the mountain. This was fucking hopeless; I stopped to let them catch up, and while I was standing there, sucking in great lungfuls of cool air, I caught a whiff of cigarette smoke. I thought to myself: I really don't need this!

My options were limited: either go back down the mountain, re-route and try somewhere else, or carry on and hope for the best. Neither was very attractive. For a start, the low ground round here seemed to be teeming with soldiers. I thought about it for a few moments and then decided: bollocks, I'm going on. I grabbed Blue and told him to stay with the group, then got hold of Mohamed, the smiling RPG-7 man, and set off slowly along the trail. After we'd covered about two hundred metres, a shape began to resolve itself in the darkness about a hundred yards off the trail to our right. It looked to be a defensive sangar of some kind. We withdrew back to the group which was out of sight of it, and I got my – slightly damp – map out to have a look.

Although the sangar wasn't marked, it was in the perfect position for such a structure, on a commanding height over-looking both the road and the river, and giving wider views over a large area of ground as well. With only a couple of hours of darkness left, I doubted whether we would be able to get safely back over the road and river and find another route. We were going to have to try to sneak past. I whispered to Blue:

'Tell them to tread soft and keep low. I'll go first and get into position to give covering fire, you send them over in pairs.'

He nodded.

It was a cold night but I was sweating like a pig as I scuttled past the sangar, now quite well illuminated by a shaft of moon-light. Although I was tensed and ready for a challenge, nothing happened; Mohamed and his loader followed me, then the others, and finally Blue. As quietly as we could, we hit the trail which led us down and away: we'd made it, though Christ knows how. I couldn't help thinking that the occupants of the sangar were going to get their throats cut some day if they stayed that dozy.

I was concerned now that we were falling behind schedule and I tried to speed us up a little. A couple of kilometres past the san-gar, we came to a plateau, eight or nine hundred metres across, covered with knee-high grass. Against SOP, I decided to pile straight across.

I realised my error when we were about two thirds of the way across. I looked back to ensure that the boys were keeping up and saw, to my horror, that we'd left a trail like a six-lane motorway through the dew-covered grass. If anyone saw it before the sun burned it off in the morning, we were going to be in the shit. Still, it was too late to worry about it now.

When we reached the other side of the meadow, I checked my map again and saw that we were now on the north side of mountain 7660, about half way to Camp Six, and close to the mouth of a re-entrant that we would have to climb the next night. We were dropping with exhaustion now and it was time to find a lie-up.

We found a place a little way off the trail and got ourselves settled in. As dawn came up, Blue took the boys off to pray while I got a brew on for everybody. When they'd finished we ate our stale bread and drank our tea while I explained the sleeping and stag arrangements. I wanted a 50 per cent alert: half the team sleeping, half the team awake. We would do four-hour shifts. It was 5.45 a.m., so I told Blue:

'Get your head down; I'll wake you at ten o'clock.'

He rolled his blanket around himself and was asleep in seconds. I looked round to see the three guys who were meant to be awake with me, but they were completely sparked out as well. I shook the nearest one, but it was like shaking a corpse: he was dead to the world. Fuck it; never mind, let them sleep.

I gave my weapon a quick clean and then sat there, thinking about a Big Mac, large fries and a chocolate milk shake. I felt my ribs, which were sticking out like a stray dog's. I'd never been fat, but this was ridiculous. My thoughts were interrupted by the sound of rotor blades. I stayed put so I couldn't see it, but I heard the pitch of the rotors change for landing. Shortly afterwards, a second one turned up but seemed to just circle around.

After a couple of minutes, the first helicopter's rotors changed pitch again and it took off, flying back over our position. The second followed it and soon the sound faded completely away. My guess was that they had either been landing or collecting a patrol, or possibly even placing an OP. Either way, the Mujahideen slept on obliviously. The rest of the stag was very quiet – peaceful really. The mountains were bathed in glorious sunlight and the only things moving were butterflies, ants, wasps and mosquitoes.

At ten o'clock I woke Blue. He was slightly pissed off that my three companions had slept through the morning but didn't make a fuss. I rolled up in my poncho and was pumping out Z's within a very few seconds.

At 2 p.m. I was shaken gently on the shoulder. I looked up to see Blue's smiling face, so everything was OK. He took the boys off to pray while I got a brew on, as had become our routine. When they'd finished, we drank our tea and ate the last of the naan. It was the last teabag as well, apart from a small brew kit I had for emergencies in the E & E pouch on my belt kit, and that was going to stay put until things got desperate. My feet felt ghastly – I couldn't accurately recall when I'd last got my boots off – and I decided I needed to clean them up and dry out my socks.

I laid out the socks on a rock to dry and replaced the boots loosely on my feet for a few minutes, then thought: fuck it; to hell with SOPs! I took the boots off as well and sat there, wiggling my toes in the warm air, looking at the map and thinking about our route. I reckoned we had about thirty kilometres (roughly eighteen miles) to cover to reach Camp Six at Bald-bagh, but that it shouldn't be anything like as difficult going as the previous evening. When my feet were thoroughly aired and my boots and socks were dry, I replaced them, and then we sat around, waiting for evening and the chance to get going again.

In fact, our approach to Camp Six turned out to be just as

difficult as the previous night's march, not because of the terrain, but because of the ever-increasing evidence of enemy activity. Throughout the night, we were plagued by patrols sending up flares as they manoeuvred through the mountainous countryside and, although we didn't come into direct contact with them, we spent a good deal of time working our way around them.

Dawn arrived with us three kilometres short of Camp Six in an area of scrub, boulders and dried watercourses; presumably some kind of run-off from the mountains all round us. By SOP we should have stopped and lain up for the rest of the day but we were low on water so we took the chance and moved on, and another half hour found us approaching the entrance to the camp.

We reached the entrance, a gap between two large rocks, and were surprised to find that we had not been challenged. This was strange, and even stranger was the odd smell that was hanging about the place. Blue had the point, to prevent any fuck-ups over mistaken identity, but I went forward to stop him.

'There's something wrong here, Blue. Where are the guards?'

'I don't know, maybe they are praying?'

'Maybe, but it fucking stinks here. What can that smell be?'

Between us we decided that we would go forward, together with Mohamed and his RPG-7, and take a look while the rest formed a rearguard and cover group behind us. Once again, Blue took point, while I followed on behind him. Although it was now quite warm, I could see that Blue was shaking like a leaf.

The track floor was hard bedrock, so there was no danger of AP mines being buried, but I kept my eyes open for tripwires and other booby-traps above ground level just in case. The smell as we got closer to the camp was overpowering, and I was close to retching even before we got to the guard position. As I half expected, it was there that we came across the first body: a heap of rags, bones and putrefying flesh; it had clearly seen its share of scavengers in the days since it had died.

In a small open area a little further on, we came across a pile of maybe twenty more dead; men and women. Again, their bodies had been ripped apart by scavengers in search of food: it wasn't a pretty sight.

There was another corpse in the main camp area, as well as signs of a firefight – or shooting at any rate. It was very clear that they'd been bumped, rolled up and killed where they were; there were no weapons around, and several of the caves bore the marks of burning, as if they'd had demolition charges set off inside them.

'Blue, nobody is to go inside any of the caves. They could easily be booby-trapped . . . and don't drink the water yet either, we need to check upstream.'

I followed the stream a little way until I got to a small waterfall, four or five metres high, just outside the camp perimeter. There was no sign that anything was wrong; indeed, it didn't look like anyone had been there for years, so I hoped the water would be good. I arrived back to find that one of the Afghans had taken a long drink from the stream. He didn't keel over immediately, so I decided that we would watch him for thirty minutes, then if nothing had happened, we could assume that it was safe. In the meantime, I had a good look about to make sure that nothing usable had been left behind. Regrettably, it hadn't.

Thirty minutes passed and the Afghan who'd drunk from the stream was still hale and hearty, so I decided that it was safe for the rest of us to take some. We sank gallons of it. Our problem now was food: we'd been relying on Camp Six for resupply and we hadn't got it. The only food we had was my emergency supply in my E & E pouch, and there wasn't much of that. Nevertheless, we had to eat, so I fished out a packet of soup and some tea and brewed it up.

When we'd eaten, the Afghans wanted to pray. There was no reason why not, so I left them to it and walked down to the pile of bodies. Taking a closer look, I could see that they had all been shot – and probably at close range where they were lying. The way I saw it, the camp had been captured and the fighters then rounded up, centralised and massacred. Big boys' rules, I suppose. I bent over and picked up one of the many spent cartridge cases that were lying around; it was a 5.45 x 39. Undoubtedly the Mujahideen had been killed by Russian troops. To some extent, this was a relief: I had a nagging fear that another Mujahideen faction might have done it, despite the ceasefire. 'Fortunately' I was wrong.

I walked back to the boys, who had now finished praying, and organised a stag roster, then got my map out to work out a route to Camp One. As I was doing this, Blue came over to ask whether they should bury the dead.

'Well, Blue, I think it's your decision, but what I would say is that there are a lot of them, they're all past caring, we have a long way to go, and we don't have any food. My advice is to leave them as they are: it would be a good gesture, but better to get them to send a team from Camp One to do it.'

Blue went off and the Afghans had a discussion about it: they seemed to come to the same conclusion that I had and nothing more was said about it.

From the map I could see that it was about twenty-five kilometres as the crow flies to Camp One via Naway, hopefully no more than one night's march if all went well. Well, that would be good news to tell the lads when they woke up.

My turn came and I got my head down for a couple of hours, only to be woken by the distant sound of a muezzin making the call to prayer, followed by the voices of two of the lads who'd come with us from the ambush at Tirgari. I presumed the summons was coming from the mosque in Bald-Bagh. The sound of their voices woke the rest of the group, but I hadn't a clue, with my limited command of Pushtu, what they were saying.

'What's the matter, Blue, what are they talking about?'

'They say they must go to pray.'

'You don't mean they want to pray in Bald-Bagh do you?'

'Yes, Tom.'

'That's madness; if they go there, they'll compromise us.'

Blue spoke sharply to them, but I could see they weren't having any of it.

'I'm sorry, Tom, but these four say they are going, and they want to have some money to buy food.'

'All I've got are American dollars and Pakistani rupees. If they take those they'll attract a lot of attention and someone is bound to follow up . . .'

The situation looked like it might be about to turn nasty, so I gave in and gave them some Pakistani money, but I was absolutely furious and so was Blue. We made them agree to return by 17.30 hours, otherwise they would find us gone, then they simply upped and walked out, making no attempt to conceal their movements. It seemed as if they'd decided that the adventure was over for the time being. We were now down to just four.

There were still several hours before we could safely move and I decided that it would be a good idea to try to get some more sleep but, despite the fact that I was on my chin straps, I just couldn't settle down. I was desperately hungry, of course, but more than that, the anxiety and tension of the last few days had got me so jumpy I was like a cat on a hot tin roof. Looking around, I think it was the same for the others.

By 5 p.m., there was still no sign of the return of the errant four and we began to make our preparations to leave. It occurred to me then that we would have to drastically change our route: the four who'd left definitely knew where we were going and how we were planning to get there. If they were captured, I didn't see them holding out all that long, so it seemed to me that we should make a big detour, even though it would add half as much distance again to our route. Looking at the map, I decided that we would make our way firstly towards Tatang, then follow the course of a small river towards Gandamack, before finally heading south-east into the mountains and towards Camp One.

At a quarter past six, we moved out. You didn't need to be Einstein to know that the others weren't coming back.

I took the lead as we set off, but no sooner had we got to the trail than Blue stopped me: I realised I hadn't briefed him on my change of plan. When I did, there was a major sense-of-humour failure and the good old Chinese parliament made its reappearance with a vengeance. The three Afghans were rabbiting away when: bang! A flare shot up into the sky from hill 6990, the peak at whose base Camp Six was sited. I hit the deck like a sack of spuds and the Afghans followed.

I realised then that there must be a sangar or fort at the top of the hill, and that the flares that had plagued us the night before had probably come from hill 7660, rather than patrols out on the ground. Actually, this was good news, but I wasn't going to let the Afghans know. Better they felt obliged to do what I told them. I motioned to Blue and he came over.

'Listen, Blue. They're soldiers up there. If they spot us, then in minutes we will have artillery, helicopters and troops here. If we go my way, we'll be OK, but if we fuck around, then they'll kill us all. Understand?'

Blue nodded glumly.

EIGHT

By midnight we had passed Tatang and were well on our way towards Gandamack. Once more we had a road and a river to cross, but with just four of us, we were burning up the miles faster than we'd done throughout the entire operation. We filled our water bottles at the river, and I set a course to hit the road running between Gandamack and Sorkh Pol. I wanted to give Gandamack a wide berth because it was a big place with a considerable military presence.

We had a good ten kilometres to cover, and it began to hit me just how hungry I was. My legs felt leaden, and I had a sort of light-headed dizziness that was markedly affecting my concentration level. In my E & E pouch I had a big bar of dark Bourneville chocolate – classic emergency food – but if this wasn't an emergency, I didn't know what was. I pulled it out, and used my pocket knife to cut away the polythene and masking tape I'd used to waterproof it. The four of us sat down, and I shared it out. We washed it down with water, and I sat and watched the Afghans smiling as they ate it.

Odd as it may seem, the fact that I was prepared to share out my emergency chocolate cemented the bond that had grown between the four of us. They never again queried or disputed any of my instructions; it seemed that I'd earned their respect and trust (they didn't know it, but they'd earned mine by not fucking off with the others at Bald-bagh!).

We tabbed off again after a short break but after only a few minutes, we saw a bright light in front of us: a searchlight of some sort, sweeping around the countryside. It stopped, there was a pause of five minutes or so, then it re-appeared, five hundred metres or so to the left, apparently patrolling along the road. I was beginning to wonder whether the Soviets had something personal against me; how many soldiers are out there, for fuck's sake! In this kind of situation, it's easy to become paranoid. At the end of SAS training comes the combat survival course with its E & E exercise, then called Exercise Hard-nut Wanderer. On this exercise, you know that everyone is out to get you, but now we couldn't be sure. Most likely, the massive increase in troop levels was the result of a pre-planned counter insurgency operation, but in my slightly dazed state, I was beginning to wonder if maybe, just maybe, they knew about me, and were trying to find me. Certainly, what should have been a relatively straightforward three- or four-hour march was shaping up to become a two- or three-day epic.

We got up close to the road and I had a good sniff around, but I was pretty certain there were no troops about, just the vehicle with the searchlight and that was now a good two clicks away. We crossed over and moved into an area of thick scrub, which was giving way to sandy, desert-like terrain. Time was now against us: although we were moving fast, we'd had to waste a good deal of time avoiding Russians, recceing crossings and so forth, and I was concerned that we would be right out in the middle of nowhere at daybreak. We really started to push it now, taking risks that a month ago I wouldn't even have considered.

In the early light of dawn, we were crossing rolling scrubland when we heard the sound of rotor blades again. We found a fold in the ground and got down as five Hind Ds roared over us, flying steadily on towards the mountains. We stayed put as they evidently found a target and began to take it apart, shredding it with heavy machine-gun and rocket fire. They came back over us and then turned about, taking another run in at whatever they were attacking.

This carried on for a good quarter of an hour, and throughout we had no option but to stay down, faces pushed into the dirt, knowing that if we made any move at all, they would almost certainly spot us. I could feel nervous sweat pouring off me, and Blue looked like his eyes were about to pop out with anxiety, but there was nothing for us to do but wait it out.

Eventually the noise faded, and when I was sure that the helicopters were clear, I raised my head enough to get a good look round. There was smoke rising from the mountains in front of us, but otherwise nothing much to see. I turned to Blue.

'I think it would be a jolly good idea if we fucked off from here as soon as possible.'

He didn't take much prompting to agree with me and we carried on, picking our way through the scrub and keeping as close as we could to the little folds and ditches which offered the only real cover from the air.

As we got closer to the slopes of the mountains, we could hear occasional outbreaks of shooting from somewhere in front, which seemed to be getting closer and closer. After one particularly fierce exchange, which seemed to be fairly nearby, I decided that we should get ourselves into cover and see what emerged. We found a crevice between two large rocks and while I kept watch, the boys took the opportunity to say their prayers. We'd spent a few minutes there, and I was studying my map when a movement caught my eye. As I watched, twenty-seven men rounded a large boulder and crossed in front of us, using a well-defined track. They looked like Mujahideen – they were dressed in Afghan clothes but carrying AKs – but I thought it wise to stay hidden, and I didn't do anything to alert Blue and the boys who were still praying. We'd got into enough shit by hooking up with stray Mujahideen groups on this trip already!

As the first group disappeared from view, a second group appeared. This time it consisted of four mules: two carrying wounded men and two with some other load, followed by two men with Kalashnikovs. As this group crossed in front of me, there was another outburst of heavy firing, and from very nearby now. Blue crawled over and asked what was happening, and I told him about the Mujahideen I'd seen. This pissed him off. He was annoyed because he might have known them and been able to get us food but I managed to reassure him by saying that I simply hadn't wanted to disturb their prayers. So we sat there quietly, trying not to attract any attention as a fierce firefight continued around us.

After half an hour or so, things began to hot up. By now we could hear shouting and yelling, as well as gunfire, and it was apparent that the centre of the fighting was moving closer to us. I needed to find out what was happening, but when I stuck my head round the edge of the sandstone, there was fuck all to see. This was getting confusing.

I got the map out to try to plot a route out, when suddenly there was a burst of fire very close by, and then Blue was up and returning fire with his AK. Shit, we were compromised; map away and let's rumble!

I crawled over to Blue to find out what he was shooting at when another burst came in and we both got showered with dirt and gravel: fuck that! I took a quick look round, in time to see the muzzle flash and smoke of a weapon fairly nearby, then some movements. I fired three aimed double-taps and the movement stopped, to be followed by shouting and screaming. The fire slackened off near us, but there was still plenty going on.

'Blue, who the fuck is out there?'

'It is the Kalkh's army. The Communists!' he shouted back.

'Then we have to go, these bastards will have air support coming in any time!'

There didn't appear to be any activity in the direction we were going in anyway, so I told the boys that I would cover them while they moved off one by one, then they could cover me. Unfortunately, none of them were too keen to be the first across.

'OK, well, I'll fucking go while you cover me then.'

Blue agreed and I set off, zigzagging, running like fuck for a depression in the ground thirty yards away. I dropped in and looked around, only to find that Mohamed had followed me in. If it had been Junior Brecon, I'd have bollocked him, but I let it pass. We got down and began laying down fire, and the other two crossed. There was no incoming, and I began to feel a little more confident.

'Okay, girls, let's try that again.'

I managed to get a laugh out of Blue with that one.

I set off and found some more cover with no problems, then the others followed, one by one. Still no incoming fire, but now we could see more of the area from where we'd been fired at. Lying huddled in the dust was a body, but from his clothing, I would have said he was a Mujahideen, not a soldier.

'Are you sure these are the army, Blue?'

'Oh yes.'

We carried on along a gully, and when we were about five hundred metres away from the firefight, we came across the body of a dead Afghan next to an equally dead mule, complete with its blanket-covered load. I didn't want to get too close at this stage, and we boxed around them, putting a clear hundred metres between us. We were now beginning to climb into the mountains and I was finding it hard going. We'd had no proper food for four days and I was finding it so hard to concentrate, I needed to stop what I was doing and sit down, rather than attempting to make a decision on the move. We stopped for a water break and to check our position.

I reckoned we had about five or six kilometres to go before we got to Camp One. We were going to make it. But I was worried by the firefight we'd just got caught up in. I simply didn't believe that it was the Afghan army: we'd seen nobody in uniform and they hadn't called in air support or artillery. I was too confused to come to any definite conclusions, but there was something wrong.

It was now about 2.30. Blue and the boys prayed for fifteen minutes, then we pushed on. This last effort was incredibly difficult. I was dizzy with hunger and exhaustion and anxious not to miss the hidden path into the camp. After two hours, we saw in front of us a group of eight men; they were evidently heading in the same direction and we followed them in. I allowed Blue and Mohamed to go first; I didn't want to be mistaken for a Russian at this stage of the game.

Almost the first person I met when we entered was Abdullah. I was delighted to see him, I was sure he'd been killed or captured at Tirgari and it turned out he believed the same thing about me. We sat and talked as hot tea was brought for us; in my confused state, I had a strong urge to clean my rifle, but as I sat there, I realised it could wait an hour or two: it had worked that morning anyway!

Suddenly, Abdullah remembered something.

'Tom, I have something of yours!'

He nipped off and came back five minutes later with my bergen. It was an emotional reunion, even though my spare, clean-ish clothes had acquired a touch of mildew. It was nothing a good night's airing wouldn't sort out.

It turned out that Abdullah had had just as lucky an escape from Tirgari as we had. In the confusion after the ambush he and a small group of his men had tabbed the twenty kilometres from Tirgari to Zirani in four hours – a feat that would be a source of admiration in the Paras, let alone the Mujahideen – and then worked their way through to Camp One, travelling by night and lying-up by day.

He mentioned that he'd seen soldiers occupying the summit of hill 6990, and I told him what we'd found at Camp Six. He was shocked; when he'd passed through, everything had been OK. I suppose the soldiers in the sangar must have noticed the general comings and goings. It was bound to happen.

The mullah now began his evening call to prayer and I took the opportunity to clean my AKM. It was full of sand, and I was amazed that it still worked, but I hadn't had a single stoppage or misfire in three major contacts; a good measure of the quality of the weapon.

As I sat there, feeling reasonably secure for the first time in days, the women began to bring out food and set it out for the evening meal. This surprised me; normally the Afghan women kept their distance from me and the only one I'd seen close up had been the 'nurse' at Camp Five. I suppose I was now pretty much accepted by the Mujahideen as 'one of them'; I'd certainly shown I was on their side.

When the fighters came back from prayers, we settled down to eat. The food was good: goat meat, chicken, rice, salad and bread. But my stomach had shrunk and I was full in minutes. I said my goodnights, found myself a little niche, rolled up and slept like a baby.

I woke up with the dawn call to prayer at 4.45 but thought: fuck it, just five minutes more. Several hours later, Blue woke me again with a brew of fresh green tea. I sat up and drank it gratefully, while Blue squatted next to me and chatted. Eventually, he worked round to what he really wanted to know.

'Tom, there is a column going back to Pakistan tomorrow. Can we go with it?'

Actually, this was cracking news. We certainly needed to rest for a day or so but there was no point in hanging on out here any longer, and I imagined William would be pretty antsy by now.

'That's fine, Blue. By the way, is all the equipment I collected still here?'

'Yes, Tom, it's in the commander's hut.'

'Excellent! We'll need three or four mules to move it all, though. If you can organise them, we can set off tomorrow at whatever time you want.'

Blue went off to sort out the mules and I went to get myself cleaned up.

Washing now presented a slight logistical problem. Because the women at this camp were prepared to walk around openly while I was there, there was a raised danger that they might see me naked down at the washing area. I wasn't shy, but I didn't want some irate mullah ordering the Mujahideen to stone me to death for flashing at the girlies. Consequently, I had a good scout about to make sure it was all clear before I got my kit off and jumped in. It's a military proverb: time spent on reconnaissance is seldom wasted.

I couldn't believe how filthy I was. It was as if I'd been working down a coalmine. I lay in the cool water for a while, then piled my dirty gear, boots and all, in with me and gave it a good scrub out. I got out, dried off and put on the mildewed stuff I'd dried out the night before: it felt great. On my feet, I wore an old pair of jungle boots I kept in my bergen for wearing around camp. I hung my wet gear to dry on some bushes, and then went off to see what was happening.

As I crossed the camp, I bumped into Blue. It turned out that he'd had no luck whatsoever in getting hold of mules. This bothered me: I could understand why mules would be fully loaded coming into Afghanistan, but not why they would be full going out. I went to look for Abdullah, but he was nowhere to be found and, instead, I went to the cook and got some tea and naan. It was a scorching hot day, and I found a shady spot to drink my tea and eat the bread. When I'd finished, I took my mug back to the cook and saw another group of Mujahideen, who'd just arrived, unloading what I took to be sacks of yellow-ish flour from the backs of their mules. They put the sacks in caves, leaving the mules 'empty'. Right, here we go then, I thought, and set off to find Blue.

Unfortunately, I couldn't find him, nor any other members of my team, even after I'd looked almost all round the camp. At this point, I spotted the old mullah, just getting ready to begin the call to prayer. This'll flush 'em out, I thought, and I was right.

When they'd finished praying, I grabbed Blue and started to explain to him about the mules, but I began to realise that he wasn't really taking in what I had to say. I assumed he was still knackered and left him to it while I went to check over and pack up the various bits and pieces I'd collected. Most of it wasn't going to be a problem, but the sheet of armour was a real bugger, and I didn't envy the mule that was going to have to carry it. By now lunch was ready and being set out on a big carpet beneath a canvas awning and I went to join in, noticing that Abdullah was back and deep in conversation with an older man.

When we'd all finished eating, Abdullah walked over to see me and asked how things were. I told him about my problem with the mules but he already knew and instead suggested that I returned to Pakistan the next day with a large group, and he would organise the onward transport of my gear. I couldn't accept this: if anything was to go wrong at this stage, the previous month would have been pretty much wasted, and I preferred to supervise the transport of the equipment myself. I still had the very tattered and dogeared letter of authority from Hekmatyar, and although I knew it wasn't Abdullah's fault, made him read it again.

'All this stuff about the mules being full is bollocks!' I told him. I think he got the gist, even if he didn't fully understand the language. He looked worried.

'Tom, I must speak to the commander here. Maybe he will let you have some mules.'

I went back to my sleeping area for a kip, puzzled at what they could possibly be taking back into Pakistan. The obvious answer would be wounded, but there didn't seem to be too many here. I got my head down for a couple of hours, waking when evening prayers were called.

After prayers came the main meal. All this food! I'd eaten a good deal more in the past twenty-four hours than I had in the previous week, and I was beginning to feel almost bloated. When we'd eaten, Abdullah came over to tell me that he'd got me one mule. I was to get as much as possible on to it, and anything else would have to come back later. Well, one was better than nothing, and I accepted.

Happy that I'd agreed, Abdullah suggested that I might like to come with him to one of the closed caves. One of the fighters he was with looked completely pissed: a big sloppy grin on his face and unsteady on his feet. This surprised me; I'd taken these boys for strict Muslims, but if they were up for a bit of moonshine and were happy to share it with me, then I was game on. Lead me to it!

We got to the cave and they led me in, and I found where my team were hanging out. But I was wrong: it wasn't booze. In the centre was a big pot and the Afghans were sitting around it, passing long, thin pipes to each other. So not booze: opium.

I sat with Abdullah and after a few minutes the pipe got round to us. He had a go, passed it to me, and I took a draw. Jeeesus! I'd never even smoked a cigarette, and I spent the next ten minutes coughing up my guts while the Afghans laughed at me in a somewhat mellow fashion. When I'd recovered, I sat there talking with Abdullah and Blue, but I could see that the lights were slowly going out in their heads, and after a little while, I made my excuses and left to get a proper sleep.

I woke up with the call to prayer and sat eating hot naan and drinking tea while they made their devotions. When they'd finished praying, I made sure that my team had got plenty of

176

breakfast down their necks and then walked over to where the mule-handlers were beginning to get everything loaded. More than anything else, I was anxious that they didn't forget about my cargo. Seeing me, the mule boss – the older Afghan whom I'd seen talking to Abdullah the day before – walked over and in perfect, almost accentless, English told me:

'Don't worry, old boy, we'll get your stuff loaded up in a minute.'

This place was full of surprises.

I stood watching as the mule handlers carried sacks of flour out of the caves and hooked them onto the backs of the mules, before carefully covering them with tarpaulins to waterproof them. I suppose they use it to make bread in the refugee camps, I mused, though they'd be better off transporting it as grain: you can't dry flour if it gets wet.

Then the old light bulb went off again: of course, this isn't flour; it's fucking opium! There weren't any mules because they were all jam-packed with drugs. Fucking hell! Suddenly, the big firefight on our last day on the trail fell into place: an attempted opium hijack. I knew it couldn't have been the army because they didn't bring the gunships in, but a big robbery made sense: no wonder Blue didn't want to tell me.

I didn't say anything but watched as the mule-handlers expertly lashed the armour plate and my bergen on to the unfortunate creature. We were pretty much ready to go, in a convoy of fifty or so fighters and fourteen mules, including mine. There was obviously a lot of cash value in this lot, and the Afghans were anxious that it should get through, to the extent that everyone was milling around like a mothers' meeting when we pulled out. Feeling fit and refreshed after a couple of days' good food and rest, I was looking forward to the walk, with nothing to do but tag along at the back.

Around mid-morning, we arrived at the foot of Spin-Ghar, ready to begin the long seven-thousand-foot climb (from our current altitude) to the top which was shrouded in cloud. At this point, I said goodbye to Abdullah, who accompanied us for this part of the journey, and promised to return with the equipment he'd asked for. Then we started the long haul to the summit, walking, staggering, and pretty much crawling through the increasingly thin air. By mid-afternoon we'd reached the top and I sat, soaked in sweat and caked in dust and dead flies, drinking water and eating bread as I kept guard over the praying Afghans. As we started down the other side, we were in the relative safety of Pakistan. Thank fuck for that.

The journey down was, if anything, harder on the feet than the trip up and it was late at night before we reached the caravanserai where we'd halted on the way. The mules were unloaded and fed, and tea and bread were brought round for the rest of us, then I found a spot outside to basha down, away from the farting, snoring Afghan guerrillas, and I lay there watching as guards were placed on the mules and the opium, before dropping off into a deep sleep.

After the morning call to prayer, we breakfasted on tea and bread, and then got ourselves ready. As we were doing this, five of our group took off at relatively high speed in the direction we were travelling in, though when I asked Blue why this was, he told me he didn't know. As we got ready to pull out, the mule boss brought the 'landlord' over to me with the bill: thirty-five US dollars for food and accommodation for the entire convoy. Notwithstanding the millions of dollars' worth of narcotics we had, I was happy to pay. Just as before, I thought it was bloody good value.

About three in the afternoon, we reached a point I recognised just outside the village of Mangel Post, where a group of men were waiting for us, including the five Mujahideen who'd left earlier. These, it turned out, were Pakistani Inter-Services Intelligence (ISI) officers, sent to escort us into the Mujahideen base at Parachinar and ensure that we didn't have any problems with the Frontier Police. We continued a little further and then stopped to wait for darkness, after which the Pakistanis took us straight into the camp. The opium mules were taken into a special wired-off compound, complete with guards, while the rest of us went to the Hezb-i-Islami section of the base. It was clear to me then that the Pakistanis were involved at a high level with the opium smuggling.

After we'd stopped, I supervised the unloading of my gear into a tent, after which I gave my AKM and the AK-74 a good clean and oiling. Then I followed the lads over to the Hezb cookhouse. I was pretty tired after a hard day, so I got my head down for a couple of hours before our transport, a Toyota pick-up, came to collect us at midnight. Blue sat up front with the driver while I sprawled in the back with Mohamed and Iqbal, making myself as comfortable as possible amongst the piles of military kit.

Everything went fine until we reached the big army–police checkpoint outside Parachinar. On duty tonight was a keen young officer, a classic Sandhurst type (I don't imagine he'd been to Sandhurst, but the Pakistani army is more British than the British army, if you see what I mean) who was damn well going to do everything by the book. This meant he insisted on everybody getting out while he checked our papers and destinations and so forth. A bit nonplussed by this, I told him I was Thomas Jones from Wales, a worker for a medical charity making an assessment of conditions in the refugee camps along the border. I was wondering what I could tell him when he found all the Russian stuff under the tarpaulin in the back of the truck.

After a bit of chitchat, he led me off to one side and in a frightfully pukka and earnest undertone, told me:

'Listen here, old chap, I do think you should be careful travelling around at night with these fellows. A lot of them aren't awfully nice, if you see what I mean.'

I assured him I knew exactly what he meant, at which point a soldier came up with a message for him. When he'd read it, he turned to us and said:

'Well, your stories check out. I'm sorry to have delayed you, goodnight.' And we were free to go. Obviously, the fix had gone in.

We had no further checkpoint problems during the night and at around 6.30 a.m., we finally pulled in to the Hezb headquarters at Fackeyrabad. We stashed all the gear in a storeroom and I went to say hello to Mangel Hussain, one of the Hezb leaders and a good guy. After the usual hugging he asked how I'd enjoyed my tour of his country.

'It wasn't Club 18–30, but not bad.'

'I will come to your hotel later and we can talk.'

'Come to lunch . . .'

With that sorted, I went out to find Blue. He was waiting with Mohamed and Iqbal, so we hitched a lift from a jeep to the hotel and went in.

At reception, I discovered that William was somewhere up in north Pakistan having left me a contact phone number in case I got back while he was away. I got William's room key so I could get hold of my duffel bag with my clothes in, and then checked me, Blue, Mohamed and Iqbal in, paying in advance with some of the remaining dollars from the ops fund.

I told Blue that I was going to get a bath and get changed, and advised him to do the same, as we all stank to high heaven. I told him to take the other two to the little shop next to the bank counter in the foyer of the hotel and to buy new clothes and sandals and charge them to my room number. Then to meet me in the coffee shop at 9.30 for breakfast.

I had a shower and put on fresh, clean clothing for the first time in weeks. At half past nine, the four of us duly assembled in the coffee shop and began to work our way through the menu. By the time we finished, it looked like the remains of a chimpanzees' tea party. I also paid them: a hundred each for Mohamed and

Iqbal, a hundred and fifty for Blue; and fifty dollars each as a bonus. I could afford it; the Tirgari fuck-up had cut the wages bill by 50 per cent. Not a lot of money by Western standards, I suppose, but a lot for them in those days, and worth every penny.

We went back to our rooms and I tried to sleep, only to be continually interrupted by the cleaning staff who, being largely illiterate, couldn't read the 'Do Not Disturb' sign. I decided instead to go and lie by the pool and was just getting up to do so when the phone rang. It turned out to be Blue. He'd been contacted by the Hezb and told that he had to go back to Fackeyrabad a.s.a.p., so he and the others were just off down to the lobby to meet their transport. I quickly dressed and headed down to see them off, and when they'd gone, went back up to my room to collect a towel and sunglasses.

I was just going through the door when the phone went again. This time it was London. The gist of the conversation was a series of questions. When did I extract? Had I been successful? Where was my report? Where the fuck was William?

I wasn't really in the mood for this, so I covered my and William's arses with a few little obfuscations: I'd just got back so I was still putting the report together; William was up-country meeting another Hezb group (actually the address he'd given was a resort hotel in Chitral) and he had the codebook with him. The response was to '. . . make sure bloody William phones in as soon as he gets back.'

And on that note, I headed down to the reception desk to tell them that I would be by the pool, and if anyone wanted me, to put them through to me there, without telling them what I was doing.

I spread out my towel in the shade of a large palm tree and dived into the pool for a quick twenty lengths, then I ordered a nice big glass of freshly squeezed orange juice, drank it and settled down in the afternoon heat to push out some more Zs.

I was woken by a female voice:

'Excuse me, you are Tom Carew, aren't you?'

I struggled awake and sat up. Standing over me was a tall, thin and very attractive English girl, with blonde hair and a deep sun-tan. I wondered momentarily if I was dreaming.

'Er, yes, I am. Who are you?'

'I'm Kathy Blake from Islamabad.' She produced an ID card. 'Mr Loughlin in London asked me to come and debrief you about your trip over the border.'

Loughlin was William's boss in London, but there was no way I could just start yapping to her without clearance from William. After all, I had no easy way of verifying who she was.

'I'm sorry, you've had a wasted drive. What will you do now?'

'I'd better ring in for instructions.'

Obviously, she wasn't giving up that easily. Having said that, she still wasn't going away with my after-action report, not least because I hadn't written it yet. I watched her as she sashayed away towards the reception desk then lay down again to resume my sleep.

A few minutes later I was disturbed by a waiter. Would I mind going to reception?

I pulled on a T-shirt and a pair of flip-flops and padded in. The girl handed over the telephone and a voice – apparently from London – launched into a routine about how there was no problem, and that I could give my report to 'Miss Blake' either in writing or verbally (they'd obviously twigged that part of it). I still wasn't wearing it; none of these people were in my chain of command. I told London that I wasn't reporting to anyone until I'd either spoken to William, or received his instructions in writ-ing, confirmed by telex from London. It was a stalemate and, actually, I was in the right. London told me they'd get back to me, and ordered me not to leave the hotel.

I turned to Miss Blake.

'They're going to get back to me. What are you going to do?'

'I'm not driving back to Islamabad tonight; it isn't safe for lone women. I'll check in here and wait for instructions.'

We agreed to meet for dinner at nine.

'Oh, and Mr Carew . . .'

'Yes?'

'My name's Kathy.'

I went back to my room, showered and changed, and at 8.45 arrived back at the bar, clutching my 'sin permit' which would enable me to buy alcohol. I ordered a beer – my first since I'd crossed into Afghanistan – and got it down without it touching the sides. Ah, that's better. As I ordered my second one, Kathy arrived.

Just as before, we couldn't take alcohol into the restaurant, but you could have your meal served in the bar, so we did that. Once again, the menu showed an interesting and exotic list of different dishes but the reality turned out to be somewhat more mundane – although better than the average Mujahideen camp, it should be said. The food and beer were taking their toll, so at about ten I decided to hit the sack and escorted Kathy back to her room, a couple of doors down from mine. As soon as I was back in my own room, I flaked out completely, only to be woken by the phone at half past midnight. At last, it was William.

'Tom, you're back! Thank God for that . . .'

He sounded as if he'd had a few drinks but I explained the situation to him anyway.

'Oh shit! Look, try to keep it all on ice 'til I get back. I'll call you in the morning at about 8.30 to tell you when I'll be there.'

I met Kathy at breakfast and explained to her that William was on his way back. She wasn't too fussed.

'That's fine, I've spoken to Islamabad. London are sending confirmation by telex now, and I'm to stay here until the report's completed.'

'Fine.'

'I shouldn't tell you this, by the way, but everyone's pretty cross at the moment about the delay in getting this report out . . .'

'I shouldn't worry, just blame me.'

'I already have.'

Smart work by Kathy, but I wasn't too bothered: I was planning to pass the blame on to William.

After breakfast Kathy got a notepad and we went to sit by the pool while I dictated the report to her. By midday, I still hadn't heard from William so I assumed he'd got held up somewhere. We went in for lunch and had just sat down when William finally stomped in, complaining about telephones, planes and just about everything else he'd come into contact with that day. He stopped short when he saw Kathy and I introduced her.

'Tom, can I have a word with you in private?'

'Sure.'

I excused myself and went out into the lobby with him.

'Who's the bird?'

'One of your gang from Islamabad. Loughlin sent her down to debrief me . . .'

I gave him a run-down on everything that had happened since I got back.

'Well done, Tom, thanks for covering my arse . . . Christ, you can't imagine how much I've been worrying about you!'

'I can see that. You were so worried, you took a holiday in Chitral to calm down, you wanker!'

He laughed and we returned to the restaurant.

After lunch, William went off to change and then came down to join us, not least so that he could catch up on what had happened to me. Kathy was writing away, so William asked to see what she'd got down so far. She handed him a notepad covered in squiggles: shorthand. Instead, I gave him a quick verbal rundown on the insertion phase: the route, use of mules and all the rest of the bollocks. After a couple of hours, the area around the pool began to fill up, so we went back to William's room and worked on until 8 p.m., which got me to the point in the operation where I encountered the opium convoy. Somehow, I got the impression from William that this wasn't exactly news to him. As I started to go into detail, he changed the subject and suggested we go out for dinner; I wasn't sure if he didn't want me to talk about it, or if he was just hungry.

We took Kathy's car and went to a Chinese restaurant down the mall, then afterwards returned to the hotel bar for a few beers. Around midnight, William went off to his bed and Kathy and I went for a walk around the golf course next to the hotel. One thing led to another, I suppose, and we wound up back in her room in bed. Christ, I hadn't slept with anyone in well over a month, so I don't suppose I was that great, but she was lovely, and I felt like a little kid let loose in a sweetshop.

We were woken next morning by her phone ringing at around 7.30. It was William, wondering if she'd like to join him for breakfast; apparently he'd called my room and got no answer, so he assumed I'd gone for a run or something. She took a quick shower and went off downstairs, and I gave her ten minutes and then followed.

When I arrived at breakfast, William was looking nervous and uneasy while Kathy was her normal composed self. I'd obviously arrived at the wrong moment, although I couldn't think what they'd been talking about. William finished up and went back to his room to sort out a telex for London, and Kathy and I returned to the poolside to complete the report.

I started off about the opium again but Kathy interrupted.

'Don't worry about all that, Tom. William says just cover the operational side and the collection of the Russian equipment.'

I thought: Whoa! Back up the fucking truck.

'No way: the opium is central to the whole thing. You don't need to be a rocket scientist to see that's how the Mujahideen are paying for all this.'

We argued back and forth for a few minutes, and she eventually agreed to include it all. When we'd finished, and she was packing away her stuff, I picked up her notepad and said:

'I hope you don't mind but I want to take a copy of this.'

I walked across to reception and photocopied everything she'd written. Although I couldn't read the shorthand, I didn't doubt that I'd be able to find someone who could, if necessary, and I was sure it was a good idea to keep an independent version of the report. We ate lunch together, and after I'd got her phone number in Islamabad, Kathy left to return to the office.

I went up to William's room and found him wrestling with a telex and his codebook. The latest message from London was apparently telling him to supply an AK-74 to the Chinese Embassy in Islamabad.

'Are you sure? We've only got one AK-74 and I'll be fucked if I spent all that time collecting it just to hand it over to the Chinese.'

'That's what it says here . . . Look, maybe the Hezb have got another one that they'll give you.'

'I've got to go over there this afternoon to get them to cut up the helicopter armour. I'll ask then.'

I got a taxi out to Fackeyrabad a little later and went to see Mangel. Cutting the armour plate was no problem: he'd get it done right away. As we were chatting, Hekmatyar himself came into the office. Although we'd only met once, he recognised me and asked how my trip went.

'It was fine thank you, sir. Everyone was very helpful and we got almost everything we needed.'

'Is there anything else we can help you with?'

'Well, now you mention it, I've been asked to obtain an AK-74.'

Hekmatyar didn't know what it was, but when I explained he was very helpful. He had a quick discussion with two of his aides and then said:

'There may be one at my house. These two will take you there, and if we have one, you may take it.'

'Thank you, sir, that's very kind.'

We hopped in a jeep for the five-minute drive to Hekmatyar's compound. The place was surrounded by heavily armed guards,

Afghan and Pakistani, but we were allowed straight through. I followed the two Afghans across a small courtyard to an out-building.

When they opened the doors, I could hardly believe my eyes. The place was an Aladdin's cave of weaponry and ammunition: there were dozens of Kalashnikovs, together with Dshks, RPGs, grenades and everything else you could think of. I had a good look through the AKs, and eventually found an RPK-74, the light machine-gun variant of the AK-74, together with one magazine but no ammunition. I wrapped it in a blanket and the Afghans drove me back to my hotel.

I took the RPK straight up to William's room and dumped it on his bed.

'Jesus Christ, what's that?'

'Its an RPK-74. Hekmatyar gave it to me.'

'Fucking hell, you can't leave it here.'

I took it to my room and shoved it under my bed to stop him bitching, and then went back down to see him. It turned out that he'd got confirmation that we were to deliver the RPK to the Chinese Embassy, and that we were to take the rest of the gear to the Islamabad office the next day. I went to my room to pack a few things, then we went down to the bar for dinner. As we ate, I brought up the subject of the opium again. I knew now it was a subject that William didn't want to talk about.

'Tom, there are some things that it's better not to know,' was all he had to say on the matter.

I drove up to Islamabad the next day in a Hezb-i-Islami pick-up truck and off-loaded the gear I'd collected – minus the RPK which stayed behind my seat, still wrapped in the same blanket. My next move was to go on to Rawalpindi where I had to meet William, who was flying there, and drop off the RPK. My original plan had been to spend a few days in Islamabad, chilling out with a few beers, some decent food, and, of course, the lovely Kathy, but just before I'd left Peshawar, William had informed me that we were both to fly to London the next day. Things were going to be tight.

I got to the Intercontinental Hotel in Rawalpindi and found that William had beaten me to it: he was already ensconced in a room on the fourth floor. I nipped up the stairs, RPK tucked under my arm, and got to his door, knocked and turned the handle: it was locked. I heard a voice from inside; it didn't sound too welcoming.

'William, open the fucking door; it's Tom.'

I heard the lock turn and the door opened.

'Ah Tom, right . . . er, come in.'

I went in, to find he had company: a tall, well-built American called Bob Osborne.

'Er, Bob's just flown in from South Africa.'

We shook hands, but I could see that they weren't comfortable with me around. William had his papers spread out all round him and they had obviously been discussing something that I didn't need to know about. I left the RPK with William, told him that I was planning to stay at the Holiday Inn in Islamabad and left them to it.

I was pleased to be rid of the RPK: carrying a machine gun around in a foreign country is rarely the best way to ingratiate yourself with the locals, but I was still puzzled about why we should be passing it over to the Chinese. I wondered idly whether someone in our organisation was working for them, but concluded that couldn't possibly be true. It turned out to have a fairly simple explanation: we and the Americans were secretly buying a lot of Chinese-made weaponry from Norinco, the Chinese weapons export company, to supply the Mujahideen. The Chinese wanted to get hold of an AK-74 to test and evaluate, to see whether they should bother copying and manufacturing it, and, as a quid pro quo, we'd agreed to get them one. Fair enough.

I checked into the Holiday Inn and phoned William. He apologised for not being able to talk to me earlier, and arranged to meet me the next day at 10.30 a.m. to discuss our travel arrangements. Now the night was mine.

I phoned Kathy to tell her where I was. She wasn't surprised.

'Don't go anywhere, I'm coming over.'

We spent the evening in the Marines' club at the US Embassy compound, sinking a few beers and having a good time, and then relocated back to my room for an even better time. It was a Friday, so Kathy had the day off, and we were both sound asleep when someone came hammering at the door.

I got up, blearily, and opened the door to find William standing there. He saw Kathy in the bed behind me, but rather than making any comment, just grinned and said:

'I'll see you downstairs in the coffee shop.'

I woke Kathy to tell her what had happened, and to my surprise, she didn't seem too put out.

'It doesn't matter, Tom,' she told me, sleepily, 'I've had to tell my boss anyway.'

'What did you tell him?'

'Everything . . . it's the rules.'

'Bloody hell! Well, I hope he enjoyed it.'

She curled up under the sheets while I grabbed a quick shower, got dressed and went down to see William. I found him sitting in the corner of the crowded coffee shop, reading a three-day-old copy of *The Times*. He winked at me as I sat down, but said nothing else about Kathy.

'Okay, Tom. We're flying to London this afternoon for a debrief on your mission, and then on to the States on Monday.'

'Will we be coming back here?'

'Yes, all your gear from Peshawar is being collected by the Hezb and they'll store it at Hekmatyar's compound. You need to get your stuff together now because we need to get to the airport sharpish.'

I went back up to my room to find Kathy in the shower. I chucked my stuff into my bag and told her:

'I'm sorry, I have to go now. I'm off to London.'

'I know, see you soon.'

I was beginning to realise that Kathy knew more about the operation than I did. I checked out of the hotel, and William and I got a taxi to the airport.

NINE

The flight was routed via the UAE and, for the first leg,
was crowded as fuck with Pakistanis travelling there
to work, but once they were off-loaded, things were a bit
quieter and I was able to get my head down for a few
hours' sleep. We arrived at Heathrow at about eight on
Saturday morning, and we were met after passport control
and taken out via a side door to a waiting car. We had a
fast, easy run up the M4 into west London and, by 9.30,
we were in Stag Place being shown into a large conference
room in Roebuck House, the same office building where
we'd had our original briefing.

There was quite an audience. Some I recognised: Loughlin and
John Miley; others were introduced, like a US Marine Corps
colonel called Fred Fox; the rest remained anonymous. For the
first couple of hours, William spoke and answered questions
about his side of the operation: liaison with the Hezb; logistics;
and a number of areas which I had no knowledge of. Then it was
my turn, describing conditions on the ground inside Afghanistan,

how the Soviets were operating, Mujahideen tactics and so on. Late in the afternoon, I got to the opium shipments, but almost as soon as I said the words, three of the anonymous men got up and left the room. I stopped talking in surprise but Loughlin told me to carry on.

'Don't worry about them, Tom. They don't want to know about this part of the operation.'

I carried on, and by the time we were all finished, it was pushing 8.30 p.m. After we'd wrapped up the discussion, Loughlin told William and I that he'd got us booked into a small family hotel nearby. This was good news; I was in real need of some sleep and food. Loughlin was keen to meet us for lunch the next day but William said he would prefer breakfast, and that was better for me as well: I wanted to drive up to Hereford – if possible – to see my wife and our daughter.

We met at nine the next morning over bacon and eggs in the hotel dining room. Loughlin was a good talker, and from what he said, I got the impression that he'd been involved in this kind of operation before. He seemed interested to know why I believed it was opium the Mujahideen were transporting, rather than flour, for example. I talked him through it.

'Firstly, the gun battle near Camp One – that was an opium hijack; secondly, the seriousness with which the Mujahideen guarded it; thirdly, the Pakistani protection at Parachinar. None of that would have happened for a few sacks of flour.'

I didn't mention that I'd tried some.

'But I also noticed while I was on the move that very few of the fields had any obvious crops in them, and that's because they had already harvested the poppies. Farmers grow crops to sell, and that's what the Mujahideen are doing, I guess. That's how they're financing the war.

'But the Russians are going to realise this as well. Don't forget, the poppy is a weed and all the Sovs need to do is get some crop-sprayers and they're half way to winning the war.'

'But crop-spraying aircraft will be sitting ducks for the Mujahideen,' Loughlin interjected.

'On their own, maybe, but they'll come with Hinds as back-up. Remember, I was only there a month, and even in that time the Russians were getting their act together. Soon they'll have proper forts on the hilltops, with proper observation and sensor equipment; then they'll begin to control and pacify larger and larger areas; then they'll seal the border. If the Mujahideen don't make a big leap forward, they're going to be wiped out.'

We continued discussing things in this vein for fifteen or twenty minutes, while William listened intently. Then Loughlin dropped a little bombshell.

'We're just about to reach the stage where we'll start to supply them with SAM-7 anti-aircraft missiles. That should even things up with the Hinds a little.'

This was a surprise, though I was still sceptical.

'It might, but the SAM-7 is a tail-chaser. It homes on exhaust emissions and is quite easy to deflect with decoy flares and so on. I've even heard of chopper pilots bringing their aircraft home after being hit by them: it's not going to solve the Mujahideen's problems.'

It was 9.45. William and I collected our bags and we started to walk back with Loughlin to his office.

'Loughlin, I assume that I'll be going back to Afghanistan?'

'Yes, Tom, this operation will be continuing for the foreseeable future.'

'Look, is it possible that I can have some help out there? It's bloody hard work on my own; if there were, say, four of us, we'd get a lot more done and it would be safer as well. I can't say I was entirely happy with a handful of Mujahideen for protection.'

'I hear what you say, Tom. But you will never get three. Four Brits out there would stick out like a sore thumb. Ask for two and you may get one. Do you have anyone in mind?'

'Yes, I do.'

193

'Okay, give me his name on Monday morning before you leave for Washington. By the way, do you have a US visa?'

'No.'

'Okay, give me your passport and I'll get it sorted.'

We were back at Roebuck House. Loughlin gave me a set of keys for one of the pool cars, a 2.3 Cortina.

'OK, Tom, be back tomorrow by 10 a.m.; your flight is at noon, so don't miss it.'

I slung my bag in the back of the car and pulled out into Stag Place, then threaded my way through Victoria towards Sloane Square, then up to Knightsbridge and onto the A4. When I'd made my way through Hammersmith and Chiswick and got onto the M4, I put my boot down and red-lined the Cortina out into the West Country, arriving at my home near Hereford just before 1 p.m.

Unfortunately there was nobody there. There was no reason why there should have been; Debbie didn't know I was back in the country. I phoned her best friend but she was out as well. Bollocks.

I drove into Hereford and parked outside my old friend Sparky's house. I'd known him since I joined 7 RHA, when he was in 9 Para Squadron, Royal Engineers. At Christmas 1973, my first after joining the Regiment, we'd been the only people in the squadron basha – we were completely skint, having blown all our money on horses and beer – so we'd cooked up a compo curry on a camping-gaz stove for our Christmas dinner. But when I knocked on his door, his wife answered and told me that he was overseas. Instead, I went next door to the Red Lion, and found some of the Iranian Embassy mob from B Squadron – Rusty, Max and Snapper – propping up the bar with old Jock the Clog. I had a beer with them, listening to Pete – Snapper – in full motormouth mode, before I noticed Paddy Egan in the corner.

I knew that Paddy was at a temporary loose end. He'd been in the process of leaving the Regiment because his marriage was suffering, but it had broken up anyway and he'd been left high and dry. But I'd worked with him out in Sri Lanka and knew he was a sound operator, well suited to this kind of task. It turned out that he'd just got back from doing a job in Holland, but when I told him that I might have some work for him 'out east', he jumped at it.

'Listen, Paddy, I can't tell you anything about it now, but give me your phone number and I'll be in touch in a week or so.'

I went into the town centre and soon spotted my wife's car. It turned out she was having lunch with our daughter and some friends at a restaurant, and as I walked in, my face sun-tanned dark brown, she did a double take and almost fell off her chair. I drove back with her and explained that I had to leave again at seven o'clock . the next morning. She was pissed off, to put it mildly.

I spent the afternoon playing with my daughter and helping out around the house, but to be honest my mind was on the trip to Washington and the debrief at the Pentagon. Funding for the operation was being largely provided by the DIA, and they would want to know they were getting their money's worth. I slept poorly that night, and by next morning at seven o'clock I was really ready to go.

I reached Stag Place at 9.45 and reported in to Loughlin. He returned my passport, complete with a colourful US visa, and gave me a large sealed brown envelope which I was to hand personally to a Special Forces major called Norman Blakelock. It turned out later that he was the chief planner for this operation. William strolled in half an hour later, while I was drinking tea with Loughlin, and collected a major bollocking for being late, much to my amusement. Then we went down to the car and headed for Heathrow Terminal 3, and the British Airways Washington flight.

I didn't get any sleep on this flight either and by the time we landed at Dulles airport, I was in quite a state of nervous anticipation. We were met by a plain-clothes army officer who escorted us quickly through customs and immigration to a car which took us directly to our hotel, the Marriott Twin Bridges opposite the Pentagon. We checked in and had a coffee together, then I went to my room to unpack and get a shower. No more than ten minutes later, the phone rang and William was on to tell me that we were wanted to begin the debrief straight away. I dressed quickly and went down to the lobby, and William and I then went out, to find the same car waiting for us.

We were met at the entrance to the Pentagon by another plain-clothes officer. He took us to security, where we were issued with visitor passes, and then escorted us along hundreds of yards of corridors, past walls hung with photos of distinguished generals, paintings and divisional signs, until we arrived at another security checkpoint and went in to the DIA section.

We were taken to a large conference room where some twenty or thirty people were waiting for us, some uniformed, some in civvies. It was one of those occasions when I was glad I had William with me. Whatever else he could do, he could certainly talk.

On this occasion he did things slightly differently, though. He had written a script, from which he read for twenty-five minutes or so, explaining what I'd done. Then he produced large blow-ups of all the photographs I'd taken during the operation and placed them in piles on the table in front of me. Then it was my turn: for the next three hours I spoke, partly in response to questions, partly narrating my tour inside Afghanistan. At one point I was asked whether I'd seen chemical weapons being used.

'Jesus, no! If I had, I doubt I'd be here now; I didn't have any NBC protection with me. All I saw were the Mujahideen who'd lost their body hair . . .' and I went on to explain what the Mujahideen had told me about them.

Next up were the air force people, wanting to know about the operation of the Hinds: were they effective, what counter-measures did the Afghans have and so on. This led us on to the question of SAM-7s. Did I think the Afghans could use them?

'I don't think it would be a problem to train the Afghans how to use them; they aren't stupid! It seems to me that the problem is whether they would work. I don't know what countermeasures the Hinds have against heat-seekers, and I don't know whether the SAM-7 has an IFF system which might disable it against a Soviet helicopter. Also, you have to remember that to get them into the operational area, you'll have to transport them across country on mules, and that means they'll get a good old battering.'

That got them thinking.

'Finally, anyone who fires a missile at a Hind is really going to piss the Russians off! They are going to work damn hard to nail him whether he hits or misses; and if he misses, he's going to piss the Mujahideen off as well. They might decide to carve him up too!'

A lot of heads were nodded.

We got onto weapons now. Were the AK-74s used a lot?

'From what I could see, most Russian soldiers seemed to carry them, but none of the Afghans.'

From there we began to look at how the Russian troops on the ground were operating, their tactics and so on. I noticed William was beginning to nod off; I was feeling pretty knackered as well. Luckily, at this point sandwiches and coffee were brought in.

When we'd finished the refreshments, William and I were asked to wait where we were for twenty minutes or so, and the first group of people filed out, leaving us on our own. We were both tired, and I think we both dozed off. Certainly the next thing I remember is being gently shaken awake by a US army colonel as the room filled with a completely different group of people, once more in uniform and civvies.

This group seemed to be particularly interested in the extraction of equipment: would it be feasible to get more out?

'Getting the kit isn't a big problem. If you tell me what you want, the chances are that the Mujahideen will have captured it at some point, or can be persuaded to try to. The biggest problem seems to be getting the stuff out, because every single mule is loaded up to the eyeballs with opium.'

The room went completely silent at this point.

'Why do you think it was opium?'

I explained about the gun battle and the fact that they were guarding it like gold dust. Once again I left out the bit about having tried it. Then came the big, stupid schoolboy question.

'What do you think they were doing with it?'

'Do you really want me to answer that?'

They all just looked straight at me.

'OK, I believe I saw more than one thousand kilograms of opium being taken from Camp One near Wazir to Parachinar in Pakistan. Once the opium was inside Pakistan, it was escorted by the Pakistani military to a special section of the Mujahideen camp, which was undoubtedly under Pakistani military control. My conclusion is that the Mujahideen are using the opium to fund their operations and obtain co-operation from Pakistan, and that the Pakistani military – or somebody in it – is taking a significant cut.'

There were a couple of guys in civvies at the back of the room who were looking at me as if I'd just dropped my kecks and shat on the floor. Fuck them! They asked for it.

I was shown a few satellite photos of areas in Afghanistan that I'd visited, including one of my mule convoy on the day of our exfil. I couldn't identify myself in the picture, but I was undoubtedly there; the wonders of modern technology!

The meeting began to break up for the day, and as William and I got our kit together, Norman Blakelock, the SF major, came over, introduced himself and invited us to go to dinner with him and his family that evening. He'd arranged a car to take us back to our hotel, and another one to take us to his house. It was a kind offer and I was glad to accept.

We arrived back at the hotel to find that London had sent William a long list of irritating questions as well as a request for a sitrep. He immediately started bitching about the extra work, and how they didn't understand about jet lag.

'William, mate, just tell 'em to fuck off! We've got too much to do over here to worry about those tossers. Nothing has happened here that won't wait for a few hours.'

I felt this was sound advice but William didn't seem to agree and went off to his room to compose a telex. In the meantime, I took a shower and got changed for dinner.

The driver arrived at six o'closk and we set off for Norman's house. I was feeling so jet-lagged I'd dozed off within minutes of leaving the hotel, and the driver had to wake both of us when we got there. We had a nice supper with Norman and his family but I didn't get the chance to talk to him alone as I'd wanted. At 9.30 we returned to the hotel so that we could get some sleep before the next round of briefings began at 7.15 the next morning, but my body clock was beginning to readjust itself and I didn't fancy bed just yet.

I happened to know that an old G Squadron mate, Dave Kerry, was working as a bodyguard in DC, and knowing that he liked a few beers when off duty, I decided I'd do a recce round some of Washington's nastier bars to try to find him. I grabbed a cab and asked the driver where to go for the best nightlife. He took me to Georgetown.

I spent the next three or four hours going from bar to bar vaguely looking for Dave but slowly drinking myself into a pleasant stupor. Round about 1 a.m., pissed as a fart, I headed back to the hotel, only to find people heading down in the lift to a disco-bar in the basement. I followed.

Round about 5 a.m. I headed back to my room and collapsed into my pit. At 6 a.m., William rang. Breakfast?

I was feeling like shit now, of course, but I poured myself into the shower, got dressed and headed on downstairs to hit the black coffee. William gave me a funny look as I sat slurping it down.

'Tom, you look bloody awful. Did you have trouble sleeping?'

I opened my mouth to respond and he caught a whiff of the beer. Surprise, surprise, he went ape-shit, yacking on about irresponsibility, stupidity and all the rest of it. Typical officer class; and like the good little squaddie I was, I sat meekly, ignoring him, letting it go in one ear and out the other as I wondered whether I would get the chance of a few more coffees during the morning.

The car arrived on time and we were soon back in the same conference suite. I took the opportunity to go to the bog where I had a good, long puke and after a couple more coffees from a machine, I was beginning to feel back on form. This morning followed the same format as the previous day: Q and A with a series of intelligence specialists. Lunch came in the form of sandwiches and more coffee and while I was sitting alone eating it (William was in another room at this point) two guys in civvies I'd seen the day before approached me.

'So, Tom, how was the food out there?'

'Oh, not so bad. Very ethnic, if you see what I mean.'

Then it came: the opium. What else did I know about it? Who owns it? Where was it going? Was I sure about Pakistani involvement? What were they going to do with it?

These kind of schoolboy questions pissed me off.

'Look, they aren't going to make aspirins out of it. My assumption is that they're going to sell it and use the profits to buy weapons. This isn't my world, but from the way they protected it, and from the involvement of the Pakistanis, I assume that it has real value.'

They both looked somewhat ill at ease.

'Did you, ah, report all this in your debriefing in the UK?'

'Yes, why not?'

'We at the, er, Agency would prefer it if you were not to mention this again. In fact, if you do see anything connected with opium again, just ignore it completely.'

I nodded my head without saying anything. If anything, that confirmed to me that the Mujahideen were moving the opium with, at the very least, the tacit co-operation of the CIA. Well, fuck them: if I see it, I'm going to report it; in my UK report at any rate.

After lunch they began their briefing to me of items required during the next phase of the operation. They showed me slides of various different types of AK-74, the AGS-17 grenade launcher and its ammunition, the RPG-18, together with a whole bunch of items from the downed Hind. The chemical boys wanted various NBC items as well as pictures of unusual body-hair loss and chemical agent burns, and – if possible – any unexploded chemical weapons I could obtain. I managed to keep a straight face at that one: I didn't have enough room for NBC gear with me and the only way I was going to go anywhere near a chemical weapon would be if one was dropped on top of me.

At long last they finished and I got the chance to talk alone with Norman. One problem that I had was a lack of worthwhile operational intelligence on the Russians so Norman gave me his standard briefing. His estimate was that there were about eighty-five thousand Soviets in the country, together with a small number from other Eastern Bloc countries; the Russians were in the process of increasing the numbers of Hind gunships and Hip transport helicopters, and he also thought they might have two further squadrons of Mig-23 fighter bombers moving in.

'The other thing, Norman, is that I need extra help on the ground. It's really hard work on my own and just a couple of guys would make things a lot easier.'

'I understand, Tom. I have no problem with increasing the size of the ground team, but it has to be a UK decision. There are a lot of political reasons why we can't put our guys on the ground right now.'

With everything wrapped up, Norman took me downstairs to the Pentagon PX which was in the basement and I bought presents for my wife and daughter. Then he dropped me back at the hotel.

The return flight to the UK was next morning so when we'd packed and eaten in the hotel restaurant, William and I hit the downstairs disco for a few more beers. I woke up next morning with a stonker of a hangover, but I managed to sleep for 85 per cent of the return flight and arrived in London in good shape. We were met at the airport and driven straight to Roebuck House for a debrief on the Pentagon visit. With that completed, Loughlin told me:

'We've got the green light for you to take Paddy. Your flight out to Pakistan is next Tuesday afternoon, so I'll want you and Paddy here Monday morning at ten. In the meantime, you've got a few days' break so make the most of it.'

It was Thursday evening, so I had three days with my family. Oh well, better than nothing.

I spent Friday getting Paddy briefed up and scouring the stores at Bradbury Lines for various bits and pieces I wanted to take with me. I picked up a much larger medical kit, as well as four boxes of field dressings and some cartons of Paludrin and paracetamol tablets for the camps. I also got a bundle of green windproof smocks, which were much needed, a few Para smocks and five old A-frame bergens, filled with belts, ammunition and water-bottle pouches; and a few ponchos, as very few of them had any waterproof clothing.

I collected Paddy at 6.30 on Monday morning, and we drove up to London, arriving in good time. After I'd introduced Paddy to Loughlin, I told him that I thought we needed some cutting gear so that we could dismantle the armour of the helicopter. Loughlin agreed and gave me some cash, and Paddy and I went down to a power-tool shop in south London where we bought a large, petrol-driven, chainsaw-type, German-made Stihl disc-cutter and a set of metal cutting discs. The shopkeeper obviously thought we were a pair of security van robbers, particularly when I pulled out a roll of twenty-pound notes to pay him, and after he'd shown us how to operate it and packed it back in its protective case, I'm sure he thought the next time he'd see us would be on *Police 5*.

In the afternoon, we made sure that all the gear was securely packed in big 'GQ' Para bags and in the evening we went out for a last big English dinner and a couple of beers, before heading back to the hotel for a relatively early night. In the morning we reported back to the office to pick up our travel documents and kit, together with some cash to cover the excess baggage charges (which came to £300). William arrived while we were doing this, looking like shit. It turned out that he'd been on the piss in some nightclub until the early hours. Loughlin sent Paddy and I to get a coffee while he bollocked him, and then at 12.30 we left for the airport.

Once we'd checked our baggage in, we went through to the departure lounge to wait our call. Paddy and I went down to the duty-free shop, Paddy to load up with the world's supply of cigarettes and me to get a big bottle of scotch for an old Pakistani guy I was cultivating. He'd served in the Royal Indian Navy during the war and was a useful source of gossip and information about who was who in Peshawar. I also called in at the bookstall to get some reading matter.

The flight was crowded, as usual, with lots of Pakistanis heading for home. I'd managed to get a window seat, so at least I wasn't being disturbed by some old dear wanting to get up for a piss every five minutes, and I settled down with my book. William was up the front in club class, once again, while Paddy was off poisoning himself in the smoking section. After the meal had been served and then cleared away, I got my head down for some sleep, but no sooner had I done so than I was woken again by the plane landing at Amman in Jordan. Cobblers! When we continued, I did manage to doze a little, but I can't say I felt all that refreshed when we finally rocked up in Islamabad.

The first problem to confront us after we arrived was that the connecting shuttle flight to Peshawar only had one place left on it. William took that, and Paddy and I loaded up our kit, and some of William's too, into a taxi for the five-hour drive. When we arrived at the Intercontinental, dusty and aching after the usual bone-rattling journey, we found William lounging in the bath reading a book. I suppose that's the difference between management and workers.

Over dinner we set out our agenda for the next few days: priority was to arrange the next infiltration to get to the Hind, now that I knew precisely what we needed to get from it and had the means to do so. Everything had gone pretty smoothly last time, but this time there was a hiccup. We couldn't do the infil without Hekmatyar's say-so, and he was away somewhere.

We kicked our heels for the next couple of weeks, touring Mujahideen bases round Peshawar to acquire information and captured Russian equipment, but it was an intensely frustrating period, made worse by some aspects of the task we were doing. The least pleasant job was visiting the hospitals to talk to the wounded Mujahideen fighters. They were a grim sight, full of men with missing limbs, and dreadful wounds on their bodies and heads, lying in conditions of absolute filth. At one camp we were taken to a shed which had been converted to a ward for 'special cases'. These turned out to be men with chemical injuries.

Some of them had appalling burns from mustard-gas attacks – like something from the First World War – while others had the injuries I'd seen before on the first infiltration: their hair had gone, their skin seemed yellowish, burned and a little 'cheesy' in texture and they were as sick as dogs. We took photographs of their injuries and got them to describe what had happened, asking them to pinpoint the exact locations on our maps.

Most of the chemical attacks apparently came from helicopters using big sprayers but a few told us about shells or aircraft bombs. Whatever: it was chilling to see the effects that these weapons had; and dreadful to think what effect they would have had on the dense European battlefield if we had ever had to fight the Soviets there.

After a few days of this, Paddy and I were so depressed that we decided to do something to help them. The problem was that once they were out of action, the big chiefs weren't interested in them; they had no value as fighters. We drove into the Peshawar bazaar and loaded up with goodies for them: everything from tea to soap, lemonade to towels. We took them back and distributed them round the hospitals. It was a moving sight; most of the fighters were close to tears of gratitude. When we got back to the hotel, we did a quick check and found that we'd spent $272, a good deal of cash in 1980.

That same afternoon, after Paddy and I had been for a run around the golf course, we got back to the hotel to find two attractive young English girls sitting by the pool. We started chatting with them and discovered that they were Pauline and Mary, British Council teachers based in Islamabad. We gave them our cover story as aircraft ground crew and arranged to meet them for dinner that evening. I went up to my room for a nap, but I was called down by William who was in a rage of frustration. He had still had no luck persuading the Hezb to take us into Afghanistan without Hekmatyar's personal say-so, and now London was getting antsy, even though we were supplying them with good-quality information from the Mujahideen in Pakistan. I knew also that William was very busy fixing incoming weapon resupply flights into Peshawar; though I didn't at that stage realise quite how busy. Among other things, he had to organise paper-trail-free refuelling for aircraft and Swiss-bank letters of credit for the Hezb to buy ammunition and weapons from Eastern Bloc countries, and bribe customs officials to let the weapons in – all in an area under intense scrutiny by the world's press and intelligence agencies. In fact, over the next few years a few stories did appear in the press about mysterious flights into Pakistan, but the journalists who wrote them soon found their access disappearing, and one or two who got onto the Mujahideen's black list didn't ever return from cross-border forays into Afghanistan.

William wanted to have another go at persuading the Hezb the next day, even though we knew that Hekmatyar still wasn't back. I wasn't sure it was worth the effort, but we agreed to go together and take a chance. I told him that we had two additional guests for dinner, and although he was naturally slightly wary, I think he was too distracted to be bothered too much.

We had a pleasant enough evening and I got my head down early, ready for another tedious session with the Mujahideen. Sure enough, the next morning brought more frustration: William closeted himself with the head-sheds for several hours but got absolutely nowhere. Instead, I went up to see old Mangel Hussain and drink tea with him in his office.

Quite a few of the senior Mujahideen guys in Peshawar were on an ego trip: whenever the press showed up, they'd be wrapping themselves in bandoliers of ammunition and toting around Kalashnikovs with triple-taped magazines, ready for the inevitable photo shoot. But, of course, when any real fighting needed to be done, they were straight back behind their desks.

Mangel wasn't like that. He never pretended to be a fighter: he was a teacher from Jellalabad; a clever man with a good brain and a sound grip on reality. He was head of information for the Hezb and so quite influential, and when I'd explained the nub of our problem to him, he promised to see what he could do.

When I'd finished my tea I went down to the courtyard to wait for William and chat with some of the lads who were there – mostly in sign language. I was pretty well fully accepted by the Mujahideen fighters now and they were happy to joke and take the piss with me; so much so that somebody came out to tell them all to shut up. But it was back to grim faces when William came out: I knew he'd got nowhere.

I told him Mangel was on the case but that I wasn't holding out any great hope, and he told me:

'I've got to go back to London for a few days on another matter. I need to get you over the border before then, otherwise I'll really be in the shit. These fucking Afghans are beginning to piss me off!'

Paddy wasn't around when I got back to the hotel so I went down for a swim in the pool, where I found the two girls eating ice-cream. After I'd done my forty lengths, I persuaded Mary to rub some sun oil into my back, which was nice, then sat shooting the shit with them. Paddy showed up after half an hour or so and we ordered sandwiches and juice for lunch and then, when the girls had gone off to do some sightseeing, settled down for an afternoon siesta in the sun.

I'd been there an hour or so when a waiter came out to tell me that Mangel Hussain and another Afghan had arrived. We ordered tea and sandwiches and sat by the pool to talk. It appeared that things were moving fast: Hekmatyar had returned at lunchtime and Mangel had got in quickly to see him, securing his agreement that we could cross the border as soon as possible. This was good news, but when I phoned up to William's room to tell him, he wasn't there. Mangel asked me to bring William to the Hezb headquarters that evening to collect him, and we were then to go on to Hekmatyar's house to confirm arrangements.

William turned up twenty minutes later looking very pissed off. He'd been told to return to London the next day and was fully anticipating being deeply in the shit for not getting any further with phase two of our operation. I told him what had happened and, at first, he didn't believe me; I suppose he was getting used to having the piss taken by now. But once I'd persuaded him it was true, he began to cheer up a little. An hour or so later, we headed off for Fackeyrabad, leaving Paddy to baby-sit the girls in the bar.

Surprisingly enough, Mangel was ready to go as soon as we arrived at the HQ, and directed us the short distance to Hekmatyar's compound. Once we were through the guards, we were shown up to the offices on the first floor and ushered into the great man's presence, where tea was served.

It transpired that he was puzzled at the delay in our operation. As far as he was concerned, he had already given us authority to travel in Afghanistan with his fighters. I suspect he didn't realise that most of his staff were afraid to take a piss without a direct order from him. The only problem he foresaw was the onset of winter. It was getting on for the end of November now – though still bloody hot as far as I was concerned – and soon the first snow would come to the White Mountain. When the path over the top was blocked, the route round would add five days each way to the journey. It was Sunday now: Hekmatyar would have everything ready for us to go on Tuesday.

By the time we got back to the hotel, William was his old self again. We went over our arrangements for the trip then went down to the bar to join Paddy and the girls. After a few beers we headed downtown to the Chinese restaurant and then back to the hotel where, to everybody's disappointment, we discovered that the bar was closed. William was obviously feeling very pleased with himself because he now revealed that he had a couple of bottles of scotch in his room 'for medicinal purposes' and some cola in his fridge. We needed no further invitation, and all of us wound up getting heavily pissed; so much so, in fact, that when I woke up the next morning, I was in bed with Mary in her room.

After we'd hit the fruit juice in her fridge, I found my watch and saw that we just had time to make it down for breakfast. But somehow, watching her soaping her breasts in the shower made me think of other things, and we didn't actually emerge until mid-afternoon.

TEN

My third infiltration into Afghanistan was Paddy's first, and the first one I'd done with a properly trained helper. I'd expected it to be much easier, but in fact it turned out to be a huge waste of effort.

We arrived at Fackeyrabad on the Tuesday evening with our kit – including the disc-cutter – loaded into big GQ para bags. It had started to rain so once we'd got it all loaded up, we clambered into the back of the truck ourselves, and settled back as far as we could under the slightly leaky canvas tilt. There was nothing for us to do now until we reached Parachinar. We were in the hands of the Afghans, so we made ourselves as comfortable as possible on top of the bags of kit and got our heads down for the journey.

We rolled into the Mujahideen camp at 5 a.m. It all looked much the same, and the same enthusiastic young commander was still running the Hezb-i-Islami section. Quite a few of the Afghans came over to give me the traditional hugging and kissing greeting, much to the amusement of Paddy.

'Very friendly people, Tom . . . are you sure you haven't

forgotten to tell me something?' he enquired, in his dry Irish brogue.

'Fuck off, wanker.'

After the Afghans had finished their prayers, we settled down for a breakfast of naan and green tea, and then one of the lads brought weapons over for us: brand new AKMs, still packed in their maker's grease, together with as many magazines as we needed and a screw-on rifle-grenade launcher with a few grenades. Ammunition came from the same big box as last time.

Our escorts rolled up around midday; eight of them – several of whom spoke a little English – armed with AKs, an RPK and an RPG-7. I'd originally asked if Blue could come along as well, but apparently he was on different business now. Now it was our turn to give some kit away. We gave each a windproof smock, a belt, a water bottle with a pouch, ammunition pouches and a poncho. We also wanted to give out the bergens but there were no takers, at first anyway. In fact once we'd put extra food, water, magazines and waterproofs into them, they couldn't have weighed more than fifteen or twenty kilograms, and we did eventually persuade them to carry them.

Although we weren't going to cross the border until the next morning, the Afghans wanted us to move up closer to the border. Apparently, they told me, the Russians had 'eyes' in the camp. Well, maybe, but I thought it much more likely that they were trying to keep us away from the opium store. We loaded our kit and our escorts into a couple of old Toyotas and set off along the track towards the border.

We were still inside the camp when someone caught my eye in the Jamiat-i-Islami compound: Darkie Davidson. We made eye contact but no move to speak or communicate with each other. It was SOP; we didn't need to know what the other was doing.

Close to the border, we arrived in a small village with a bazaar composed of lock-up type shops which were to be our home for the evening. A meat curry was brought for us, together with bread, but soon just about every swinging dick in the village had heard that two English soldiers were going over the border with the Mujahideen, and we became the star attraction. As the evening wore on, a group of old-timers came over to talk to us, and more food was brought. It turned out that several of them had served in the old British Indian Army during the Second World War and one, the headman, wore a chestful of British medals to prove it. We listened to their reminiscences, in broken English, of the war against the Japanese in the jungles of Burma, and told them a few stories of our own. As we all chatted, I asked the headman if we could pay for the food. He wouldn't hear of it, we were the guests of the village.

The conviviality was continuing in full flood when a small boy shouted something from outside. The lights were put out, the door kicked shut and we were plunged into darkness. I reached for my AKM and grabbed Paddy's hand by mistake, his response:

'Not now, darling, I think we're about to be busy.'

We were probably only ten kilometres from Ali Mangel's Post on the border, but I was sure we were still inside Pakistan, and I couldn't imagine the Russians would cross this far over. In fact, it turned out to be Pakistani Frontier Police, a paramilitary force tasked with dealing with bandits and smugglers in the border areas. They were trying to clamp down on the bandits, who were being paid by the GRU to prey on Mujahideen groups crossing the border. The bandits would ambush convoys of wounded Afghans, disarm them, kill them and remove their ears, for which they were paid a bounty. Theoretically they received a bounty for the weapons as well but they got better prices in the bazaars in the Pakistani tribal lands, so they went there instead. The Police came in, waving torches about and demanding to see papers. This was a problem: we didn't have any.

I was sitting in shadow, and anyway my skin was fairly dark right now, but one young policeman spotted Paddy's pale face and walked over to him, flipping back the blanket he had draped over his knees and exposing the AKM he was holding, covering the group of Frontier Police. Everything went quiet. Nobody knew what to do.

I realised I needed to grab the initiative.

'Hey, leave him alone. Do any of you lot speak English?' I shouted in my best officer voice.

A voice from outside sounded out:

'Yes. And what are you doing here?'

It turned out to belong to an officer who was sitting outside in a jeep. I went out to talk to him.

'Look, sir, do you have access to a telephone?'

They didn't, all they had was an insecure PRC 10 radio.

'Sir, my colleague and I are here to monitor Russian activity on the border, and to do that we have to cross over occasionally . . .' I let him work out the significance of what I was saying for himself.

His response – in perfect English – was:

'How do I know that you aren't Russians yourselves?'

'Have you ever met an Irish Russian? Say something, Paddy.'

It turned out that the officer had been brought up in England and only came to Pakistan after he'd finished his college exams. He was now serving in the Thal Scouts – a specialist mountain reconnaissance unit – and we had an interesting chat over fruit-cake and tea which the headman brought in.

As the police left, the officer warned us again to watch out for bandits, and we settled down for a comfortable, warm night.

Next morning a man appeared with some mules for hire and we did a deal for several to carry our gear. As we were leaving, giving the traditional hugs, I was able to slip a twenty-dollar bill into the old headman's pocket. It made me feel better about all the food they'd given us from their meagre resources.

We'd been on the move for an hour or so when I did a map check and realised that we were heading east of the route over Spin-Ghar. I asked our guide what was going on.

'We can't go that way, it's snowed.'

This was a pain in the arse. The low-level route added about seventy kilometres to our journey, but it would be a serious risk to try going over the top. We didn't have proper cold-weather gear with us, and if we got caught up there, nobody was going to come and rescue us. Instead, we plodded on through torrential rain, parallelling the border, heading towards the alternative crossing point.

We spent that night in another village, just over the border in Afghanistan and still fifty kilometres short of Wazir. This was getting ridiculous and I had the distinct impression that our escorts weren't trying very hard. Our mule man was unwilling to go further into Afghanistan – or so he said – and headed back with his animals, though I noticed that they were now loaded with suspicious-looking sacks. I asked our guide whether we would be able to get some more mules.

'Yes, they'll be here in two days.'

This was taking the piss.

'Look, we either sort something out now, or we can go back to Peshawar and you can explain to Gulbuddin Hekmatyar why you aren't carrying out his orders.'

The guide smiled and said something in Pushtu to the chief escort, who laughed. I had a feeling that things were about to turn nasty. I half turned and gave Paddy a wink to alert him that something was going on, but he'd picked up the bad vibes already. I took out the letter of authority we had from Hekmatyar and passed it over. The escort's face literally turned a pasty grey-white colour and his lower jaw trembled: he evidently hadn't realised what we were about. He knew that by fucking us around he might well have signed his own death warrant. The Mujahideen didn't piss about with agreed disciplinary procedures: you fuck up, you die. I was worried now that he might decide that the only way out of the problem was to kill us and claim that the Russians had got us.

'Look, this probably isn't all your fault. We'll try to get it all sorted before it's too late and we have to turn back.'

The colour began to return to his face.

'Now we need to get to Wazir today, and it's a long march. So we need mules – or a mule anyway – to carry our equipment. Now see if you can arrange one from this village and we'll move on, OK?'

There was a discussion between our escort and some villagers. There were no mules, but eventually someone produced a donkey which we had to buy as its owner declined to come with us. We loaded the cutter and some fuel on to the donkey and prepared to set off, at which point several of our escorts downed tools: apparently their bergens were too heavy. This was getting annoying.

'Look, if you don't come now, I won't be able to pay you.'

It worked last time out and it worked this time; we were soon on the road.

We tabbed on through the day, stopping for occasional breaks and prayers for the Afghans. At the village of Pachir we were able to hire four mules and I gave the escorts the donkey to sell, which they did, much to their evident delight.

We finally arrived at Camp One at about 1.30 a.m., and I was fucked off, to put it mildly. As I got myself sorted out, I saw that our guide and the chief escort were involved in a fierce argument with the camp commander, and it was only while I was sipping the mug of tea they'd brought me that I realised what it was about. It appeared that a group of Mujahideen from Peshawar had arrived the day before, bringing me a message from Mangel at Hezb HQ. They'd come over Spin-Ghar, which was still perfectly passable, and were puzzled and worried that we hadn't made it yet. Now our escort's life was in the balance: if I didn't get him off the hook, he was going to be deeply in the shit. I told the commander that it had been my decision to go round Spin-Ghar rather than over it, that when we discovered that it had snowed, we decided not to take the risk. The tension subsided.

I didn't want to spend too long hanging around at Camp One; time was against us and we'd fucked around too much already. So when we were fed and watered – and Paddy had treated one of the Afghan cooks who'd spilled boiling water all over his sandal-clad feet – we moved on, back into the torrential rain.

We'd been on the move for a couple of hours, making our way through the thick early-morning mist, when out of nowhere a series of shots rang out, and I heard voices shouting something like:

'Rus! Rus! Rus!'

Paddy turned to me, looking a little alarmed.

'Are these fucking Russians or what?'

We couldn't see them and they, it appeared, could no longer see us, but I would have to own up to being a tad concerned. At this point our RPG man jumped up, an OG-9 round fixed to the front of his launcher. I leapt up, grabbed him by his shoulders and pulled him back down before he could fire: no point in wasting our secret weapon. The shouting had moved round to our left flank, and Paddy and I were trying to organise some kind of defence, but as we were doing so, our boys started to shout back, letting their weapons hang by their sides. My immediate reaction was that they were surrendering. Jesus! I thought. I am not going to fucking Moscow! Then I noticed some figures appearing through the mist: they were undoubtedly another group of Mujahideen.

It turned out they were Hezb, from Wardak province, on their way to Pakistan for R & R and to try to trace their families. Paddy and I got a few funny looks from them, but the atmosphere relaxed and they bumbled happily off into the mist.

Late in the evening we reached the village near where Camp Six had been. It had been more or less completely flattened; not a single building had been left standing. There were no animals, no chickens; not even any dogs. I remembered reading about how the Russians had poisoned wells on the eastern front and told the boys not to drink or touch anything as we carefully threaded our way through.

We cut through some fields and reached the crash site. There wasn't much left: it had been more or less cleaned up by the Russians. The shell of the helicopter was still there – or big chunks of it anyway – and the rotors, but anything else of interest was long gone. We cut up the rotors with the disc-cutter and loaded the bits onto the mules, then about-turned and headed back the way we had come.

We arrived back at Camp One in the early evening, absolutely knackered and starving hungry. Food was brought for us, and while we were eating my eye was caught by what looked like a bunch of shiny black grapes hanging from the roof of the hut we were in. This was odd because I hadn't seen any fruit at all growing round us. All was explained a couple of minutes later. One of the cooks needed some more meat and to get it he hit the grapes with the handle of his cleaver. The 'grapes' then flew off, before settling back on to the big joint of goat meat. They were the biggest, fattest bluebottles I'd ever seen.

We got our heads down that night in one of the sleeping caves. I dropped off quickly, but was woken by the sound of Paddy squirming around. I watched as he extracted himself from his doss-bag, tore his trousers down and hung his arse out of the cave, a great squirt of diarrhoea whooshing out of him. I was getting into my stride taking the piss out of him, when I got the thirty-second warning. In seconds I was next to him, both of us squatting and squirting.

Next morning we were woken by a good deal of disgruntled cursing from outside. Looking out we discovered we'd both crapped on somebody's cooking pot. Oops!

It was time to decide what to do next. We still had a lot of kit to collect and, although the first helicopter had been disappointing, there were bound to be others. Paddy and I were discussing options when I remembered the message from Mangel.

Shit, how could I have been so stupid? I'd completely forgotten about it and I had no idea what it was about. I went to look for the commander and found him staring disgustedly at his shit-covered cooking pot.

'Ah, sorry about that. Don't worry, we'll clean it up. Look, I forgot to get the message from you. Do you still have it?'

He went back to his hut and fetched a polythene bag containing an envelope. I opened it and inside was a single small slip of paper. It bore a short message:

ABORT. RETURN. W.

This changed everything. I couldn't think what had happened but I assumed it was serious. I went to tell Paddy.

'We've got to go, mate, a.s.a.p. I'll get the maps geared up and clear it with the commander, you get the guys ready.'

I looked around for the commander but couldn't find him, and Paddy only managed to locate one of our team. I couldn't work this out.

'Where the fuck have they all gone?' I asked Paddy.

'Beats me, mate, but I saw someone moving around up the back of the camp over there.'

This was an area of the camp I'd always steered clear of because it was where the fighters' families lived. I didn't want to get involved in any fights with the Mujahideen over their womenfolk.

'Shit, we'd better take a look . . .'

We went up there and soon found them all, sitting around getting stoned out of their brains on opium. Oh great.

My thought process was complicated at this point by the urgent need to take a crap, but when I'd finished, I went back to try to explain to our guide that we needed to leave as soon as possible. Unfortunately, I might as well have been talking to a brick wall for all the good it did; he was so far gone he just

217

nodded at me stupidly, not understanding a word I said. This was ridiculous, and I lost my rag with him.

'Right, you fucking stay here and get stoned: we're off.'

I walked over to where Paddy was cleaning himself up after another tumultuous dump, and told him:

'Get your bergen, mate. It's time to go. These cunts can follow when they've sobered up.'

The route wasn't going to be a problem but we just had to pray that we didn't bump into any Mujahideen coming the other way as we stumped off together down the track.

I suppose we'd travelled about a kilometre when we heard shouts behind us and looked back. Two Afghans were running after us, waving their arms. One of them was a member of our team; neither was armed. We stopped to let them catch up. They jogged up to us, panting:

'Please come back, we will leave in the morning. There isn't enough time today to get to the next village.'

'There is no "next village", just the mountain and the border.'

'But there's snow, you have to go around the mountain the way you came.'

I'd already made my mind up that we were going over the top. I'd never been in the Mountain Troop, who get specialist training for such things, but I was reasonably confident that I could handle conditions on Spin-Ghar in late November, even though we only had our relatively lightweight windproof smocks and I, stupidly, was wearing completely non-waterproof jungle boots. We had forty-eight hours' worth of food in our belts and bergens, which would certainly be enough for the journey. The problem was that if we ran into Mujahideen on our own, they would almost certainly mistake us for Russians and kill us before we had any chance of explaining ourselves. All in all, it was better to travel with an escort. Except these tossers had proved themselves so completely untrustworthy. I was also worried about how delayed our timetable was. William would have been expecting us back several days ago, and would, no doubt, be having kittens by now. We thought about it for a few minutes and then turned back. William would have to wait twenty-four more hours.

It snowed a little that evening at our relatively low level, and when we set off with our now straightened-out escorts, we found ourselves slipping and sliding around on the steep path up the mountain. We stopped that night at the hut we'd used the first time I came into Afghanistan and huddled inside together with the mules for warmth. Next morning we moved off into snow that was now ankle-deep, and by mid-morning was up to our knees.

I started to worry that we'd made a miscalculation when we were about three-quarters of the way to the top and the snow was waist-deep. Paddy and I were now taking it in turns to do five minutes each at the front of the group, breaking a trail through the thick, virgin snow, but it was desperately hard work. Suddenly, from behind us we heard the bleating of goats, and very soon a large flock was pushing on past us, following our trail towards the top. This was a godsend; the goats now took over from us, breaking the trail and giving us a clear, if slippery, path to follow.

We reached the top but it was too cold to stop and we continued on down the other side. We were now 'safely' in Pakistan. Thank fuck for that. We slept that night in the old caravanserai, doing a good deal for food, a bed-space and plenty to drink while a full-scale blizzard blew outside.

Next morning the snow was waist-deep at our level as well, but by the time we'd finished breakfast, enough camel and mule trains had been past to clear a virtual motorway, and we had no difficulty in making our way towards Parachinar. Until, that is, we bumped into an army patrol near Ali Mangel's Post.

There were a few tense moments. Frontier guards in this area have been waiting for a Russian invasion for about one hundred and fifty years.

'Is there an officer here?'

'I'm an officer. Who are you?'

'We're British . . .'

Things began to calm down a little and we were escorted to the border post although, to my surprise, they hadn't disarmed us yet. We were escorted in front of a captain of the Pakistan army.

'Who are you, what are you doing here and why are you carrying weapons?'

There was a big crowd of curious Pakistani soldiers hanging around.

'Perhaps, sir, we could discuss this in private?'

'No. Say what you have to say now.'

'Fine. You ring this number and you will be given instructions. I'm Tom Jones, this is Mickey McMurphy, and that's all you're getting.'

His face went bright red. I passed over a slip of paper which had our 'Get Out of Jail Free' phone number printed on it. The Captain didn't bother to look at it. 'If you won't tell me, then I have no option.' He gestured to one of his NCOs. 'Take them away and lock them in the storeroom.' Which they duly did, although, bizarrely, without disarming us.

We'd been there for a couple of minutes when they came to collect the only Afghan they'd actually arrested with us. As far as I was concerned, he wasn't going anywhere.

'Fuck off. Go and tell your fat captain that unless he calls that telephone number you and he will spend the rest of your careers cleaning lavatories.'

A few minutes later, the captain appeared and shouted at the Afghan through the door. We'd really got up his nose and I had a nasty sinking feeling about the outcome of all this, but now wasn't the time to back down.

'Hey, fatboy! Either you use the telephone and call that number, or you can fuck yourself. Either way, our friend stays with us, got that?'

A few minutes later they were back in force. A Pakistani corporal kicked the door open and they shouted for the Afghan to come out. They saw I was covering them with my AKM. Panic broke out. The captain stared at me.

'What are you doing?' He sounded almost puzzled.

'GO AND RING THAT FUCKING TELEPHONE NUMBER!'

The captain backed away. Paddy chipped in:

'Honestly, sir, you'll have big problems with Islamabad if you don't.'

About ten minutes later a young lieutenant appeared, wearing a camouflaged smock. He showed us that his hands were empty.

'The captain has called the telephone number. Everything is OK, you can come out.'

We emerged from the room. The captain was standing there waiting for us. I went up and held out my hand to shake. He took it firmly.

'I'm sorry but we were told nothing . . . I had no idea you were here.'

He was very, very pissed off; he'd lost a lot of face. Tough shit, really. If he'd made the phone call in the first place, none of this would have happened.

The young Pakistani lieutenant gave me, Paddy and the Afghan a lift into Parachinar in an old jeep. As we drove along, he asked:

'Would you really have fought them back there?'

'Yes, we would have.'

'That would have caused terrible problems, you know.'

'I can imagine . . .'

At Parachinar, we discovered that a pick-up was departing for Peshawar almost immediately and we rushed to get our gear – including the rotor blades – loaded aboard it. We set off still soaking wet, filthy and stinking from twelve days of humping around Afghanistan. We'd had no opportunity to change.

The trip back went fine until we hit a roadblock at Thal. For some reason they took it upon themselves to give us a really hard time, demanding papers, permits and all sorts of shit, even though they knew we didn't have them. Eventually they told us that because our road tax was out of date, we would have to wait until the next morning before we continued.

It so happened that the roadblock was located next to a bus parking lot, where the owner-drivers would sleep in their buses. I was so pissed off I walked across and woke up one of these characters.

'How much to Peshawar, mate?'

He looked out and saw there were just five of us.

'Fifteen US dollars each, but we can't leave until the bus is full.'

'You don't understand. How much to hire the whole bus and take us now?'

We haggled for a while before settling on a figure of three hundred and fifty dollars. We unloaded the pick-up and stashed all our gear on the bus, much to the irritation of the Pakistani soldiers at the roadblock. It occurred to me, rather late in the day, that they'd simply been holding out for a bribe. Never mind.

About half an hour down the road, we hit another roadblock shakedown. I'd had enough of this. As the NCO in charge sauntered up to the bus, I got down.

'If you don't fucking let us through right now, I'm going to call ISI and get them down here to sort you out.'

The NCO's jaw dropped. He snapped up a smart salute and waved us on. Paddy gave me a quizzical look.

'Do you actually know anyone in ISI?'

'Nope, not yet.'

We arrived in Peshawar around dawn. I paid off the remaining members of our escort and Paddy and I manhandled the rotor blades up to my room. Rather than wake William, I shoved a note under his door, then I ran myself a deep, hot bath and lay in it, thinking about what a complete waste of time the whole operation had been.

Paddy and I had breakfast with William that morning. The

222

operation had been aborted because US satellite imagery had revealed that the helicopter had been stripped down. I knew from examining the wreck that this had happened at least a month before we'd got there. There were grass and weeds growing through it in places but for some stupid reason, this intelligence hadn't been passed to William until after we'd left. William's next statement provided welcome news.

'We're going to pack up for the moment until the weather gets a bit better. We're booked on a flight back to London tomorrow but if we can check out of here by lunch-time we'll spend tonight in Islamabad.'

Something occurred to me.

'Oh William, I saw Darkie up at Parachinar. Should we send our gear up there for him to use?'

'Best you forget you saw him, Tom. He's on another job.'

Fair enough.

As usual, William got the hopper flight to Rawalpindi while Paddy and I hard-arsed it back in a taxi, with our civvy kit in our holdalls and the rotor blades wrapped in blankets. Our military gear was left in a storeroom we'd hired at the hotel. We checked in at the Holiday Inn and spent a while getting sorted out. I'd just stepped out of the shower when Paddy came to my room.

'Come on, Tom, let's go and find something to eat. I'm fucking starving!'

We got some sandwiches in the coffee shop. As I was chewing my way through them, I remembered Kathy. I found a phone and called her.

'Hi, Kathy. It's me, Tom.'

'Hi, Tom, I heard you would be in town tonight. Do you fancy dinner, or will you be out with Mary?'

Oh shit. It seemed that she played tennis with Mary once a week. Oddly enough, she didn't seem too bothered, and in the end she, Mary and Pauline turned up, together with William, when he finally appeared from Rawalpindi, and we had a pleasant evening together. At the end of it, Kathy and I decided that we would keep our relationship strictly professional from now on. I was married and she had a long-term boyfriend in addition to being married to her job.

Next morning, slightly hungover, we flew back to London, and after a short debrief it was time to go home.

ELEVEN

After my first Christmas with my family for four years, I was given instructions to move to the US Air Force base at Ramstein near Munich, where I would be staying for a few weeks. By now I knew that I was going to be with the Afghanistan operation for the time being, which gave me – and my wife, for that matter – a certain sense of security which you don't get from normal life at Hereford.

At Ramstein, the whole Afghanistan operation was housed in a special, secure compound. We were hemmed in by mesh fences topped with razor wire, by floodlights, by dogs and by armed US military policemen.

My first move, on arrival, was to get a special ID card issued at an anonymous security office and then I moved into the compound. After passing through an area packed with computer terminals – which in 1981 was unusual and space-age to say the least – I was shown into a conference room in the back end of the building. Here I met two of the original DIA briefing team, which had sent me to Afghanistan in the first place, Colonels Miley and

Fox. The purpose of this first meeting was to work out ways of moving weapons, equipment and ammunition into Afghanistan, and for the next few hours we talked through all the options available.

The great Second World War tradition of resupplying resistance movements used airdrops, the lone Dakota flying over Nazi-occupied territory while a plucky despatcher shoved small pallets of Sten guns and RDX out through the door to waiting reception parties. But even though the Americans had tried this in Vietnam, China, the Ukraine and the Balkans in the '50s and '60s, we knew now that it wasn't an option. Any flight into Afghanistan had to be launched from a friendly and discreet country – and there weren't that many of those to be found in Asia in 1980 – and it had to be invisible to radar. Driving also wasn't an option. The only roads leading into Afghanistan were now so well guarded that it would have taken a large army to get anything in. The upshot of this was that the only realistic option for moving even large quantities of material in-country was to go the way I'd gone before, on foot and by mule.

Their next big question was about training areas. Where could we take the Mujahideen to run the training programmes they would need if they were going to take on the Soviets credibly with modern weapons and tactics? My answer was straightforward: definitely not Afghanistan, certainly well away from the border, and preferably not even in Pakistan. To my surprise, Fox agreed with this and said they were looking at the United Arab Emirates or Oman. I said nothing but I'd spent enough time in Oman to know that the Omanis wouldn't be too happy about accepting a bunch of scruffy Afghan guerrillas in their country, whether sponsored by the US or not. Oman was a country keen to establish its credentials as a modern, go-ahead Gulf state and not as a haven for terrorists. However, one place which had struck me as suitable was Quetta in the south of Pakistan, as long as the Pakistanis agreed, and it had the big advantage of being fairly easy to hide any training from aerial surveillance. Fox agreed to look into it.

The other big issue was tactical, and it came from a piece of kit that I knew from my own experience the Soviets were deploying with devastating effect: the MI-24 Hind gunship helicopter. The Hind first appeared in the mid-1970s in Central Europe as part of the Group of Soviet Forces in Germany and it was a formidable beast. It was a large, fast helicopter with room in the back for a small squad of infantry, but what made it special was its heavy armour plating and the massive weapons payload which it carried on its stubby wings and mounted on the body. This gave it the ability to carry rapid-firing heavy cannons, machine guns, rockets, bombs, missiles and a wide variety of more esoteric loads, including chemical or even – potentially – biological weaponry.

With Hinds in support, Soviet ground troops and even the ragtag Afghan army could operate with relative impunity, safe in the knowledge that any opposition would be rapidly suppressed. Now, Fox told me, the Hinds were switching to search and destroy operations on Mujahideen supply routes in the mountains, aided by the snow that was falling on the high ground. The only way to cover the tracks of so many people was for fresh snow to fall but, of course, you have to rely on God – or Allah – for that, so the helicopters were having a field day.

This brought us to the next operation. Western support for the Mujahideen was still very, very covert and it was not considered politically possible, or desirable, to supply them with the latest Western hand-held anti-aircraft weaponry – the British Blowpipe or the American Stinger missile systems – but the Americans had developed a clever scheme to acquire some Soviet SA-7 Grail hand-held anti-aircraft missiles.

The fundamental problem with this was that although the Soviets had licensed production of the missiles and the launchers throughout the Warsaw Pact nations, they had retained sole rights to the gyroscope unit which had to be fitted to make the system work. Without this, the missiles were so much scrap; you certainly couldn't fire them. So although it wouldn't have been too difficult to persuade the Czechs, for example, or the Hungarians, to sell a small consignment for hard currency with no questions asked, Soviet control of gyro production meant that they would never get away with it.

But the Americans had an in. Colonel Gaddafi was supporting a rebellion in Chad which was then facing off against the French-supported government, and the Libyans were in the process of buying a consignment of SA-7s from the Bulgarian state arms manufacturer, Kintex, through a Vienna-based arms dealer. After a little persuasion, the Austrian arms-dealer agreed to add ten launchers and thirty missiles to the deal.

The original plan for the Libyan shipment was that part was to go by sea, part by air, in several different consignments, directly from Sofia to Tripoli. But we would get hold of ours by diverting one of the aircraft to Ramstein and then shipping the weapons on to Pakistan. This was pretty neat because the Libyans would wind up with all the equipment that they expected so they wouldn't complain, but our gear would be bought on the same 'End-User Certificate' as the Libyans' and, with any luck, no one would be any the wiser.

The usual Hollywood cliché for international arms deals features various sleazy characters hanging around in hotels exchanging briefcases full of dollar bills for truckloads of green-painted crates of Kalashnikovs. It rarely works out like that in real life, because you wouldn't trust anyone involved in an arms deal who came within half a mile of a briefcase full of cash, and anyway, the sums involved are too large. Instead, big arms deals work on a series of supposedly secure paper transactions.

First off comes the presentation by the buyer to the seller of the End-User Certificate (EUC). This is a piece of paper issued by the buying government which states that the particular consignment of arms is for their own use and will not be passed on to any third party. Bollocks, really; governments everywhere are supporting all kinds of armed group, but it's a formality that every buyer has to go through.

When the seller has received the EUC, checked it out and is satisfied that the deal is legitimate, a price is agreed, and payment arranged. This is done by lodging a letter of credit with the seller's bank which will release payment when the shipment is made 'free on board' (FOB); that is, passed through all formalities, loaded onto the aircraft or ship and checked against the manifest by the buyer's representative. When the buyer is happy, he gives parts seven and eight of the air waybill to the seller who goes and gets his money, the aircraft takes off and that's it.

Well, that's what we were going to do. We had a tame cargo operator – 'Ice-Cargo', a freight company based in Iceland – who had a business flying day-old chicks from the Netherlands to Teheran. They would fly their plane from Rotterdam to Sofia, with me aboard as 'air loadmaster', and then supposedly on to Tripoli. In fact, at a given time I would give the captain a codeword, the plane would develop a 'problem' over Austria and divert to Germany, giving us the chance to offload the missiles. Somewhat different to the last time I'd dipped my toe in the waters of the arms business, attempting to trace Provo weapons back to source in Northern Ireland.

While the business side of the deal was being sorted out, I began preparations for playing my part as the loadmaster. The Ice-Air plane was to be a DC-6 so I was driven to a hangar at the airbase where there was a US military version parked up, painted all over in drab grey. My instructor was a big black guy, US Air Force I guess, although he didn't wear any badges on his uniform, and over the next two or three days he coached me through the entire process of loading the aircraft, distributing the weight, lashing down the crates.

I was also given a briefing on how to check through the cargo. The international arms market, and particularly the dodgy end of it – which this definitely was – is a snakepit; and if we got ripped off, well, it wouldn't be the first time that a buyer had paid hard cash for a few boxes full of scrap metal and used tractor parts. Buyer beware! There are a whole host of people out there waiting to fuck you over, and you can't nip down to the Citizens Advice Bureau when it happens. I was reasonably familiar with the SA-7; enough at any rate to know whether I was getting the correct item or so much junk, so I hoped that side of it wouldn't present too many pitfalls.

My first task was to link up with an agent of the arms dealer who would be handling the paperwork for the deal in Sofia in order to pass on the doctored air waybill which would be accompanying the shipment. My briefing was like something from James Bond: she would be a tall woman called Magda, in her late thirties or early forties with long black hair, a black leather briefcase and a black fur coat. I was to meet her in the departures area of Vienna airport.

Next morning, I was taken to Frankfurt where I caught a shuttle flight down to Vienna. I went through customs and passport control and then out into the airport, where I bought an English newspaper and read it while having a coffee. I killed an hour or so with this, then checked in for a flight back to Frankfurt, went back through to the departures side and waited for Magda to show up.

It would be idle to deny that I had visions of the whole thing going completely tits up at this stage. I could just see myself being arrested for harassing innocent middle-aged women in fur coats throughout Vienna airport. In fact, it all went off like clockwork. From my position near the gate for the Sofia flight, I could see that there was only one possible candidate and it was, indeed, Magda. We made contact and I passed over the paperwork, and in return she gave me a large sealed brown envelope. I had no brief about this, but I didn't want to make a scene and took it. Her flight was called and off she went. Mine was called ten minutes later, and within an hour or so I was back at Frankfurt and on the road for Ramstein.

It turned out that the envelope Magda had given me was a breakdown of the entire deal, and looking through it I realised what a clever operation it was. The dealers had obviously put a great big commission on top of the whole thing, which meant that the Libyan letter of credit easily covered our little extras while the whole deal, as far as the Bulgarians were aware, was paid for from the same source. This, of course, would greatly increase their confidence that everything was going to the same destination. Meanwhile, the dealers were being paid their extra money out of secret Mujahideen funds. So everyone was happy. The Mujahideen got the missiles; Colonel Gaddafi got his weapons; the Bulgarians and the arms dealers got their money. Nobody was going to cry foul.

Next Monday morning, I flew with an escort from Frankfurt to Rotterdam in the Netherlands where I checked in at the Hilton. I was then taken back to the air cargo section of the airport and to the offices of Ice-Cargo where I was given an old flight suit, boots and a flight bag, and then taken out to see the aircraft we would be using. This was a bit of a shock. The US Air Force DC-6 I'd trained on had been in immaculate condition: clean, well-maintained and fully functional. This one was in a shit state. The floor rollers were either missing or rusted solid, it was dirty and it stank. We'd been told that it usually carried day-old chicks, but from the smell I reckoned they must have been trafficking in month-old fish.

We returned to the office where my escort, an American officer, took my passport away to get it doctored with some fake stamps to look more like the rest of the crew's, then we headed back to the hotel to meet the other members of the crew. They were a cheery bunch of Icelanders, very pleased to have a loadmaster along to supervise the cargo side of the aircraft rather than having to share the duties between themselves. My cover story was that

231

I'd been working out in Oman, loading Skyvans for engineering and oil companies, but that I wanted a change back to Europe. It wasn't very good, but it was the best we could come up with at short notice that would explain my ignorance of aircraft in general and European procedures in particular.

Having linked up with the crew, there was nothing much for me to do until we were called forward to Bulgaria to collect the cargo. I sat in my hotel room, watching the in-house movies, drinking tea and reading; bored out of my brains. From the sounds of things, the rest of the crew had developed a strategy to cope with this. I could hear the squealing and giggling of girls from their rooms. I think I had too much on my mind to want to join in. Maybe afterwards.

At breakfast on Tuesday morning, I was joined by the co-pilot, a tall guy in his late twenties.

'Hey, Tom, where were you? You missed a good party last night.'

'I was feeling a bit rough so I went to bed early.'

'Well, don't worry, we'll have some fun in Sofia at least.'

We chatted for a bit more, then I went off and got a newspaper and sat reading it in my room, out of the way.

Around midday we got the standby call and headed down to the airport, and at about 5 p.m. we were given the green light to go. We drove out to the flying fish-crate and clambered aboard, the captain started up and we began to taxi. At this point I started getting serious butterflies in my stomach. I couldn't help recalling the story of the Bulgarian dissident, Georgi Markov, who pissed the Bulgarian government off so much that they sent an agent to London to kill him. Markov was standing in a bus queue when the agent stabbed him in the leg with an umbrella which injected a poisonous capsule into him. He died a couple of days later. I couldn't help thinking: if that's what they do to their enemies in London, what are they going to do if they catch me in fucking Sofia?

We landed in Sofia in heavy snow (not a problem for an Icelandic crew) and taxied over to the special handling area, where some guys came aboard to take away our passports and paperwork. Then we sat in the plane for an hour or so, getting colder and colder, and, in my case, more and more nervous. Suddenly the radio crackled into life: apparently the heavy snow had delayed the cargo and we would not be able to load until tomorrow. My heart sank; was this an elaborate trap? I was secretly hoping that the pilot would request permission to leave, but instead he asked them to send a vehicle over to collect us all and bring us to the terminal.

Inside the building our passports were returned with a seven-day tourist visa restricting us to the area of Sofia. We got a cab into the city and checked in at a plush, new Japanese-owned hotel, the Vitoshea. I was shitting myself. I had no brief that this was going to happen and no real idea what to do if anything should go wrong. My briefing, such as it was, had been: don't worry, if anything happens sit tight, try to hold out and we will get you out of there. Inspiring at the time but short on detail, I now realised. Fuck.

Having said that, the crew didn't seem too bothered by the situation: they were looking forward to a meal and a bit of a party. We went up to our rooms to get showered and changed for dinner and soon found ourselves in the restaurant, eating some food which I couldn't taste at the time, let alone remember now. From chatting to the waiter, the captain discovered that there was a bar-casino-disco on the top floor of the hotel, and as the snow was still falling heavily enough to deter movement outside, it was decided that we would all go.

I was surprised to see how smart the casino was. I've never been much of a gambler, but it was interesting to watch serious people losing serious amounts of money. Then we hit the disco and that was an eye-opener as well: it was crowded with people, including a fair sprinkling of extremely good-looking girls. The co-pilot bought me a beer, and as we stood drinking, two gorgeous birds sashayed over and asked whether we would mind if they joined us. Well, it would have been churlish to refuse.

Call me crass, but one of the joys of the old Communist bloc was that everyone was so skint they would do pretty much anything for hard currency. As a result, the hookers were often fabulously good looking and these two were no exception. We chatted for a little before the suggestion was made: would we like them to come back to our rooms? The co-pilot didn't need a second invitation. He was off like a rat up a drainpipe, pausing only to give me a little helpful advice.

'Don't look so worried, Tom, you pay cash – Deutschmarks or dollars. It's one hundred and fifty US.'

Fair enough. I was thinking hard. Was this some kind of honey-trap? Maybe my room was rigged with cameras and microphones and I would be compromised and blackmailed; but on the other hand, shagging hookers was clearly standard procedure for flight crews on stopover, and if I didn't do it, then that might also arouse suspicion.

Well, that was my excuse, and I'm sticking with it.

We got back to my room and Anna – as she called herself – peeled off her skin-tight dress. She was a tall, athletic girl, with high cheekbones and – I soon discovered – naturally blonde hair; and if she didn't necessarily enjoy what she was doing, she was certainly enthusiastic enough to relieve the tensions of a trying day.

Even so, I didn't sleep much – even after a vigorous 'workout' – convinced, as I was, that half the Bulgarian secret police were sitting somewhere giving me marks out of ten for technical merit and artistic impression. In the morning, we went down to breakfast together after I'd given her the one hundred and fifty dollars (as good a use for operational money as I could think of), joining the rest of the crew and their girls. Anna ate a hearty breakfast, courtesy of Ice-Cargo, and ultimately, presumably, the

DIA – she needed to keep her energy levels up I imagine – and then she and her co-workers left with much giggling, waving and 'see you next time'-ing.

We spent the rest of the morning and the early afternoon sitting around the hotel waiting for news of when we could load up the aircraft and leave. While we were having lunch, the Kintex representative came to see us, apologising for the delay and assuring us that his company would cover Ice-Cargo's 'standing time' and turn-around fees in Sofia. Just after five in the afternoon, we left for the airport, sliding most of the way in a hotel minibus but getting there in good time for the loading procedure. We went aboard the freezing aircraft, and the captain began working his way through the pre-flight checks and switching on all his systems. By now, a big tractor had towed the aircraft into a special hangar where a large trailer was already waiting.

Someone outside was banging on our cargo door and I went to open it with the flight engineer. I was slightly amused to see that it was secured on the inside with a padlock and chain – very high-tech – and as soon as we got it open, a forklift began to load the cargo, crate by crate. At this stage I got out my copy of the manifest and began to open each crate to check its contents. Suddenly, the flight engineer ran up to me.

'Don't do that, we won't get paid!'

'What are you talking about?'

'If you open the crates, we won't get paid; they'll say we stole something!'

'This is the way I always do it.'

'Well, it isn't the way we do things here.'

He needed a good smack in the mouth, but I contented myself with giving him a nasty look and he retreated. But he'd only gone as far as the cockpit and soon the co-pilot was out and giving me the works.

'Listen,' I told him, 'I've been given specific instructions from the company to check every crate against the manifest.'

'Do you have that in writing?' he asked.

'Of course not.'

'Then don't do it, and that's an order!'

This was becoming a problem. The ground crew had downed tools and were listening in; everything was grinding to a halt. The pilot came out of the cockpit.

'What's going on?'

The co-pilot filled him in.

'Why do you have to do this, Tom?'

'I have specific instructions from the shipping agent: I have to check every crate.'

He gave me a dirty look, but waved the rest of the crew into the cockpit and loading resumed. In fact, everything was present and correct. I lashed the crates down and signed off the air waybill which would then release payment. The Bulgarian ground crew hooked the aircraft back up to the tractor and we were towed back out to the taxiway.

The pilot ran up the engines and we sat waiting in the swirling snow to be called forwards for take-off. Finally our turn came. We rolled up to the start of the runway, then accelerated, lifting off – I checked my watch – just before 11 p.m. hours. I can't tell you what a sense of relief I felt. So far, so good.

The flight plan was to cross Yugoslavia, then Albania, then follow the Adriatic down to the Mediterranean and cross over to Libya. Apparently the Italian authorities didn't allow over-flights of weapons and explosives from Communist countries. Or so the crew thought.

Actually, there had been a bit of an 'atmosphere' in the cockpit ever since the bust-up over the loading. Call me Mr Sensitive, but I could tell I wasn't flavour of the month with this particular set of Icelanders. Now I was really going to make their evening. Standing behind the pilot, I asked for our location. The co-pilot turned and looked at me crossly.

'Just sit down and be quiet, OK? We're busy.'

I tapped the pilot on the shoulder.

'Can you tell me when we're out of Bulgarian airspace?'

'We are now.'

The crew had been given a codeword which was to be used, either by them or by ground controllers, in the event of a hijack so that everyone would know it was for real. I gave it now: the crewmen looked at me in utter disbelief. The captain said:

'What did you say?'

I gave it again.

'Now listen, you have developed an engine problem. Head for Frankfurt, West Germany.'

There was panic.

'But they told me in Sofia that if we had any problems I was to turn back or land in Belgrade . . .'

'Forget it. Head straight out into international airspace, then set course for Frankfurt. You will be contacted when you get into German airspace.'

He was completely gobsmacked but did as he was told. We were called up by Sofia control, asking why we had changed our heading and where we were going.

'Don't answer, maintain your heading,' I told the pilot.

Crossing Italy, we were called up by a US airbase. We gave them our call sign and our new heading, and that was it. When we reached Germany, we requested permission to land at Frankfurt, but were told to make for Munich. Suddenly, Ramstein control broke in and took over directing us. We landed and were towed over to the hangars. The crew simply sat there; I think they were in shock. The pilot cut off the engines and I left my seat to open up the cargo bay. With the door opened, a team of uniformed military police got aboard, followed by a group of cargo-handlers. I confirmed that the cargo was as per the manifest and it was quickly unloaded.

In the meantime, the crew had been given coffee and sandwiches but told to remain in the aircraft. When we'd got everything off, I went in to see them. They still looked shattered, so I just gave them a cheery 'see you round then, lads' and got off. That was the last time I saw them; shortly afterwards they took off clutching a big wad of hush money.

Back at the secure compound, I was debriefed by John Miley and his sidekick, Captain Johannsen. They told me I'd just taken part in Operation MANTA, which was nice to know. Even better was a breakfast of coffee and sticky buns which one of their people brought in. When we'd finished eating, we wandered over to the hangar and watched some US army personnel de-crating the missiles. As we watched, John told me that I was to return to Pakistan the next week and was to receive a full briefing in the afternoon. For now I had the chance to get my head down, or at least to try to against the huge noise caused by huge Starlifters and Galaxies taking off all around me.

....

The afternoon after the first – and I suspect only – hijacking ever committed by an ex-member of the SAS, we convened the planning meeting for the next phase of Operation FARADAY in a conference room within the secure compound at Ramstein airbase. The other participants were all Americans, and military too, judging by their haircuts. Not that it's a particularly good guide; it was mid-January 1981 and my hair hadn't been cut since October the previous year.

The aim of the meeting was to discuss plans for training the Mujahideen. The key finding of my three infiltrations into Afghanistan had been the need to modernise the Mujahideen's methods of war-fighting. In many ways, the culture and traditions of the Afghans made them ideal soldiers: they were fiercely loyal to their tribe and religion; they were accustomed to making their way on foot over some of the most difficult terrain on earth; and they lived lives steeped in violence, vendetta and blood feud. But the remoteness and backwardness of their country – which had been an advantage in the days of the 'Great Game' stand-off between the British and Russian empires – was now a disadvantage in the confrontation between the West and the Soviets. The Afghans' traditional guerrilla techniques, which saw them operating from secure and unassailable bases in the mountains, preying on supply routes and lonely outposts, had been superseded by modern technology and, in particular, air power and helicopters.

Where it might have taken the nineteenth-century British army five days to get reinforcing troops to a mountain outpost under attack, the Soviets could be there with a flight of Hinds in twenty minutes. Air power gave the Soviets an advantage that the Afghans weren't going to be able to overcome without embracing modern techniques and weapons. They could no longer scamper through the mountains safe in the knowledge that they had height advantage over their enemies; now, whenever they moved out of cover they were targets.

The DIA scheme, such as it was, was less than impressive. US Special Forces worked out their techniques in the early days of the cold war. They foresaw a situation in which they would be training, for example, Polish, Czech, Ukrainian and Belorussian guerrillas behind the lines in Eastern Europe, much as SOE and the OSS had trained resistance movements in the Second World War. The US army is nothing if not conservative. That's how the Green Berets saw themselves working, and that was damned well what the Defense Intelligence Agency wanted them to do in Afghanistan.

What the Americans wanted was a classic 'behind-the-lines' training set-up – which fitted their tactical doctrine – but they wanted me to implement it. Their scheme saw a short period of very basic training in Pakistan, followed by a kind of 'on the job' training inside Afghanistan which would also see the introduction of the SA-7s. This was all outlined to me by John Miley.

'I'm sorry, John, it will never work. It doesn't have a chance. The Soviets are sharpening up their act while these guys are still operating at the most basic level. If you want them to operate on anything like an equal basis, you will have to give each Afghan twelve to fourteen weeks of training at least before they go back over the border. And to try to train them inside Afghanistan is madness. I told you what happened at Camp Six. In my view, it's only a matter of time before all the current Mujahideen bases are hit in precisely the same way.'

It was clear John really didn't want to hear what I had to say.

'I think it's likely that you will have a maximum of six weeks with each group of trainees. But don't forget, these guys are born warriors: most of them learned how to mount an ambush before they lost their baby-teeth.'

'John, they don't know how to fight against helicopters and tanks.'

'Shit, Tom, we've got them the SA-7s now. That will really even things up . . .'

'Yeah, once we've taught the Afghans how to use them, which will take weeks; and once we've found if they'll work against Soviet helicopters . . . The problem here, mate, is that if you pay peanuts, you get monkeys!'

It was getting late by now, and we all went out to a small German restaurant for a big German dinner, accompanied by a few beers.

Next morning saw us back in the conference room, the situation still unresolved. During the previous evening, it seemed, the latest set of satellite imagery of our proposed area of operations had arrived and we now all had a look at this. I think John wanted to use them to decide which of the camps would be best suited for the training operation, but to me they showed why we should abandon the idea of working inside Afghanistan completely. In the winter snow, the mountain tracks used by the Mujahideen showed up clearly, and each of the surviving camps that I had visited showed up as a hub on this network. It was inconceivable that the Soviets hadn't also spotted this and marked each one down for combined ground and air attack when the weather got better.

Now there was a period of waiting. We needed clearance from Washington for the operation to go ahead at all, and when it came I would be going out to Pakistan to get it all started. In the meantime, I passed some hours in one of the gyms on the base, pushing a few weights either on my own or in the company of a small group of huge, black bodybuilders who could pick up the most enormous loads with ease. The rest of the time I was reading intelligence summaries and updates, and digests of press reporting from the area. I was sorting out some of my gear one afternoon when John came to tell me that we would be flying to London in the evening, and on to Pakistan shortly afterwards where I was to await instructions.

After a tedious journey, we arrived in London on a cold, drizzling evening and checked in at the small hotel we used in Victoria. Next morning, John and I strolled up to Stag Place together and, after we received our security passes, made our way upstairs to the eleventh floor.

Once there, I received another round of briefings. The reason for this was that I was now to be running my own operation. William was too busy supervising the arming of the Mujahideen to be too involved with what I was doing and – in any case – he wasn't really qualified either. Therefore, it seemed, I was now to be trusted to look after myself, communicate with London and handle my own funds. Well, it's always nice to know you're trusted by the bosses.

My first briefing was on communications. I was issued with a telex codebook which should, in theory, allow me to communicate with the London office as if I was a simple aircraft ground-crew supervisor. Then came the brief on funding: how to access a special account with the Habib bank and a nice new corporate Diners Club card for incidental expenses, air tickets and so on. Finally, security: try not go near our Islamabad office, because everybody is watching it, from the press to the KGB, and try to steer clear of the Holiday Inn as well. This was a clear hint about Kathy and it set me off thinking: although we'd agreed to keep our relationship on a strictly professional basis, I knew she'd been asking about me through one of the girls in the London office who knew her. Hmm!

The next morning I took the Diners Club card down to the Army and Navy Stores on Victoria Street to give it a workout, buying socks, gloves and various other bits and pieces that I needed for the Afghan winter. Much to my irritation, the assistant immediately rang to check if it was stolen – the wanker – presumably because he imagined I looked too scruffy to actually have my own credit card. Nevertheless, it worked and I was able to stroll into the office at 10.45 laden down with various bags of goodies.

Unfortunately, it turned out that the London office had scheduled a planning meeting for that morning without having told me, so I walked into a scene of panic and fluster. What they wanted was to discuss the various options that I'd looked at with John Miley and his friends in Ramstein, and they'd been desperately trying to find me to do so since 9.30. Oh well; I put my shopping in a corner and we got on with it.

The big problem that seemed to be vexing them was Soviet surveillance of any training set-up that we organised. One bright young thing came up with a brilliant solution:

'You could put up a big tent and do the training in that, couldn't you? I don't suppose the Soviets would be too bothered by a tent out there?'

I looked at him in disbelief.

'Do you really expect me to answer that?' I asked him, leaving unvoiced the second clause – 'you fucking nerd' – which hung there in the pregnant atmosphere. He shut up after that, and didn't contribute any further to the debate.

The rest of the meeting was practical and run-of-the-mill: how could the operation be concealed from the Pakistanis?

'It can't,' I told them. 'Pakistani intelligence knows everything that happens in the border area. Every time I fart, three different informers report it, and they pick it up on the bugs in my room. You just have to accept that they know what's going on.'

The meeting puttered on for several hours, but I had to leave to catch my flight to Islamabad that evening and this eventually brought it to a halt. At Heathrow, I discovered that, once again, the flight was full, but now I was able to do what William did: whip out the corporate credit card and upgrade; and as a result, I got my first decent sleep in six months of doing the London–Islamabad marathon on a regular basis.

And a good thing too! Arriving in Islamabad I discovered that the flight to Peshawar was full and that I would have to wait until the next day. I called Kathy who came out to collect me and took me back to the house she shared with another girl who worked in Islamabad but who was back in the UK on holiday. Notwith-standing our mutual decision to keep our hands off each other, we had a long, hard, athletic night of it. In the morning, she drove me back to the airport.

'Tom, look, if you're in Peshawar this weekend, give me a call and I'll come up, OK?'

'That'd be great, but I can't promise where I'll be. I'll try to call though . . .'

My first job back in Peshawar was to organise an infiltration inside Afghanistan to recce the areas where the DIA thought we might be able to locate training camps. I sorted this out through Mangel Hussein and was actually back in Parachinar within twenty-four hours of arriving in Peshawar. But winter had brought big changes: the camp now consisted of frozen rutted mud and snow and there were far fewer people about. The young commander was temporarily absent, and had left his almost blind father in charge, and it took a further day there to get the personnel and equipment for my operation sorted out. There was no question of crossing the White Mountain at this time of year and we didn't try; instead, we followed some woodmen's trails towards the town of Sekanderkhet, staying well below the deepest snow.

The main findings of my fourth journey through Afghanistan were negative. The cold slowed us down a lot but, even so, it was apparent that the Soviets were trying to clear and enforce a border buffer zone. We called at one village, where our guide had relations, to find it completely empty, and when one of the younger escorts tried a door, an explosive booby-trap went off behind it, fatally wounding him. Other villages had been completely levelled and torched. We had an overnight stop at Camp One, which was still going strong, but it seemed to me to be only a matter of time before it was hit, and I slept that night curled up with my Kalashnikov.

In short it was evident, as I'd already told John Miley and anyone else who would listen to me, that we weren't going to be able to set up worthwhile training camps inside Afghanistan unless there was a real possibility of securing them, with a combination of guards, intelligence surveillance and, ultimately, a well-supported escape and evasion plan. The area that was being looked at wasn't suitable for quick assaults by the Russians; nevertheless it would be better for everybody not to have that particular millstone hanging round their necks.

I wasn't going to be able to write a paper on this in the basic commercial code that we were using and on my return to Peshawar, I phoned Kathy to arrange either for me to go to Islamabad or for her to come to Peshawar. In fact, she showed up the next day with another guy and we spent four or five hours working our way through the factors which seemed to me relevant to this task. The other guy was taciturn, but he seemed sure that the sticking point was going to be over whether the Pakistani military would think it politically possible to allow training camps on their soil and he was pretty sure that I would have to return to London once again to explain it all before they would make an approach to Pakistan.

It turned out he was right. I spent another week in Peshawar, working on the training plan we'd developed many months before in Victoria, incorporating my experience of the Mujahideen, before, sure enough, the call came for me to return to London. I managed to get myself on a Pan Am flight that was stopping over in Karachi and, thirty-six hours later, I was once again talking to a room full of people I'd never clapped eyes on in my life and idly wondering what on earth had happened to the need-to-know principle.

That evening I went to Soho for a Chinese meal with Fred Fox and John Miley. They were still in favour of training inside Afghanistan and I was beginning to appreciate why, even though I didn't agree with them. From their point of view, the arguments in favour were logistics and political sensitivity: provided the instructors didn't get caught by the Soviets, there was no danger that anyone was going to object to what was going on because they wouldn't know about it. One point of disagreement that I'd had with the Americans all along was that they were keen to teach the Afghans the techniques of urban terrorism – car-bombing and so on – so that they could strike at the Russians based in the major towns. Personally, I wasn't prepared to do that although, of course, I realised that eventually they would find someone who was. In any event, if the fact that the US was sponsoring terrorism and teaching the terrorists how to do it leaked out, there would be hell to pay. Much easier, therefore, to keep it all tidied away inside Afghanistan under the cover of the fog of war. In Pakistan, or one of the friendly Gulf States, it was much more likely that the press would get wind of what we were doing and thus scupper it.

But by next morning it was all change. When I arrived in the office it seemed that a deal had been done and that the Pakistanis were now prepared to allow very small groups to train in a remote area close to Parachinar and conduct live firing at a military range near Thal, provided that no explosives training took place on Pakistani soil. At last we were moving in the right direction.

I flew back out to Islamabad that evening, spending the entire flight working through a list of tasks I needed to do to get the training programme up and running. My mind was whirling and my body clock was on the verge of jacking its hand in after so many rapid changes in time zone. When I arrived in Pakistan, I was hoping that I might be delayed and have a chance to catch up on some sleep at the Holiday Inn but, would you believe it, for the first time in the entire operation, the shuttle up to Peshawar was virtually empty and I was able to get straight aboard.

I arrived back at the Intercontinental totally exhausted. I took a shower, had some food and a couple of beers and went to bed, only to be woken up a couple of hours later by someone from reception bringing me an urgent telex. After I'd blearily decoded it, it turned out to be an instruction to get in touch with a Pakistani Air Force colonel named Tariq Hamid, who was to be my point of contact for the training operation. I set my alarm clock for seven o'clock and got back under the blankets.

Next morning I drove, as ordered, to the headquarters of the Thal Frontier Scouts – an impressive and highly professional military unit – where I was to meet Tariq Hamid. Driving through the gates was like going back twenty years in time. As a country, Pakistan can look pretty dishevelled, to put it mildly, but this set-up was astonishing. Everything was neat and clean; grass lawns were immaculately manicured, woodwork was whitewashed and, best of all, the soldiers were faultlessly turned out, with gleaming brasses, blancoed belts, mirror-like boots and knife-edge creases in their trousers, mostly topped off by superb waxed moustaches. Most British army RSMs would die happy if they could get their units looking like this.

After I'd reported in at the guardroom, a soldier took me to an office with a closed door, knocked and led me in to see the colonel. Tariq Hamid turned out to be of medium height and build, with an intelligent face and a bright, open smile. As I entered, he came to attention and shot me a text-book Sandhurst salute (God knows what rank they'd told him I was!), ordered tea from the soldier who'd escorted me in and asked me to sit down. He spent a few minutes on the phone, summoning various people from around the camp, then we got down to business.

The meeting was a 'for-the-record' discussion on what we were, and were not, to be allowed to do with the Mujahideen inside Pakistan. The Pakistanis were happy about the training, including live firing, provided that they were given notice of everything that was going on and were allowed to send observers at any time, but on no account were we to do any explosives training inside Pakistan. Quite evidently, the Pakistanis didn't trust the Afghans not to sell off explosives on the black market, and, to be fair, neither did I. The tribal areas around the border with Afghanistan are the Mecca of illegal arms sales and a good deal of what the Mujahideen captured was being flogged off there in a fine example of free-marketeering. In fact, on one occasion, Paddy and I had gone rubber-necking round the arms market in the village of Darra and had watched somebody nip into a stall and buy a kilo of plastique and some detonators, which he'd then carried off all wrapped in the same bag (much like you'd buy half a pound of carrots and a cauliflower). It would only have required a small jolt to set off the detonators, and thus convert the Pakistani in question into about two million irregularly shaped pieces. What he actually wanted it for is hard to imagine.

With clearance from Tariq Hamid, I was free to get on with the organisation of the training programme. After several days work, I sent a long telex to London, outlining the entire programme: where it was to be conducted, how it would progress, how I would involve the Pakistanis, and so on. I envisaged working with thirty students at a time and I asked London to send me out

247

six more instructors. I knew I wouldn't get them, but I hoped they would send me some at least. With this despatched, I settled down to wait for their response.

Five days later – and seriously short of reading material – I was still waiting. At lunchtime on the fifth day I resolved that I would call in that evening, if only to check that they'd received the telex, but I was forestalled in mid-afternoon by a call from Kathy: I was booked on the hopper flight to Islamabad next morning and should be prepared for a two- or three-day stay. Fine by me.

Arriving in Islamabad, I was collected at the airport and taken to a safe house near to the High Commission. Here, among others, were gathered Tariq Hamid, John Miley, Loughlin and an assortment of suits from the various agencies with a finger in the pie. Once again, we were going through all the aspects of my plan. The main concern of the American contingent was to speed things up. John Miley queried the spare periods that I'd left in the syllabus: why did I need them?

'I may not, but these Mujahideen will be an unknown quantity. I will have to start with the real basics and work onwards from that. If they pick it up quickly, then fine, but they may not and we need a little bit of slack in the programme to allow us to play catch-up when necessary. You also need to remember that they are devout men: they need time to pray during the day.'

Tariq Hamid backed me up on this and John conceded the point, but his next suggestion was that he could give me some Green Beret instructors, operating under Canadian or Australian cover, as assistants. In some ways this was an attractive idea, but there were also big potential pitfalls. The UK and US armies go about things in a very different way and I could see confusion ahead. One significant difference, at that time, was in the contact drills we taught. The British army, being mean and poorly funded, has always been very conservative in its expenditure of ammunition, whereas the somewhat more lavishly equipped

248

Americans would give it, as we would say, P for plenty. This is fine when you have a solid logistic tail; not so good when, like the Mujahideen, you're stuck out in the middle of nowhere, carrying everything on your back. Still, it remained an option.

Finally, it was made clear that they were still desperately anxious to acquire Soviet equipment for evaluation and this was still a major priority. Again, this was going to be tricky unless I had some extra help.

'I can't be in two places at once. Either I'm training the Afghans or I'm collecting kit.'

A British civilian I hadn't met before spoke up.

'We'd like you to train the Mujahideen to collect equipment.'

I thought about this for a few seconds.

'It's a nice idea on paper but it won't work. For them, it's just something extra to carry, so they won't bother doing it; also, they simply aren't interested. This is their jihad, not some handy intelligence opportunity.'

A whispered conversation was taking place at the other end of the table, then Mr Anonymous spoke up again.

'We can't, of course, order or authorise you to go into Afghanistan again. Your task here is to ensure that our operations achieve the desired results, but you're in command on the ground, and how you see fit to achieve your aim is up to you.

'If you do go over the border, and are captured, then no one will be able to help you. Remember, you have left the army. If you end up in Moscow, then you won't be able to hold out for long. We'll look after your family but that's it.

'Think about it. You've done well out here so far but if you decide that you've had enough, you can go home and it will not adversely affect your career. Think about it and we'll talk again in the morning.'

The meeting broke up and I headed for the Holiday Inn. In the cab on the way, I took stock of the situation: I enjoyed the work, no question, but I was vulnerable on my own. On normal team tasks, you have other members of your troop with you and, if the worst comes to the worst, you're there to fight and die together as a team. If they could get me some decent instructors to work with, then I'd stick with it; if not, I'd give it a rethink.

I took a long shower and wandered down to the restaurant to get some food. I was picking at a salad when Kathy came in, looking for me. She started off giving me an ear-bending for not calling her, but she wasn't being serious. As she sat down to join me, Tariq Hamid also came in, and I waved him over and invited him to join us.

I got on well with Colonel Hamid, we were on the same wavelength, and I wasn't entirely surprised when he put a little proposition to me. As we chatted away, he started to explain to me how, as the intelligence chief for the border area, he was in a position to ensure that everything went very smoothly for me. But the catch was that the Pakistanis were also keen to get their hands on any new Soviet equipment.

This was too good an offer to turn down but it had to be done on my terms. We needed to have priority: if we got two examples of a particular bit of kit, then we'd take one and I'd give the Pakistanis the other; but if there was only one, we'd have it, and they could have the next one. In return, I wanted a twenty-four-hour 'get out of jail free' phone number, and a pass to get me through any roadblocks and checkpoints. Colonel Hamid agreed to this and left; Kathy and I went up to my room to bed. We were undressing when she said to me:

'You know, Tom, if they find out about your arrangement with the colonel, they'll have your guts for garters.'

'I don't see why. I'm not doing it for money, I'm doing it so that their operation works.'

We left it at that and went to bed.

I was woken the next morning by the telephone. When I answered it turned out to be John Miley asking if I wanted to join him for breakfast – or should he come up to my room? I looked across the bed at the naked figure of Kathy, just stirring beneath the sheets, and told him:

'Give me ten minutes to grab a shower and I'll come and join you.'

Unusually, the restaurant was quite crowded – a couple of sets of aircrew were checking out – so we confined ourselves to small talk as we drank some coffee and then went up to my room, me hoping that Kathy had had time to get out of the way. She had, but there was an unmistakable smell of sex and perfume in the air, much to John's amusement, and it was only after a few wisecracks that we were able to get down to business.

His new concern was student numbers. I'd stipulated an instructor–student ratio of 1:5 which could be stretched to 1:7 at most. This wasn't good enough: John wanted 1:10 in groups of fifty. I knew he was anxious to get sufficient bangs for the DIA's bucks, but he was experienced enough to know that this wasn't going to achieve quality results. By and large, these guys' military knowledge and weapons-handling skills were next to zero – accidental discharges were a dime a dozen – and the thought of trying safely to control a mob of fifty Mujahideen on a live-firing range was terrifying. Half of us would be dead before we got over the border!

'Look, Tom, at the end of the day, we don't want them too well trained; do you see what I mean?'

I did, but he wasn't going to have to rely on them in the field. If I was going over the border looking for Soviet equipment, I wanted to be able to trust my team. As we wrapped the conversation up, I asked him about the SA-7s.

'They're on their way. We've got a couple of Egyptian instructors coming out to run the training. They'll join you when you've set the camp up.'

At least there was some good news.

Later that morning I was summoned back to the safe house for a further meeting, minus John Miley and Colonel Hamid. I was asked whether I'd decided if I would continue or not. I told them I would, but I wanted to get everything straightened out so that there was no misunderstanding. What I didn't understand was their reluctance to give me more British instructors. It seemed to me that a good training programme now was a means to an end: if we did it properly, we would reap the benefits in subsequent operations, including equipment extractions. We argued the toss back and forth for a while, but eventually I was told: you do it our way; get on with it.

I flew back to Peshawar that afternoon and invited Mangel up to the hotel for dinner to get an update on what was happening. He arrived with a fighter who'd just come out, having taken seventeen days to get from Wardak province. Things were getting tight on the border: villages, farms and houses were being destroyed to deny shelter to the Mujahideen; the population was being moved, with young men called up for service in the puppet army; and the Russians were setting up control points on all the major routes through the region. Even worse, gunships now flew regular patrols over the area and they were also dropping little plastic butterfly mines, small enough to be quickly buried under a light dusting of snow, but large enough to take off a foot or hand if they were disturbed.

On the positive side, Mangel had given orders to the commander at Parachinar to help me set up a training camp there and everything was ready to go. I arranged with him to fix me up with transport there the next day and, after they'd left to return to Fackeyrabad, packed up my gear and sent a telex off to London giving the latest sitrep.

Next morning I was checked out and *en route* for Parachinar by 05.30. Much to my surprise, my transport was a brand new jeep driven by an Afghan and there were three more piled in the back with my kit. I made the mistake of sitting up front. A mistake because the driver was like a man possessed: he was red-lining it the whole time, overtaking on blind bends with oncoming traffic, lurching all over the road. I spent the whole first half of the journey jamming my right foot onto an imaginary brake pedal and shutting my eyes. From the feeling of knees being dug into my back through the seat, the guys in the back were doing much the same thing. About half way there I spotted a roadhouse and suggested we pull in for a cup of tea; there was an enthusiastic chorus of agreement from the back. Now was my chance: I slipped the driver twenty dollars and asked if he would mind if I drove. He didn't.

We continued at a more sedate pace, including a stop for prayers (giving thanks to God for the change of driver), until we reached the big military checkpoint. Now was the time to discover if Colonel Hamid's pass worked. I showed it to the sentry and instead of the usual shakedown, we got a big, smart salute instead. The Afghans were pleased as punch – with an English driver and salutes from the Pakistani army they felt like royalty.

The new commander at Parachinar was Syed, an Afghan I knew and liked. After the usual hugging, he showed me to the area he'd chosen for me, about two kilometres from the main camp, secluded in an area of sand dunes and scrubby trees: perfect, really.

We set up our camp the next day in a set of tents acquired from Red Cross aid supplies. I sent a pick-up into Parachinar village to buy planks, hammers and nails, and black and white paint, and went to draw weapons from the main armoury, getting a selection of brand new AKMs, RPKs and RPDs, all still in their greaseproof paper envelopes and packed with the maker's grease. Along with the rifles came a huge box of ammunition and a crate of magazines.

Unfortunately, there was no blank ammunition to be had, so we would be training dry or live, which would be fun, considering most of these guys couldn't hit a barn door at fifty paces. I decided that I would try to buy some old Lee-Enfield No.

4 .303 rifles to use as starter weapons, to try to introduce them to the marksmanship principles.

I was making a start on cleaning the grease from the Kalashnikovs with a bucket of petrol and some old rags when I saw two young Afghans walking towards me. One of them spoke excellent English and had been appointed by Syed as my student/ interpreter. He was one of the occasional Afghans one comes across with fairish hair and blue eyes – a legacy, someone told me, of the passage of Alexander the Great's army thousands of years before – and I immediately nicknamed him Ginger. The other, who spoke a little English and was just to be a student, I decided to call 'Number 1'. Numbers are much easier in this kind of training; they reduce confusion and speed up response times.

I sent the two Afghans off to collect their possessions and then set them to work soaking the Kalashnikovs in petrol to get the grease off, pulling them through and lightly oiling them. At about 14.30 they broke to wash and pray, and I decided to have a brew. I was standing there, sipping my tea and eating a chocolate biscuit, when I saw a blue pick-up truck with a taxi sign approaching. It pulled up next to my little camp and a stocky blond figure jumped out.

'Hello, wanker!'

I could hardly believe my eyes: it was Popski!

I'd known Popski since we did P Company together in Aldershot in 1969. His Christian name was Fred, but his real surname was Polish – fifteen letters and no vowels – and nobody could pronounce it except him. He was in the Para Armoured Squadron, so I'd seen him off and on around the 'Shot, and from time to time in Belfast and Derry as well. I think it would be the summer of '74 when we'd met at Hereford. He was doing selection then and, having passed, went straight out to Oman to join A Squadron on 'Storm'.

But a few weeks later, I saw him again, coming out of training wing with a face like thunder. It turned out that he'd fallen foul of an old scrote who worked there called Major Henderson and been RTU'd . In fact, he hadn't done anything wrong as far as he knew. During his vetting he had freely admitted to having relatives in Poland, but as he pointed out, he'd never been in contact with any of them and had never even visited the country. At the time, this had been accepted, but he had reckoned without Henderson.

Major Henderson had originally come into the regiment as quartermaster to sort out the logistics side, a job he'd done very well. He'd never attempted selection, but he'd been appointed a sort of honorary member and badged, and managed to weasel his way into a permanent post. When he retired from the army, he got himself a 'retired officer' job as 'Records Selection Officer' in training wing, and had set about creating an empire for himself, poking his nose into all sorts of business which shouldn't have concerned him. If he took a dislike to you, as he did with Popski, then you were out, and there was very little anyone could do to help you. Henderson came to the arbitrary conclusion that Popski was a security risk, and that was it: bye bye.

So Popski had followed a well-trodden path and gone to southern Africa to join the Rhodesian SAS in their fight against the Communist insurgents of Zanla and Zipra, along with Reg X, another Henderson career casualty. Now Rhodesia had folded and he'd returned to Britain, hoping to be able to rejoin the SAS via R Squadron, the 22 SAS reserve unit. He'd gone to see 'Paddy the Ditch', the R Squadron PSI, who'd listened to his story and sent him to see the Commanding Officer.

The Commending Officer read Popski's C Squadron release file and then sent for his training wing selection file. It was now he discovered how badly Henderson – who by this time had been put out to grass after being caught having an affair with someone twenty-five years his junior – had fucked him over: the file was marked up 'security risk' in big red letters, and an official annotation had gone on his records. The Colonel was apologetic.

255

'I'm sorry, Fred, there's really nothing I can do; you won't be able to rejoin the regiment while this is still against you, but if you want to do something on the same lines, I may be able to help.'

Ten minutes later, Popski was in the duty vehicle getting a lift down to the station, a rail warrant in his pocket and an address in Victoria written in his notebook; three days after that, he was on his way out to Pakistan.

We kicked off the first training course three days later with ten students between the two of us. I'd realised that I'd forgotten to get hold of any .303s, and being unable to find Syed, I'd driven into Parachinar to buy some in the bazaar. I'd negotiated a deal on ten of them at fifty dollars each when the shop I was in suddenly emptied out. Looking behind, I saw a group of smartly dressed men in civilian clothes. Their leader smiled at me.

'Excuse me, sir, are you British?'

'Yes.'

'Perhaps you might like to explain what you're doing and why you want to buy these weapons?'

There was no point in making a scene in the shop. I went with them back to their car and they drove me back to the police post in the town. I gave them the 'get out of jail free' number and they called it. After much discussion, the handset was passed to me.

'Colonel Hamid would like a word with you, sir.'

I put the phone to my ear. Colonel Hamid was as genial as ever.

'Tom, I'm so sorry you've had a problem, but if you needed rifles, you should have asked me: we have plenty.'

I thanked him and he gave me instructions where to meet him so I could collect the rifles. After he'd done so, he signed off:

'Well, Tom, I look forward to seeing you later. By the way, I hope your friend – er – has settled in well.'

I quietly laughed that the Colonel hadn't tried to pronounce his name either, but the point was taken; we weren't doing anything he didn't know about.

The secret police courteously drove me back to my jeep and I returned to the camp. I sat eating lunch with Popski, egg and tomato sandwiches in naan bread if I recall rightly, describing my little adventure to him.

'Right, I'm coming with you: I'm not missing this.'

We met the Colonel at an old fort near Shublan. Once again, it was a picture of military precision, featuring a well-kept parade square edged with whitewashed pebbles, evidently some RSM's pride and joy. Popski was staggered.

'Fuck me, I wouldn't have missed this for the world!' He looked a picture with his blond hair, huge bushy Elvis sideburns, squinty eyes, long nose and monster moustache. We were shown into an office where Colonel Hamid was waiting with a teapot, cups and slices of fruitcake.

When we'd taken tea, the Colonel showed us to the armoury where we were able to select ten old but immaculately maintained .303 rifles.

'Is there anything else you need? You only have to ask.'

We had a look round but there was nothing we could use.

'Now then, follow me and we'll fetch you some ammunition.'

The ammunition store was by the guardroom. We got there and the storeman showed us in and allowed us to collect what we needed: boxes of .303 ball, tracer and blank. Suddenly, Popski spotted something.

'Well, well, well! Kalashnikov BFAs.'

A BFA, or blank firing attachment, is a little device which screws onto the end of a rifle barrel and allows you to fire blank ammunition without having to re-cock your weapon after each round. We had a further look around and came up with a couple of cartons of Kalashnikov 7.62 x 39 blank.

'Could we take some of this, Colonel?' I asked.

The Colonel had a quick conversation with the storeman.

'You can take it all, Tom. They never use it.'

So we did.

After we'd loaded our jeep, the Colonel came to say goodbye.

'Now, please remember, the weapons must not go over the border. Lose everything else, but we do need to have the rifles back, if you don't mind. And please also remember our agreement, Tom.'

I assured him I did.

'Well, good luck and drive safely.'

We ran the first course through in about ten weeks, taking them from the basics of living in the field, tactical movement and so on, through application of fire with small arms, support weapons and anti-tank weapons, right up to the use of the SA-7 anti-aircraft missile, taught by the two Egyptians who John had promised would turn up. From the first course, we selected three Mujahideen, including Ginger, to act as our assistant instructors on the second course, and then we were in business. By now, London was beginning to get twitchy about our lack of progress in extracting Soviet kit and I decided, when the first course had dispersed, to do a recce of the route over the White Mountain.

Leaving Popski to get going with two assistants and the second group of students, Ginger and I, with a couple of escorts, made our way to the top of Spin-Ghar. We slept one night in the caravanserai at the bottom and the next morning followed the trail to the border at the top. It was cold, there was a light dusting of snow, but it was clear; once more, the game was afoot.

Back in Parachinar the next day, I reported in by phone telling them, in a simple word code, that I was intending to re-commence extractions shortly. I hung around for a few hours, drinking tea in a café, until I was called back for confirmation. Everything was approved, but there was a new rule: neither Popski nor I were to cross the border. I couldn't understand this: we'd given the Afghans basic recognition training but there was no way that they would be able to spot, for example, the laser sight from a Hind. I doubt if most of them could have told the difference between a compass and a fuel gauge.

I got back to the training camp feeling pissed off. I briefed Popski on what had happened and we sat down to work out how to get round the problem. There was no easy solution, other than employing Ginger as our chief collector; we didn't know anyone else who spoke English well enough for us to train.

I spent four days with Ginger, working through the collection priorities before sending him off with a small escort and one SA-7 missile and launcher. I'd given him seven days for this first trip, and I spent six of them hanging around, biting my nails with anxiety before leaving, with a couple of guys, to wait at the top of the White Mountain for his return.

We spent four days at the top of the mountain before Ginger showed up. He was on his chin-straps and minus the SA-7, which had been taken from him by some group leader he'd encountered. The only thing he'd managed to acquire from the long list of items I'd given him were several personal NBC decontamination kits.

It wasn't his fault: when I went over, it was as a foreigner personally sponsored by Hekmatyar, whereas Ginger was nobody. The commanders in the field were little warlords who wouldn't think twice about bumping someone like Ginger off if he pissed them off. I reported all this to Islamabad but was told to carry on and that the 'don't cross over' order still stood.

When Ginger had had a couple of days to rest and recover I sent him off again, giving him fourteen days this time, but once more he returned more or less empty-handed. Somehow, Syed got to hear about this and was furious: as far as he was concerned, Ginger had failed miserably. I tried to persuade him that it wasn't really Ginger's fault, but he wasn't really prepared to believe me. He ordered Ginger to – effectively – turn round and go straight back into Afghanistan until he'd collected the items on my list.

At this stage, I did manage to intervene. The problem, I told Syed, was that to get most of the stuff on my list, Ginger needed to shoot down a helicopter. This time I would give him a launcher and three missiles, but we would need at least a day to get them ready. Syed fell for this; at least I'd bought Ginger some recovery time.

The next day we readied Ginger and his ten-man group for the off. The launcher and missiles were strapped to a mule and we headed out, this time escorted by me, Popski, Tony (our QM, cook and bottle-washer – an old Afghan whom we'd named after the landlord of the Bull Ring, a pub in Hereford) and a couple of others.

At the caravanserai, we met a family group who'd only just made it out, having been robbed at gunpoint of just about everything they owned by a group of Mujahideen – they thought – on the other side of the mountain. This was worrying. We knew that a bandit group was active in the area but they were clearly now on this route, and our team might not be strong enough to fight them off. I discussed it for a while with Popski and we decided that we would escort Ginger as far as Camp One. It might be breaking the rules, but I didn't think we had any choice under the circumstances.

We set off, as usual, early in the morning and by late afternoon, we were getting close to the little hut at the foot of the mountain on the Afghan side where I'd stopped to sleep on previous occasions. About a kilometre from it, we could see signs that it was already occupied – there was a wood fire burning at its entrance – and as we got closer, having left one of the Afghans with the mules, we began to spot movement.

As far as I could make out, through the shadows and twilight, a group of about six men seemed to be escorting a larger group of men, women and children. They halted by the sleeping hut and then four of the 'escorts' pulled someone away from the large group. Creeping closer, we could hear the screams of a young girl and from about fifty metres, we were able to watch as three of the men started pulling at her clothes, revealing the skinny body of a girl in her early teens. While this was going on, two of the men were guarding the large group, while a third simply stood there laughing.

We had a quick whispered discussion and it was decided that I would nail the guys by the hut while Popski took Ginger and Tony to get the three men with the girl, and laughing-boy. By now, the girl was naked and being held down on the deck while the first of the men was unhooking his pants in preparation for raping her. Popski was just moving around to clear his sight-lines when we heard a frightened shout behind us. Kneeling up in the scrub about twenty yards away was a seventh bandit.

Popski dropped to one knee and fired a four- or five-round burst that hit the seventh man full on in the torso, lifting him up into the air and throwing him several feet backwards. I took aim on the two guards and dropped them one after the other with two rounds – not bad shooting though I say so myself – and then Ginger, Tony and Popski nailed the other four between them.

We closed up to the hut where the girl was still screaming but was now being comforted by members of her family. The bandits had been lambs to the slaughter: the two I'd shot were carrying their weapons over their shoulders, the other four had put them in a pile while they'd had their fun. The guy Popski had whacked seemed to have been praying: we found his prayer mat unrolled where we'd shot him, and now fouled with slowly congealing blood. Typical religious hypocrite: stop for a quick pray while your mates gang-rape some poor kid.

We carried out a quick search of the bodies. They had various types of banknote, some jewellery and bits and pieces of that sort, and Tony claimed he recognised them as border tribesmen – Afghan or Pakistani was pretty much immaterial. We gave the money and gold to the family who'd been attacked – they were now planning to get over the mountain as soon as possible – and then saddled up for the onward journey to Camp One. We wanted to clear this area as soon as possible; it was likely that the seven clowns we'd knocked off were a small part of a much larger bandit group.

We moved about ten kilometres away from the hut before we basha'd up for the night in a secluded spot near the trail. Leaving just after first light, we arrived in Camp One shortly before afternoon prayers. The commander was yet another new guy, and it was noticeable how many more fighters were present than before, and how alert the guards were – definitely a good sign. Popski and I sat with him that evening and he told us about the Afghan army, from which he'd deserted.

It seemed that the main cause for discontent was very simple. The Russians, being Communists, simply couldn't bring themselves to allow the Afghans time off to pray during the day and the result was massive – and entirely avoidable – discontent in the Afghan army. Ridiculously simple but a major factor in the eventual collapse of the Soviet empire.

As we chatted, the commander mentioned that they'd captured a broken Russian weapon which he'd never seen before. He sent two guys to get it and they reappeared with an AGS-17 automatic grenade launcher – one of the highest priority bits of kit on our list. The belt-feed mechanism was pretty mangled, probably from some Afghan attempting to load it the wrong way, but it was otherwise completely intact. What a result! I arranged to hire a mule to take it back with us next day and slipped the commander a hundred dollars as a thank you: we were back in business!

As usual, the trip back took three days and on this occasion was largely uneventful. I called in when we were back at Parachinar and reported what had happened, then called Tariq Hamid. He was with us very quickly, anxious to see what we'd got. Although our agreement was that we would give him the second example of any item we collected, I thought it would be diplomatic to give his guys a chance to have a look over the AGS-17, as a sign of good faith at least. We agreed that he would take possession of it for forty-eight hours and would then return it to me so that I could get it down to Islamabad.

Two days later, armed with a strangely spruce looking grenade launcher, I was back at the Islamabad safe house for yet another meeting. I was sitting at the table next to John Miley, who began to reassure me that more help would be arriving soon, when we were called to order by Loughlin who had turned up with his boss. The first part of the meeting covered aspects of the operation which I wasn't involved in, and I was drifting along with my mind in neutral when I suddenly realised questions were being addressed to me.

'Tom, what's happening with the SAM-7s? Are we getting results?'

'Not so far: on the first operation, the missile and launcher were confiscated from my operator by one of the field commanders. I've got an operation on the go at the moment, but it's too early to know what's happened . . .'

'What do you mean "The missile was confiscated"? Why didn't you stop that?'

'I can't fucking stop it when I'm sitting in Pakistan, can I?'

I looked at a row of ashen faces; I started to get a sinking feeling in my guts.

'Why didn't you go over with them?'

'Because I've had two verbal orders and one written order not to cross the border.'

I was thinking to myself: I can't have fucking misread the orders, can I? John Miley stood up and took me to one side as the meeting descended into chaos.

'Tom, there was no order not to cross.'

'There fucking was! On three separate occasions . . .'

I began to realise what had happened: the various desk officers involved had been covering their arses in case anything had gone wrong by issuing orders that they didn't expect me to obey. I suppose I'd been a bit of a twat, but it was their fault as much as mine. In reality, they didn't care what I fucking did, provided we achieved the aim; if I was going to cross the border, then fine, just don't tell them in advance.

I left the meeting and went to the Holiday Inn. I was fucked if I was going back to Parachinar today. I called Kathy and she came over to join me. We drank, ate and slept together, and that calmed me down.

I returned to Parachinar the next day and debriefed Popski over several Pakistani beers. He was sympathetic.

'Typical fucking Ruperts! They live in a world of their own.'

Five days later, I was preparing to go back to the mountain to meet Ginger when we heard voices: he was back, and once more absolutely shattered. We got him some food and tea, and he told us about their close encounter with a flight of Hinds. They'd fired their first missile, which had missed, and loaded up and fired a second, which had also gone astray; then the Hinds were on them. The mule carrying the third missile had been hit and collapsed on top of it, crushing the fragile weapon and rendering it useless. Ginger and his team had rightly decided to let discretion be the better part of valour and had legged it, being lucky to get away with their lives.

'So, what happened to the missile?' I asked.

'It's still under the mule, I suppose.'

I could have kicked myself: I'd never told them to recover all spent missile parts. Checking on the map, Ginger indicated that the action had taken place near Gandamack, and after a quick discussion with Fred, I decided that we would have to go back the next day to see if the missile was still there. Somehow, I doubted it.

We got a jeep at dawn to drive us to the foot of the mountain, which knocked a day off our journey, and made good time going over the top. We were all travelling in light order: I just had my belt kit; so we slept out in the open that evening in a big huddle to keep warm. Arriving at Camp One the next day, it was virtually empty: just a few guards and an old man.

'Everyone has gone to fight', he told us, 'it is jihad.'

We pushed on the next morning towards Gandamack. We

could hear shooting and the thump of helicopter rotors, but nothing too close, so we continued moving carefully forwards. Early in the evening, Ginger began to recognise features and, around nine o'clock, we came to an area that stank of rotting meat. In the dim, shaded light of my torch, we could see the remains of the mule, now torn apart by wild animals, but no sign of the missile or the two spent tubes. There was no obvious sign of wheelmarks or combat boots, but it was too dark to be sure, and my guess was that the Russians had come in and picked them up. There was nothing for it now but to retrace our steps and head back to Parachinar.

The journey back was a tedious, exhausting slog. I arrived back at the camp to find Popski teaching basic Kalashnikov stoppage drills to a group of new students. At lunchtime he came over to join me in our tent, and I related what had happened. Pospki had some news for me too.

'We've got some guests.'

'Oh yeah? Who?'

'Don't really know. They're sightseeing in Parachinar now, but one of them is definitely a Rupert, and a crap-hat, too, I wouldn't be surprised to find.'

'What do they want?'

'Wouldn't tell me. As they're hats, I assumed they must be your mates.'

'Well, we know they're not yours: you haven't got any mates . . .'

At about 17.00 the two men in question appeared in a shiny new Land Cruiser. The Rupert got out and walked towards me.

'Ah, you must be Carew. I'm West and this is Mr Field, and we're here to conduct trials of Blowpipe.'

'Oh yes? How can we help you?'

'We'd like you to test it out for us. We'll show you how it works, then you can go and give it a try.'

'What do you mean "give it a try"?'

'Well, try to shoot down a Hind. From our calculations, it shouldn't have any problems . . .'

I briefly considered losing my rag, but decided against it.

'Look, you know how to use it. It'll be much easier if you nip over the border and have a go.'

'I'm afraid that simply isn't possible, so I was told to tell you to do it.'

'Listen, matey, I'm afraid my diary's full just now. I've got a camp full of Mujahideen to train, and a long list of stuff that London wants brought out of Afghanistan. You'd do better to come back next year.'

He handed me an envelope. I opened it. Written orders from Loughlin: I was to 'assist them as requested'. Fuck!

Next morning I woke our two guests at 06.00 hours.

'If you're going to teach me how to operate this thing, we'd better start now.'

Except, of course, it took them half an hour to get their hot-water shave, their wash, and dressed up in their pressed uniforms with polished boots. Tony couldn't believe his eyes. Both Popski and I were sporting pretty reasonable beards by now, my hair was well down over my collar, and I don't think my OGs or windproof had ever been ironed; as far as we were concerned, they were from a different world. When we'd eaten tea and naan we set up a little area where the two new boys could instruct me.

The crucial difference between the Blowpipe and most other hand-held anti-aircraft missiles is that it's user-guided. The launcher unit has an optical sight zeroed with a radio beam and the missile rides along it, with fine tuning from a thumb joystick. When the missile is close enough to its target, a proximity fuse sets off the charge which will hopefully bring whatever you've fired at crashing to the deck. Well, that's the theory anyway. The advantages of this system are that it gives you much wider scope to engage oncoming and side-on targets, but the disadvantages are many. In the first instance, learning how to steer the missiles is a tricky process which requires weeks of work with a simulator; then there's the very real disadvantage of having to stand out of cover while you guide the missile home. If you miss, your target is going to know exactly where you are and they're going to be pretty pissed off with you. It's also bloody large and heavy: nearly twice the weight of the SA-7 in all, and damned awkward to move around if all you've got are mules. Its range and power probably made it a superior weapon to the SA-7 overall, but I knew which one the Mujahideen were going to prefer.

By mid-afternoon they'd given me about as much training as I could handle and they began to load up their Land Cruiser for the trip back to Islamabad. Something occurred to me.

'By the way, who's paying for this operation?'

'What do you mean "paying"?'

'Expenses: guides, mules, escorts, food *en route*, that sort of thing. It's all got to be paid for and you won't get much change from fifteen hundred dollars.'

This had got them.

'I'm sorry, I didn't realise. We'll leave the missiles with you and get back to you.'

At this point, the technical guy spoke up. He'd been pretty quiet up to now.

'For Christ's sake, though, don't lose those missiles whatever you do! They're sterile: no markings, but don't let them go to Moscow, OK?'

They disappeared off down the track in their truck.

I hopped into our borrowed jeep and drove over to see Syed in the main camp.

'Syed, I have to go back over in two days' time. Can you find me a team of escorts?'

'Sure, Tom, no problems.'

Half an hour later, he came back with ten gaunt-faced, hollow-eyed guerrillas. By the look of them, they'd only just come out, but they looked like my kind of soldiers: doers, not poseurs. I invited Syed and the new team to come over to dinner with us that evening for a 'get to know you' session.

Next morning I went into Parachinar to deal with our admin. We had an account at the Habib bank there and I needed to check whether we'd received any deposits recently. It turned out that two thousand dollars had been transferred from London the day before, but there was no sign of anything from West. I drew seven hundred and fifty dollars to top up the operational fund, leaving about three thousand in the account. I returned to the camp and set about preparing my operational kit.

I'd just finished cleaning my rifle when a jeep pulled up, sending a fine cloud of dust over everything. The driver got out and handed me a brown envelope. I opened it and the first thing that I found was a copy of a bank deposit receipt for fifteen hundred dollars, dated the day before. Fine, the Blowpipe mission was paid for. The second thing was yet another fucking stupid order from some arse-covering twat at headquarters: apparently it was too sensitive for me to actually fire the missile; I must get an Afghan to do it and observe the results. What complete bollocks. I burnt it and crushed the ashes into the dirt.

I slept that night like a condemned man awaiting the hangman. My sleep was so disturbed I had to get up twice to make myself brews. In the end I did get a couple of hours' fitful kip but I didn't feel rested. In the morning, I left Popski scoffing breakfast like a horse and went over to the main camp to get a pick-up for the Blowpipes. We loaded them up then piled aboard for the trip to Ali Mangel's Post.

We took an early lunch at a tea-stand before we reached the trail and also managed to hire some mules. Then we flogged on through the heat of the spring afternoon, making our way towards the caravanserai at the foot of the mountain. We arrived there soaked in sweat and covered in horse-fly and mossie bites – warm weather brings its own problems – and settled in for the night.

Next morning we set off bright and early – after an enormous breakfast – and began to climb the mountain in the most glorious sunshine I'd encountered. It was cool when we started, but by 10 a.m. it was scorching, and the sweat was pouring from all of us. We reached the top at midday and moved into the cool shade of a rock to rest. After we'd had a brew and the mules had shared a bucket of water, we carried on down the other side, with me making a note to take a salt tablet that evening to counter painful leg cramps I was getting.

We came to the hut where we'd had the shoot-up with the bandits in the mid-afternoon, to find that someone had started to clean it up again, but there was nobody around and we continued on for several more hours before we lay up for the night.

Next day, after the usual early start, we reached Camp One at about noon and found that it was back up to its usual complement of between thirty-five and forty inhabitants. I unloaded the Blowpipes with the help of a tall, Mongolian-looking Afghan and the mule driver and we put them in the cave where I was intending to sleep.

My plan was to spend the next day at Camp One, and then push on to a likely area where we might get the chance to use the missiles, but the camp commander had a better idea: he was sending a couple of mules to a camp in a neighbouring province and wanted us to escort them. Fair enough. We stayed the night at Camp One and the next afternoon married up with the commander's little group ready to go. The rule now was no movement beyond Camp One in daylight: there were so many gunships about now that the risk wasn't worth taking. Of course, I did actually want to run into some gunships, but I wanted to do it on my own terms.

We marched all through the night and, as day was breaking, came to the blown-up remains of an old farmhouse. To my amazement, there was a group of Mujahideen living within it, operating it as a kind of way-station for travelling members of the

Hezb. They'd camouflaged their presence by carefully draping old carpets and sheets of tin about while the mules were taken down into a kind of basement. This was actually a normal arrangement for Afghan farms: they live above their animals in the winter because the heat from them rises, but the stink does as well, and I can't see it becoming popular in Britain unless heating-fuel prices really go through the ceiling!

It was a long, scorching hot day on the plains. Sleep was virtually impossible because of the cramped conditions in the shade and the flies which were everywhere: in our mouths, our noses, our eyes and just buzzing around for the hell of it all. We heard the occasional thud of rotor blades and the distant thumps of artillery, rockets, bombs and cannon fire, but nothing came close to us. Even so, it was evident that any attempt to move in daylight would have been suicide: Russia was certainly in control of this part of Afghanistan by day. Perhaps the SA-7s or the Blowpipe might change that.

We repacked and moved out at last light and tabbed on to yet another bombed-out village to rest up another day. There was nobody in this place, apart from a few chickens, scratching forlornly around in the dirt, and the bloated decomposing corpse of a dead donkey. The smell of burnt explosives was too strong for me: I didn't like the thought that we might still be on some artilleryman's target list.

We spent another hot, dry day being eaten by insects, but this one was enlivened by the appearance of a flight of Hinds. Too far away to be worth engaging with the Blowpipe, they were close enough to cause near panic amongst the fighters. I had a Blowpipe ready for use but the helicopters stayed resolutely out of reach and eventually departed.

That night our journey was shorter. We travelled for about three hours until we reached a ravine in which a number of people, Mujahideen and civilian, were sleeping in dug-outs and caves. This was the destination of the commander of Camp One's convoy, and we helped unload the mules there, before taking a quick meal of cold goat meat and drinking tea by the bucketful. Then we about-turned and headed back to the same burnt-out village to lie up again.

I'd been asleep for several hours when I was woken by the sound of rotors. I looked out to see an MI-8 Hip – a large transport helicopter – cruising along reasonably slowly at treetop height, apparently following our trail from the night before. Like an idiot, I didn't have the Blowpipe ready – this would have been a sitting duck at about four hundred metres' range – as it slowly cruised past and disappeared out of sight. Twenty minutes later we heard heavy firing from some distance away, so it evidently found what it was looking for. The sound faded and everything went quiet again.

We moved out at dusk and made off in the direction taken by the Hip during the day. We soon found what the shooting had been about: we reached a pen containing a number of dead and dying goats and cows, evidently wiped out as part of the Russian scorched-earth policy for the border areas. They could no longer be used by the Mujahideen for milk or meat.

We spent the next day sheltering in yet another burned-out building, desperately attempting to avoid the attentions of flies and mossies, while I tried to work out what we should do next. It seemed to me possible that we would have to put out some kind of bait for the helicopters – maybe light a campfire or something – rather than hope for a random appearance when conditions were right, but certainly we needed to be in an ambush position which we could safely occupy for several days, if necessary, rather than roaming across the plains of Afghanistan at random. Fortunately, we found a place that very evening.

Much of the area we were crossing was abandoned farmland. The owners had either fled, been killed or called up by the Afghan army. But there were still many traces of its former use. As we headed out that evening in the general direction of Camp One, we came across a small stand of trees and bushes through which an irrigation stream flowed. There were the remains of some dry-stone walls which would give a certain amount of protection from fire and view, fresh grass for the mules, water and shade. In fact it was ideal in every respect but one: as isolated cover, it would be an obvious place for someone to hide. Still, I felt that the other advantages outweighed that defect and we settled ourselves in.

The first day was pretty much quiet, apart from the farting of the mules caused by their unaccustomed rich diet, and the second was similar until about 4 p.m.. Then we heard the whine of a spotter-plane engine, followed by the heavy throb of Hind rotors. As we watched, a flight of five Hind Ds appeared and began to attack a target maybe four or five kilometres from our position. As they circled, we heard the staccato hammering of their rotary cannon and the whoosh! bang! of the rockets. But they remained tantalisingly out of reach and I resigned myself to not being able to use the missile. Even so, I crept down to the edge of our cover, taking the Blowpipe with me, just to watch the tail end of the attack.

And then it all changed. Darkness was falling quickly now but I suddenly realised that the helicopters were coming closer and closer. The only problem was, I couldn't really see them: none of them were using navigation lights (which would be madness in wartime) and they were all staying close to the deck where the black sky merged with the shadowed ground.

The sound of the rotors was deafening and I had the Blowpipe on my shoulder now, desperate to locate one of the Hinds silhouetted against the sky. Then I saw one, and a second; maybe six to eight hundred metres from me. Now I had to pick them up in the optical sight as well. I strained my eye against the rubber cup, desperate now to pick up any visual clue . . . yes, I'd located one . . . I put my finger on the trigger and settled the bulky assembly comfortably on my shoulder. Suddenly WHOOSH!

Fuck, fuck, fuck! The fucking missile fucking launched itself! I still had line-of-sight on the helicopters but . . . there was a big flash, followed by a loud bang . . . had I got one? I couldn't see – I didn't think so. Suddenly the sky was alight with flares, the whole area lit up like Guy Fawkes night. There was no wreckage on the ground, I must have missed.

What the fuck had happened? As far as I was concerned, I'd barely touched the trigger. I couldn't understand how it could launch like that. Whatever, there were some pissed off and frightened Hind pilots around now, and it was time to make our excuses and leave.

The darkness which had prevented me from getting a clear shot at the helicopters was now our friend. We quickly got the gear loaded aboard the mules and moved out at a rapid rate. There was no further follow-up for about four hours, when we were maybe two clicks short of Camp One, when we heard the crack of flares igniting behind us. We watched as, in the distance, the little copse was again lit up, then heard the whistle and thump, and saw the flashes, of falling iron bombs. We hadn't heard any helicopters, so I assumed it was fixed-wing aircraft, bombing from well above us.

We made it back to Camp One, and from there to Parachinar, without any further incident. Popski laughed his balls off when I told him what had happened.

'First ever Blowpipe fired in anger and you have an ND, you fucking arsehole! Jesus, talk about sending boys to do men's work!'

I must admit, I could see the funny side as well, but it struck me as daft that they were prepared to risk sending me off with their missiles after only one day's training.

Next morning I took the used Blowpipe tube back to Islamabad. There was a meeting scheduled for that afternoon at the safe house so I would be able to give my after-action report then. I was pleasantly surprised, when I arrived at the house, to find William there – it was the first time I'd seen him in months – and we had a quick and somewhat guarded chat about how life was treating the pair of us.

The meeting kicked off at three but lasted well into the evening, going around and around the whole Blowpipe operation and what I thought had gone wrong. I was feeling tired and irritable and eventually lost my temper.

'Right, I've fucking had enough of this. I'm going to write down what happened, photocopy it and then you won't all have to ask me the same fucking bone questions!'

It wasn't normal for me, but I was feeling run down and I was pissed off that they wanted me to go straight back to Parachinar to set up another Blowpipe mission. I thought fuck 'em, called Kathy and arranged to meet her at the Holiday Inn. As we were eating, I began to feel a bit feverish, hot and cold at the same time, and thought: bollocks, I'm going down with a dose of malaria here. We went to bed, but I was feeling ghastly, and by morning I was completely drained.

The trip back to Parachinar was a nightmare. By now I had the galloping bumsquirts – it was coming out so fast I could shit through the eye of a needle – and I frequently had to get the driver to stop. I guessed I must have got food poisoning: not difficult considering some of the shit I'd eaten inside Afghanistan, and when we got to the camp, I just went straight to bed and slept.

Next morning, I felt so bollocksed I couldn't get out of bed. Popski was up early to teach a class but I just couldn't move. Instead, Tony brought me endless mugs of tea, which went straight through me, and I just lay there, wrapped in my poncho liner, feeling like death.

Popski got back to find me still in much the same position as he'd left me. He took one look at me and told me:

'Jesus, you look like the Incredible Hulk: your skin's all green and your eyes have gone yellow. You gonna split your shirt or what?'

He got out the medical kit and took my temperature.

'Sorry, old mate, you're fucking sick. It's off to bed with you.'

I alternated between bed and the bogs for the rest of the day, but I wasn't getting better and Popski decided that he had to move me to Islamabad for medical treatment. He got a pick-up and driver from Syed and I was driven to the safe house, from where I phoned Kathy. She got a doctor to me within the hour.

'Well, Mr Carew, what do you think you've got?'

'I guess food poisoning, and maybe a touch of malaria as well . . .'

'I think not. My guess is hepatitis, certainly jaundice, and probably malaria too. You need to go home and get some treatment there . . .'

Kathy made the arrangements – everybody knew about us anyway – and within three days I was back between clean sheets in an isolation ward at Hereford General Hospital.

EPILOGUE

The operation continued for a short period after I left, with Popski running the show, and was then wound down for a while. When they revived it later that year, with different personnel, the whole thing went to rat-shit. I never heard the full story, but in conversation with Loughlin some years later, he briefly related how two Brits had gone over the border on another extraction mission, only to walk into a Russian Spetsnaz ambush on the way home. Both Brits and all their Mujahideen escorts were killed and, of all things, the Russians found some kind of British ID card on one of the bodies. That, not surprisingly, brought the operation to an abrupt close.

Training inside Pakistan was then taken, more or less completely, into the hands of the CIA. Groups of Afghans were brought to Scotland for training by ex-members of the regiment. It didn't take long for the Western intelligence agencies to realise that, in the Hezb-i-Islami, they were backing the wrong horse. The rank and file fighters were fine but the leadership, it became clear, was more interested in jockeying for power and making money from drug sales than in fighting the Russians. Instead, when the covert military support effort was stepped up again in the mid-'80s, and modern US Stinger missiles were introduced into the equation for the first time, support was targeted at the group led by Ahmed Shah Massoud in the Panjshir Valley.

I spent about twelve miserable weeks in Hereford General Hospital, recovering from a wide portfolio of exotic diseases before I eventually discharged myself in protest at Salvation Army band practice, which took place close to my ward. After I'd taken some time to recover, I rejoined the army. Poor old Popski was killed on a different operation: he never managed to properly rejoin the SAS. I went back to training wing in March '83 and from November the same year was back on training duty in Sri Lanka.

It was there that it all went wrong for me. In April 1984 I was helping to conduct an advance-to-contact training exercise for the Sri Lankan army when we ran into a group of Tamil Tigers. They weren't supposed to be anywhere near, but then they hadn't read the intsums. As the exercise broke down into a full-scale firefight, I got hit in the left knee by a fragment from an 82mm mortar round.

After a period in Stoke Mandeville hospital I resumed duty, on a round that, during the late '80s and early '90s, took me to Namibia, Mozambique, Northern Ireland on several occasions, as well as the wilds of the commuter belt south-west of London where I was involved in training one of the TA SAS squadrons. At the start of the Gulf War I went out to the UAE for another training task but by then my time in the army was short: twenty-two fun-packed years were over.

Some people get a gold watch when they retire; I got a call from Loughlin. In 1991, the fragile stability of the Balkans broke down completely as Croatia and Bosnia-Herzegovina sought to secede from the Yugoslav federation, with the encouragement of various

Western governments. A vicious fratricidal war erupted between Croatia and Serbia, which had retained control of the federal Yugoslav National Army (the JNA). Was I prepared, Loughlin wanted to know, to go to Croatia and make an assessment of what equipment and training they would need in order to stabilise the situation? I was.

Most of what went on at that time remains highly classified. When I arrived in Croatia in November 1991, the country and its defences were fragmented. The defence of Croatia was, at least in part, in the hands of town councils and mayors and their weapons were anything they could lay their hands on, including stuff taken out of military museums (I never saw it myself, but I was told that somewhere in Croatia, a Second World War German Tiger tank was being used!).

Once I'd made an initial assessment of their needs, I was tasked to organise shipments of weapons, clothing and equipment, and to begin the process of creating a cadre of Croatians capable of using it all.

One of the strangest aspects of the job was sourcing the gear. The great majority of the uniforms and vehicles we acquired came from the British army, from the Rhine's surplus sales centre at Rheindahlen. I was given a little office there from where I bought up ton after ton of British army DPM combat uniforms; huge crates of boots, shirts, pullovers and socks; bales of webbing belts and pouches; all of which were loaded on to newly acquired Bedford trucks and Land Rovers and driven down from Germany to Croatia by a small team of Belgians I'd recruited.

Weapons, on the other hand, were embargoed and to get these through required a more convoluted method. Our main source was a Syrian arms dealer who was part-owner of a factory in Poland which manufactured a wide range of weaponry. Although he was *persona non grata* in much of the West because of his connections with Palestinian and Islamic terrorist groups, he was regarded as a friendly contact by the agencies I was working with.

He had no problems supplying the weaponry we needed on the basis of an End-User Certificate that was dodgy, to say the very least.

My first meeting with him took place at his home in Spain. I had to go there to give him a large quantity of cash as a deposit on the first shipment of weaponry and ammunition. From Split, where I was based at that time, the easiest option was to drive, using the Range Rover which I had as my runaround and mobile office. Having crossed Italy and France, I was south of Barcelona on a major road when a small car driven by a woman pulled alongside, and I saw her and the two men who were accompanying her gesticulating at me and pointing at something on my car, indicating, I supposed, that there was something wrong. I pulled over and they did the same.

I was tired at this point or I wouldn't have been so stupid. I got out of the Range Rover and walked over to the attractive, dark-haired, olive-skinned girl who was jabbering at me in a language I didn't recognise. As I got close to her, I looked around and saw that one of her companions had nipped out of their car and was reaching in through the passenger window of the Range Rover to steal my briefcase!

Duh! I suddenly realised I'd fallen for one of the oldest tricks in the book. I whirled round, grabbed the guy by his hair and smashed his face against the side of my vehicle. He collapsed to the ground, but as he did so, I felt an enormous whack on the back of my head. Slightly dazed, I turned round to see that the girl had hit me with the heel of her shoe and was about to do so again. Bollocks to that! I nailed her with a punch to the throat and she went down like a sack of spuds.

Under the driver's seat of the Range Rover, I kept a 9mm Browning Hi-Power for medicinal purposes and now seemed a good time to bring it out, but as I was reaching for it, the third guy managed to get their car in gear and fuck off down the road. I gave his two mates a couple of kicks and got back into the Range

Rover, blood pouring from the back of my head. Having checked that the money was still intact, I set off again until I got to a Spanish police patrol which was waiting by the road twenty minutes further on. I stopped and told them what had happened and they nodded sympathetically.

'It's bloody gypsies, sir. They'll steal anything.' They helped me clean up the cut and get a dressing on it and I carried on, somewhat wiser. The cash handover went without a hitch.

My operation in Croatia, and later Bosnia, continued into the second half of the '90s before it was eventually wound down and I was able to return home. A couple of years later Loughlin asked me to begin planning a similar operation for Kosovo but, as things turned out, we were overtaken by events and nothing came of it. Life has been quieter since then.

When I think about Afghanistan now, it's with a sense of sadness and regret. The Afghan war was Russia's Vietnam: they couldn't sustain the losses they received there and maintain the arms race with the Americans; something had to give and in the end it was the Communist system. The ragtag irregulars of the Afghan resistance kept the Soviets fighting for ten years but then let their victory slip from their fingers as the country fell under the control of the Taleban – a fundamentalist sect who were, in effect, the last men standing at the end of the war. At least the Taleban are Afghans, I suppose.

The legacy of our intervention has been somewhat more dubious. The need to pay for the war led the Mujahideen to increase the production of opium tenfold, and Afghanistan is now one of the most important sources of raw material for the illegal narcotics trade. They no longer have to spend their profits on weapons and they are reaping vast rewards.

There is also the problem of terrorism. The jihad in Afghanistan attracted Muslim volunteers from all over the world, all of whom received military training and fundamentalist indoctrination, and many of whom are now using their knowledge and experience to wage war on everything else they hate: Americans, Jews, Sunnis, Shias; whoever. It's a sad irony that bogeymen like Osama bin Laden acquired their skills as a result of the CIA's training programmes.

Sometimes I'll hear a snatch of Pushtu on a city street or the thud of helicopter rotor blades, or catch the smell of naan bread cooking in an Indian restaurant, and it will all come back: the towering mountains; the heat and dust; the exhaustion; the fear. It was a strange time on a wild frontier.

I was only three years old when my Dad died and now I can't really remember him at all, no matter how hard I try. Perhaps my life would have been much the same if he'd lived, but I doubt it.

AN UNORTHODOX SOLDIER

PEACE AND WAR AND THE SANDLINE AFFAIR

Lieutenant-Colonel Tim Spicer OBE

Tim Spicer has always led a controversial life. Once one of the leading commanders in the Falklands, Belfast and Bosnia, he rose to the rank of Lieutenant-Colonel. His military career provided him with the background that later led him to set up Sandline International – and walk into some of the most controversial events of the decade.

In this fast-moving account, Spicer describes the events in Papua New Guinea when he was held at gunpoint but came away with his life and his men – and $36 million dollars – and gives the full truth about the 'Arms for Africa' affair which lead to accusations over a broken UN arms embargo to Sierra Leone. Spicer's account of modern soldiering looks at the creation of private military companies – the legitimate version of the old mercenaries – and concludes with a troubling forecast about an endangered world. *An Unorthodox Soldier* is an essential guide to life as it is lived in some of the world's trouble spots and provides a glimpse into the intrigue behind the British political scene.

Tim Spicer has served in Northern Ireland and in the Falklands.

ISBN 1 84018 349 7
£7.99

ALSO AVAILABLE FROM MAINSTREAM PUBLISHING

SOLDIER AGAINST THE ODDS

FROM THE KOREAN WAR TO SAS

Lofty Large

What is real military experience? Can it be gained in a few short hours, or over a period of many years, in a variety of situations, in different environments and countries?

Lofty Large has known the exhilaration of victory and the terrible despondency of defeat, the satisfaction of seeing his enemies go down and the horrific stinging crash of bullets smashing into his own body. In this book he discusses the paradox of army life, from the great parades and military bands, to months of silent movement, every nerve at full stretch, with only the muzzle of your rifle or machine-gun between you and the enemy.

Lofty Large has served in the mind-numbing cold, in the blazing desert heat and in sweat-drenched jungles. He has faced minefields, traps and ambushes, bombs, bullets, rockets and napalm. He has also been a prisoner of war.

This book details why he would not give up on his army career and defied the odds, passing the SAS selection course and going on to enjoy an illustrious career in the Special Air Service. Military experience in this soldier's case was always against the odds.

ISBN 1 84018 346 2
£7.99

THROUGH FIRE AND WATER

ARDENT: THE FORGOTTEN FRIGATE

Mark Higgitt

The average age of the 199 men on board HMS *Ardent* was 23 in May 1982 when she came under the most concentrated attack of any ship taking part in the Falkland landings. She was hit 17 times and one in four of her crew was either killed or wounded. She lost a greater proportion of her men in 22 minutes than any other fighting unit in the entire war. So why has the British public forgotten her name?

Through Fire and Water tells the frigate's story, from Christmas 1981 to her sinking in Falkland Sound – and beyond. It follows the families who waved sons, lovers, brothers, husbands and fathers off as *Ardent* left the docks. It describes the sickening fear of being in a defenceless warship singled out for destruction, the feeling of despair as those on board tried to save their ship and their mates while bomb after bomb came crashing down. It's the story of men from Britain who joined up to see the world, but instead became the focus of its attention. In a war so well documented, this is the first time their story has been told, the first book to explain why it all happened, the first to tell the true story of the forgotten frigate.

ISBN 1 84018 356 X
£20.00

ALSO AVAILABLE FROM MAINSTREAM PUBLISHING

ENIGMA VARIATIONS

LOVE, WAR AND BLETCHLEY PARK

Irene Young

Enigma Variations takes its name from the Enigma enciphering machine at Britain's top-secret intelligence headquarters. Here, at Bletchley Park, Ultra – the most vital intelligence of the Second World War – was controlled. And it was here that Irene Young worked. Enigma also refers to the disappearance of her husband while on service with the SAS. These variations on the theme are entwined in an intensely moving story of one woman's destiny – and fate.

In *Enigma Variations* the truth of life at Bletchley is revealed. It is a story about the grim conditions endured by the supporters of the brilliant cryptanalysts. It is also a story about a secret that Irene Young kept from her husband – in the interests of national security.

Enigma Variations, a portrait of life in the shadow of war, reveals the humour and tragedy surrounding the mysterious intelligence community.

Irene Young was educated at Edinburgh University and served in the Foreign Office throughout the Second World War.

ISBN 1 84018 377 2
£6.99

THE DAMAGE DONE

TWELVE YEARS OF HELL IN A BANGKOK PRISON

Warren Fellows

Think about the most wretched day of your life. Maybe it was when someone you loved died, or when you were badly hurt in an accident, or a day when you were so terrified you could scarcely bear it. Now imagine 4,000 of those days in one big chunk.

In 1978 Warren Fellows was convicted in Thailand of heroin trafficking and was sentenced to life imprisonment. *The Damage Done* is his story of an unthinkable nightmare in a place where sewer rats and cockroaches are the only nutritious food, and where the worst punishment is the *khun doe* – solitary confinement, Thai style.

Fellows was certainly guilty of his crime, but he endured and survived human-rights abuses beyond imagination. This is not his plea for forgiveness, nor his denial of guilt; it is the story of an ordeal that no one would wish on their worst enemy. It is an essential read: heartbreaking, fascinating and impossible to put down.

'The picure that builds is gross, a horrific contemporary version of *A Day in the Life of Ivan Denisovitch* . . . If you've ever had even as much as a spliff on a Ko Samui beach, you must read this book'
JAMES BROWN, *GQ*

ISBN 1 84018 275 X
£7.99

ALSO AVAILABLE FROM MAINSTREAM PUBLISHING

TEN-THIRTY-THREE

THE INSIDE STORY OF BRITAIN'S SECRET KILLING MACHINE IN NORTHERN IRELAND

Nicholas Davies

This explosive book reveals the conspiracy between British Military Intelligence and the gunmen of the UDA who targeted and killed both Republican terrorists and ordinary Catholics.

The secret partnership was sanctioned at the highest level of the British government and full details of planned operations, including killings, were passed directly to its Joint Intelligence Committee in London.

Ten-Thirty-Three was the codename given to the agent who was fed with all the details necessary for Loyalist gunmen to carry out their murderous activities. But somewhere along the line the power went to Ten-Thirty-Three's head and he became increasingly unpredictable. It wasn't long before he was completely out of control, and his Military Intelligence bosses had the makings of a major catastrophe on their hands . . .

This extraordinary true story lifts the lid on shocking abuses of power in Belfast in the 1980s and 1990s.

ISBN 1 84018 343 8
£6.99